CW00369674

SHOW RING STYLE

CONTENTS

Author's Note
This photoguide portrays the best of show ring dress. It emphasises style and elegance. There is a dress code for each class and I have included a few tips. But rules can change and, if you are in any doubt about what you should wear, I recommend you ask the relevant organisation – *The British Show Hack, Cob & Riding Horse Association* (TEL: 01675 466211), *The British Show Pony Society* (TEL: 01487 831376). *Sport Horse Breeding of Great Britain* (TEL: 01732 866 277), *The Side Saddle Association* (TEL: 01858 575 300).

INTRODUCTION

Cole Porter's famous song, 'Anything Goes', was a Broadway hit in 1934 when Sir Walter Gilbey was judging 'the most suitably dressed boy and girl' at Richmond Royal Horse Show. To Sir Walter, a stickler for tradition in riding dress, 'anything goes' was anathema. He condemned the low standards in Rotten Row and his views were widely reported. Letters asking for his advice poured into his office, often with photographs which he divided into 'Graces' and 'Disgraces'.

Sir Walter's legacy today is that there are very strict rules as to what should be worn at a horse show. I shall refer to these, but this photoguide is really about 'Graces', the riders of today who would, I trust, have delighted Sir Walter Gilbey's eye. Well, what the eye doesn't see... It is wise to check clothes before the show (*right*)!

LEADING REIN AND CHILD'S FIRST RIDDEN PONY

LEADING REIN

These classes have become a fashion parade. There is a strong military flavour in the choice of styles and colours for Mum, who must remember she has to run. Hats are worn. Although such outfits seem more suitable for a wedding than taking a child for a ride on a leading rein, this is show business.

Red is the favoured colour: it may be right for guardsmen, buses and pillarboxes, but be very careful with it in the show ring, and especially with small children. Use it to catch the eye, but sparingly please. And clashing browbands will not do. Keep it plain and simple.

AUTHOR'S TIP

In lead-rein classes a bitless bridle is not allowed. The lead-rein must be attached to the noseband.

CORRECT DRESS FOR LEADING REIN AND SHOW PONY CLASSES

Jacket: Plain dark coat. Tweed or cord is permitted for leading-rein classes but not for show pony classes
Jodhpurs: Cream or fawn
Boots: Black or brown jodhpur boots with straps to fit under the boot holding the jodhpur legs neatly over the boot
Gloves: Leather or string
Shirt: With collar and tie
Hat: Dark coloured hunting cap or crash hat with black or dark blue cover to current approved BSI or European Standards

(*right*) Sir Hardy Amies said of the tie: 'It comes into the room almost before the man'. Here we have matching ties with large spots combined with a plait bow which is perhaps rather big. Note the dark double-breasted suit and good bowler hat correctly worn, straight, just above the eyebrows.

CHILD'S FIRST RIDDEN PONY

(*below*) A well-cut coat (if a little short in the sleeves, but child riders grow fast), a single plait and a first-rate look. There is an overall impression of confidence gained from the well-fitted hat worn straight, the high collar with pin, jodhpurs fitting snugly over the boot and the hair perfectly arranged.

HUNTER PONIES

(*left*) Tweed coats for a Show Hunter class at Ponies UK.

AUTHOR'S TIP

Remember that earrings are not allowed or indeed any body piercings.

(*below*) Attention to detail… another immaculate figure, this time at Windsor.

CORRECT DRESS FOR WORKING HUNTER PONY CLASSES

Jacket: Tweed (plain dark blue or black are permissible for final judging at major shows)
Jodhpurs: Fawn or cream
Boots: Brown or black jodhpur boots or riding boots with garter straps
Gloves: Leather or string
Shirt: With collar and tie and plain tie-pin
Hat: Hunting cap or crash hat with black or dark blue cover to current approved BSI or European standards
Cane: Not to exceed 75 cm (30 in)
Spurs: Not permitted

SHOW PONIES

(*right*) Well-fitting jodhpurs and highly polished brown jodhpur boots – note how the jodhpur fits well down over the boot.

(*above*) Leather chaps worn for riding-in keep jodhpurs clean. Note these chaps are of plain colour and have no frills. If you want to look good in chaps, the keep-it-simple rule applies – and choose the colour carefully to go with jeans or jodhpurs.

(*right*) A perfectly cut coat and a performance to match.

HUNTERS/COBS

Two examples of hunter/cob class dress. The white collar with blue shirt, following the everyday wear of the bowler-hatted City gent of forty years ago, still looks good.

CORRECT DRESS FOR HUNTER, WORKING HUNTER, RIDING HORSE, COB AND HACK CLASSES

DAY
Jacket: Tweed coat (men); tweed coat or blue or black jacket (women)
Breeches: Fawn or buff
Boots: Plain black or brown with garter straps
Gloves: Leather or string
Shirt: With collar and tie and plain tie-pin
Hat: Bowler (men); bowler or hunting cap (women). For the jumping phase of Working Hunter classes a hunting cap or skull cap to current approved BSI or European Standards must be worn with a navy or black cover
Cane: Plain malacca or leather-covered not exceeding 81cm (32in) for hack, cob and riding horse

EVENING
Jacket: Scarlet or black hunting coat (men); dark blue or black (women)
Breeches: White (men) with scarlet coat, white or fawn with black hunting coat; fawn (women)
Boots: With brown tops and white garter straps or black patent leather tops when a top hat is worn with a black coat (men); plain black (women)
Shirt: collarless with white stock
Hat: Top hat (men); bowler hat or hunting cap (women) (top hats are permitted for women in cob, riding horse and hack classes)
Whip: Hunting whip
Note: In riding horse classes in the evening men wear a black tail coat with fawn breeches

ALSO WORN IN THE EVENING
Breeches: Fawn or buff
Boots: Black
Gloves: Leather or string

(*above*) The equivalent style for ladies. The hunt cap looks neat (a bowler does not suit everyone) and dark brown gloves, rather than a lighter tan, do not draw attention to the hands.

(*above right*) A scarlet swallowtail coat for a hunter class? Surely not, unless it is a championship at the Royal International or the Horse of the Year Show. But we are in Dublin and this competitor relishes the chance to dress for the big occasion.

(*right*) The velvet hunt cap with a high crown. Styles vary so choose one with the weight and width that suits you best. Note the neat tab collar, tie and pin.

HACKS

(*below*) A rather stylish coat in a hack class. A waistcoat is not worn and a tie pin becomes desirable or the tie may flutter at the canter. Note the skyblue tones of collar and tie.

CORRECT DRESS FOR HACK CLASSES, as on page 7.

AUTHOR'S TIP

Your horse's mane must be plaited, tails pulled or plaited and remember to keep numnahs as small as possible. Coloured browbands are allowed. Choose with care.

(*above*) A hack class in the main ring at Windsor and a more formal look, tweed gives way to the dark blue coat.

(*right*) An even more formal style: the top hat takes over for the Championship judging at major shows such as Windsor, the Royal International Horse Show or the Horse of the Year Show. Blue showing coat with velvet collar, cream silk stock and cream-coloured breeches. Boots with black patent leather tops add a gleaming touch.

(*below left*) Championship style: the rider wears a single-breasted cutaway coat more often seen in side-saddle classes. The expanse of breeches visible at the waist means a waistcoat must be worn. Here, it works well, but it is risky unless you have the figure to suit the outfit.

(*below right*) A more conventional coat. No waistcoat, midriff covered, probably a safer bet, and here worn to perfection.

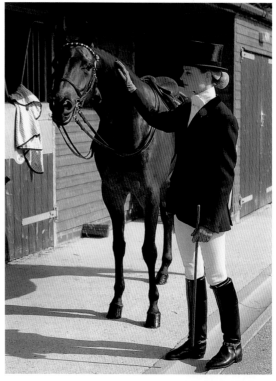

(*left*) Another form of Championship dress for gentlemen in a hack class, and the most elegant, is a black morning coat with overall trousers.

(*below*) The equivalent dress for ladies: a black swallowtail coat with black buttons, for the Hack Championship at Windsor.

SIDE-SADDLE

CORRECT DRESS
FOR SIDE-SADDLE CLASSES

DAY
Habit: Dark blue, black or tweed
Gloves: Leather (never black)
Shirt: With collar and tie and plain tie-pin
Hair: In a bun (false if necessary)
Hat: Bowler with veil
Cane: Not more than 1m (39in)

EVENING
Silk hat with veil, white or cream hunting
stock with dark habit and long black boots

(*above*) A child rider at the annual Side
Saddle Association Show. Her sense of
style – white collar, blue striped shirt, black
tie and grey waistcoat – is eclipsed by the
compulsory and cumbersome safety helmet.

(*left*) Dublin winner: a dark blue habit and
a good example of junior side-saddle style.

AUTHOR'S TIP

Children riding in side-saddle classes must
not wear spurs.

(*left*) A magnificent silk hat and a vintage habit still in service. If you can find a genuine tailor-made side-saddle habit which fits, or can be altered to fit, do not hesitate to make an offer for it.

(*right*) A black habit, another fine top hat and a rider whose graceful figure is perfect for showing a hunter side-saddle.

(*below*) The bowler hat denotes less formal style. A collar and tie is worn. The buff waistcoat adds a dressy touch. Note brown gloves and leather-covered cane, perfect bowler hat and veil. The judge for the ladies hunter class at Windsor.

(*above*) An immaculate example of today's show style. In the Edwardian era, fashionable habits were either black or very dark grey. Some hunting ladies would ride 'in pink'. In this case the bodice only was made entirely of scarlet cloth, usually with brass buttons.

(*left*) A bicycle seems a curious choice for a lady in a side-saddle habit…

IN-HAND

(*right*) The Blue Riband for showing in-hand, but this winner deserves a rosette for her carefully chosen outfit in tones of brown.

(*below*) An immaculate in-hand outfit at Dublin, and another first prize for the well-tailored coat, with touches of blue: shirt, pristine denim trousers and a hat to catch the eye.

AUTHOR'S TIP

Nylon headcollars are not allowed for in-hand hunters, they must be shown in leather head-collars or bridles.

(*above*) A traditional outfit for show-ing in-hand – the Englishman's suit. Single-breasted, three buttons, well-cut. It may be out of date but here it is not out of style. Note the bowler hat correctly worn and cornflower buttonhole.

(*right*) Variations on the theme: a soft felt hat and a coat that is a near match. For showing in-hand, keep the colours low key, aim for comple-mentary tones. Remember the horse is the star but you are, as the lawyers say, 'constructively present'.

BOOTS

(*right*) Jodhpurs and highly polished brown jodhpur boots – note how the jodhpur fits well down over the boot.

(*above*) Well-fitting breeches and highly-polished black butcher boots with garter straps for showing. The boots are cut high, essential to show 'a good leg for a boot'. Note the length of the coat which has two side vents, as opposed to a long centre slit which has a slimming effect. Beware of riding coats which are too short.

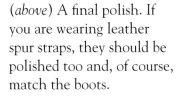

(*above*) A final polish. If you are wearing leather spur straps, they should be polished too and, of course, match the boots.

(*above*) A showing boot, kept for the occasion and you can see your face in it.

JACKETS

(*right*) An Oxford shirt with a collar cut with space for a tie. Show riders should pay special attention to the fit of the collar and tie and the choice of tie pin. This plain pin is a good example, simple, functional, elegant.

(*below*) Bespoke tailored tweed showing coat with dark blue velvet collar and fox's head buttons. The outfit is one of carefully studied elegance, note the tie and the treatment of the hair, and the dark gloves and hat of just the right hue.

(*right*) A dark blue coat denotes classic formal show pony style. The white collar with the dark tie and a matching hat adds to the formality and the overall stylish effect.

(*below*) What a comfort to know there are still cutters like Michael Smith, Director of Bernard Weatherill Limited, at work in Savile Row. In the context of overall showing costs, a well-made coat is a small investment, but one of the wisest.

HATS AND HAIRSTYLES

(*right*) Hair in a pony tail, tied back in a 'scrunchie' which matches the tie. Note deep-crowned hat.

(*below left*) Long hair tied in a single plait; this is time-consuming but the effect is simple, eye catching and traditional.

(*below right*) Hair treatment seems to vary but the small single bow provides the answer and this is a first rate example.

(*right*) KISS, standing for 'Keep It Simple Stupid', is the theory behind this unobtrusive bun contained in a hair-net – simple, effective, perfect style.

(*far right*) A brown hat for a change and it is nice to see it. And the short plait, with the brown colour-matched ribbon, is understated and elegant.

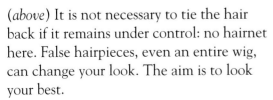

(*above*) It is not necessary to tie the hair back if it remains under control: no hairnet here. False hairpieces, even an entire wig, can change your look. The aim is to look your best.

(*above*) Top hat and black veil for a side-saddle show hunter class. The stock is natural silk, a warmer colour than white. Note plain pin fastened horizontally.

JUDGES AND COSTUME

(*right*) Judges confer at the Royal International Horse Show; tweed coats, buff breeches, black butcher boots with garter straps, bowler and hunt caps.

(*below left*) A discerning judge studies conformation at Windsor. He has dressed up for his part, but his elegance is discreet and relies on fine tailoring, the traditional hallmark of the horseman.

(*below right*) Preliminary judging at Windsor – a tweed habit is less formal but if you wear one, be sure that it fits. Note how the shoulders of this coat are cut. A dark coat can hide some short-comings, but a tweed one must be right in every way, and fitted sitting on a saddle of course.

(*right* and *below left*) Grooms and helpers in the ring should look the part. These photographs show different styles but both are effective.

(*below right*) Costume side-saddle classes offer limitless scope for style icons to shine.

British Library Cataloguing-in-Publication Data.
A catalogue record for this book is available from the British Library

ISBN 0.85131.785.5

Published in Great Britain in 2000 by
J. A. Allen an imprint of Robert Hale Ltd.,
Clerkenwell House, 45–47 Clerkenwell Green,
London EC1R 0HT

Design and Typesetting by Paul Saunders
Series editor Jane Lake
Colour processing by Tenon & Polert Colour Processing Ltd., Hong Kong
Printed in Hong Kong by Dah Hua International Printing Press Co. Ltd.

GENERAL EDITOR: CAROLINE BOISSET

SELECTING PLANTS

CAROLINE BOISSET AND JOHN WALKER

**OVER 1,000 TREES, SHRUBS, FLOWERS
AND FOLIAGE PLANTS FOR EVERY
GARDEN SITUATION**

MITCHELL BEAZLEY

THE GARDEN DESIGNER
SELECTING PLANTS

First published by Mitchell Beazley in 1993 as
The Garden Sourcebook

Mitchell Beazley
An imprint of Reed Consumer Books Limited
Michelin House
81 Fulham Road
London SW3 6RB

Editors Emily Wright, Simon Ryder,
    David Joyce, Richard Rosenfeld
Designers Jeremy Roots, Geoff Fennell
Senior Art Editors Larraine Lacey, Mike Brown
Editorial Assistant Jaspal Bhangra
Production Controller Sarah Schuman

Commissioned Photography Sue Atkinson,
    Paul Barker
Commissioned Artwork Tony Graham, Andrew
    Macdonald, Coral Mula, Gillie Newman, Sandra
    Pond, Will Giles
Picture Research Christine Rista

Executive Editor Sarah Polden
Design Director Jacqui Small

A CIP catalogue record for this book is available
from the British Library

ISBN 1 8573 2488 9

The publishers have made every effort to ensure
that all instructions given in this book are accurate
and safe, but they cannot accept liability for any
resulting injury, damage or loss to either person or
property whether direct or consequential and
howsoever arising. The authors and publishers will
be grateful for any information which will assist
them in keeping future editions up to date.

Typeset in Plantin by SX Composing Ltd,
Rayleigh, Essex

Colour reproduction by Mandarin Offset,
Hong Kong

Produced by Mandarin Offset, Hong Kong
Printed and bound in Hong Kong

A note on plant hardiness
Extensive information on the appearance, size and cultivation requirements of every recommended plant is given. A hardiness zone
is also included in each instant (denoted by "z" followed by a number). This relates to a range of average annual minimum temperatures and should be used as a guide to the best plants for a particular area. The temperatures are as follows: zone 1: below
-45.5°C/-50°F; zone 2: -45.5 to -37°C/-50 to -35°F; zone 3: -37 to
-29°C/-35 to -20°F; zone 4: -29 to -23°C/-20 to -10°F; zone 5: -23 to
-20.5°C/-10 to -5°F; zone 6: -20.5 to -15°C/-5 to 5°F; zone 7: -15 to
-12°C/5 to 10°F; zone 8: -12 to -6.5°C/10 to 20°F; zone 9: -6.5 to
-1°C/20 to 30°F; zone 10: -1 to 4.5°C/30 to 40°F. Most plants will
succeed in warmer zones than the given zone, and it can pay dividends to grow a more tender plant than the hardiness zone might
suggest in a warm microclimate (for example, a sheltered corner of
the garden).

Contents

SELECTING

PLANTS

TREES AND SHRUBS

The design of every garden, whatever its size, should include trees and shrubs. Even in the smallest plot there will be a suitable location for a tree, which will introduce the valuable element of height, and there are good compact selections of many shrubby species which will give substance to the overall composition. In addition, trees and shrubs create shade and a superstructure which allows a whole new collection of plants to be grown.

The choice of plant depends on the function it is expected to fulfil within the design. It is important, particularly in small gardens or where a single specimen is required to create a focal point, to be certain that the plant will justify the space it occupies. Size and shape are factors that should be considered for year-round effect: there are small compact strains of many plants as well as larger, vigorous ones; forms range from tall and columnar to pendulous. The foliage, flowers and fruit, bark and colour of young twigs all influence the visual scene while fragrance is always an added bonus.

Larger species should be positioned with care as they will create shade and block out light as they grow. Some of the most vigorous ones may interfere with the foundations of buildings and nearby drains if sited too close to them. For example, *Populus* species can be particularly problematic.

Left: Evergreen conifers – including cultivars of abies, chamaecyparis, cupressus and picea – create a stunning picture in golden- and blue-greens all year round. Changing light and atmospheric conditions will show the wide range of shapes, sizes, colours and textures to good effect. The flowering heaths used here add a bright seasonal note. A pleasing pattern, enhanced by the healthiness of the plants.

If blocking out an undesirable view outside the garden or breaking the linearity of a wall is a priority, then use quick-growing species. These plants often make large trees when mature, so a strict pruning regime will need to be carried out regularly. Quick-growing species are also very useful in creating an air of maturity early in the life of a garden. Often, as in forestry, a quick-growing tree is planted alongside a slower-growing species as a nurse and is removed as the latter gains size. I have seen balsam poplars (*Populus balsamifera*) coupled with a beech tree. The poplars grew quickly and, as the beech gained height, the lower branches of the poplars were removed. Once the beech had made 15ft (4.5m), the poplars were felled. Another slow-growing species which benefits from a nurse is English oak (*Quercus robur*).

Left: Three birches make strong vertical accents as they snake up through an understorey of ceanothus. Even in winter the trunks will remain arresting features of a simple composition.

Right: The appeal of this planting relies on contrasts of habit as well as of flower and foliage colour. The pink flowers of the hibiscus and foreground heather harmonize with the maroon foliage of *Cotinus coggygria* 'Royal Purple'. In habit and leaf shape the cotinus contrasts with the *Eucalyptus gunnii* behind it. Spiky heather and rosemary contrast with the broad, variegated leaves of the impressive dogwood.

Above: The foliage of the fine, spreading *Acer pseudoplatanus* 'Brilliantissimum' opens pink and later turns bronze and then greenish yellow. Here the lobed leaves make a sharp contrast against the tight, controlled shapes of clipped *Chamaecyparis lawsoniana* 'Fletcheri' behind.

Left: The bright red autumn foliage of *Acer palmatum* makes a strong focal point in a relaxed planting of shrubs, ferns and perennials. A well planned seasonal effect.

Large trees already present in the garden can create considerable shade. Try to work with rather than remove the tree; it is possible, through careful pruning, to significantly reduce and raise its canopy, letting in light without markedly altering the tree's impact.

There are many shrubs and small trees that are adapted in the wild to growing in the shade of taller trees and require these conditions to thrive in the garden. These include both evergreen and deciduous species: *Aucuba japonica*, *Juniperus × media* 'Pfitzeriana' and *Prunus lusitanica* provide good, all-year-round dense foliage. To this quality mahonias, some viburnums and many rhododendrons add blossoms in winter and spring. *Acer palmatum*, *Philadelphus coronarius* 'Aureus' and *Pieris* species are also grown for their foliage which colours spectacularly for extended periods, adding an additional season of interest to that provided by the flowers.

When designing a garden it may be that a plant is needed that is of interest throughout the year. Alternatively the garden, or a specific section of it, may need to be designed to be at its best during one season of the year. Many trees and shrubs have interesting features in at least two seasons and there are some outstanding ones that are attractive in three seasons. Among the best are many viburnums, particularly *V. opulus* 'Aureum' with its beautiful golden foliage, large panicles of white flowers in late spring and bunches of translucent red berries from late summer into the autumn. Other outstanding plants are sorbus, crataegus and prunus species that combine good foliage with flowers, fruit and bark; dogwoods with flowers, autumn or variegated foliage, and fruit; and witchhazels with winter flowers and autumn colour.

In winter the main feature is the bark. This may have a shiny, polished appearance as in some cherries;

a peeling or flaking texture that reveals layers of differing hues as in birches, *Acer griseum* and *Pinus bungeana*; or brightly coloured twigs from the previous season's growth as found on many willows (*Salix* species) and shrubby dogwoods. To get the best effect from willows and dogwoods it is necessary to prune them hard in early spring at least every other year.

There are many trees and shrubs that flower in early or late winter when frosts are at their worst. These always perform most successfully if planted in a sheltered spot away from the morning sun which can damage frozen flowers by thawing them too quickly. Remember that the blooms will be shown to their best advantage against a solid backcloth, so grow winter-flowering species near conifers or broadleaved evergreens or in front of a wall of a contrasting colour.

Spring is the time for flowers. They range in colour from the pale yellow racemes of *Stachyurus praecox* to the bright pinks of the flowering cherries. Choose the most garishly coloured ones with care so as not to clash with other spring-flowering plants. Young foliage can also have an impact, with delicate cream, pink and coppery leaves unfurling in the sun.

In summer the vegetation is at its height. Flowers are at their most abundant with lilacs, mock oranges and buddlejas covered in a mass of blooms. The dense cover of leaves makes a rich background to all the other plants in the garden. Colours range from the dark maroon of *Cotinus coggygria* 'Notcutt's Purple' or 'Royal Purple' to the blue-green of *Cercis siliquastrum*, the grey-green of *Pyrus salicifolia* 'Pendula' and the yellow-green of *Robinia pseudoacacia* 'Frisia'. The shape of the leaves – varying from the perfectly rounded to very narrow and feathery – and their size – they may be large or very small – are characteristics that affect the visual impact of the garden and can be used in very effective juxtapositions.

Autumn is the time when the canopy thins out and the garden begins to wind down, but still there are late flowerers such as *Abelia* × *grandiflora* and *Hydrangea paniculata; Clerodendron trichotomum* and *Callicarpa bodinieri giraldii* make a show with many berries that complement their startling foliage colour. Pyracanthas, cotoneasters and berberis are also good in berry, while maples, amelanchiers and euonymuses have beautiful foliage.

Right: Quercus coccinea 'Splendens', the only named form of the scarlet oak, colours gloriously in autumn. Arboreta and the many other plant collections throughout the world are often the best places to evaluate the ornamental qualities, speed of growth and ultimate size of trees when assessing their suitability for the garden. This oak will eventually make a tall tree in excess of 90ft (27m).

Quick-growing

Acer negundo z 3
Ash-leaved maple or box elder
This rapid-growing deciduous tree can reach 30ft (9m) and has pinnate ash-like leaves, 8in (20cm) long, and a bushy habit. The bright green young shoots carry hanging clusters of pale pinkish-brown flowers before the leaves in spring. Cultivars include 'Variegatum', with irregularly white-bordered leaflets, the golden-yellow leaved 'Auratum' and the less-vigorous 'Flamingo', which has pink young leaves that mature to green with white and pink markings. Will tolerate some shade.

Ailanthus altissima (*above*) z 5
Tree of heaven
This deciduous tree rapidly reaches 45ft (14m) with a spreading habit. The ash-like leaves are 1-2ft (30-60cm) long and turn yellow in autumn. Female trees bear small panicles of yellow-green flowers in late summer and early autumn, followed by bunches of bright red, winged fruits. It grows from seed in most soils and in some areas is rather a weed. For a tropical-looking bush cut back hard each spring; the strong shoots carry leaves over 3ft (90cm) long. Resistant to atmospheric pollution.

Alnus glutinosa **'Aurea'** z 4
All alders grow easily in virtually any soil and are especially suited to moist conditions. This cultivar has pale yellow leaves, which are most conspicuous in spring and early summer, fading to pale green as the summer progresses. With similar features is *A. incana* 'Aurea', the grey alder, the young yellow shoots contrasting well with the bright, red-tinted catkins during spring. It makes an attractive shelter-belt subject for an exposed garden. Alders bear woody cones which stand out in winter.

Aralia elata z 3
Japanese angelica tree
A tall, suckering deciduous shrub or a small, thinly-branched tree, the doubly-pinnate leaves are the main attraction of this plant. These are up to 3ft (90cm) long and form ruffs at the ends of the branches. 'Aureovariegata' has yellow margins and splashes on the leaves, and 'Variegata' has creamy-white margins and blotches. The variegations turn silver-white in autumn. Plant in deep fertile soil, in a sheltered spot to protect the leaves from strong winds. The cultivars stand out best when grown against a dark backcloth.

× *Cupressocyparis leylandii* z 6
Leyland cypress
This forms a noble tree of a dense, columnar habit. It is one of the fastest growing of all evergreen conifers, capable of reaching 100ft (30m) when mature. It makes a fine specimen in a large garden providing it is correctly sited and tended. The foliage is borne in irregular, slightly drooping sprays and is aromatic if crushed. Useful as a screen or windbreak, it grows well even in poor soil and tolerates alkaline soils and coastal conditions. 'Castlewellan' has yellow foliage.

Liriodendron tulipifera (*above*) z 5
Tulip tree
Fast-growing and deciduous, this tree can reach 40ft (12m) in 20 years. The peculiar leaves are four-lobed, glossy green in summer, turning to clear butter yellow in autumn. The tulip-like flowers are greenish-yellow with orange centres and are sometimes followed by woody fruits. Young trees flower less readily. The leaves of 'Aureomarginatum' have greenish-yellow margins. Succeeds in all fertile soils, including chalky.

Pinus sylvestris z 3
Scots pine
Characterized by its red-brown young bark, this fast-growing conifer will reach 100ft (30m) after many years. For the smaller garden choose 'Aurea', slow-growing with golden-yellow winter foliage, or 'Nana', a bushy, slow-growing dwarf form. Trees are densely conical when young, losing their lower branches as they age. The leaves are dark greyish-green, stiff, needle-like, and held in pairs. Small brown cones stand out against the foliage. Avoid damp, acid or shallow, chalky soils.

***Populus* × *serotina* 'Aurea'** z 3
Golden poplar
Also listed as *P.* × *canadensis* 'Serotina Aurea'. Like many poplars, this species is a rapid-grower and can reach 150ft (45m). It requires a fair amount of moisture to grow well; searching surface roots can damage drains and foundations so plant away from buildings. The pyramidal, juvenile shape develops into a densely branched, rounded canopy. Pointed leaves open golden-yellow in spring, turn greenish-yellow, and then golden-yellow again before falling in autumn. This cultivar is useful on wet sites.

Ribes odoratum (*below*) z 2
Buffalo currant
This ornamental currant is a vigorous, deciduous shrub that grows to 5ft (1.5m) with a loose, erect habit. The shiny, dark green leaves are carried on upright stems, along with golden-yellow, clove-scented flowers during spring. Shiny black currants contrast with the rich orange-yellow autumn foliage. Prune out some of the oldest shoots in late winter. Suitable for most types of soil.

Shade tolerant

Acer palmatum (*above*)   z 5
Japanese maple
This plant will slowly make a small tree
of 20ft (6m) with a low, rounded crown,
but is best treated as a shrub. The
species has palmate leaves, 2-4in (5-
10cm) across, with five or seven lobes;
these turn scarlet in autumn. Small,
purplish summer flowers are followed
by winged fruits. 'Senkaki' has coral red
winter bark; 'Atropurpureum' is
smaller, growing to 6ft (1.8m), with rich
purple-red summer foliage. Grow in
cool, moist loam, possibly in a tub or
raised bed, sheltered from cold winds.
Succeeds in dappled shade.

Aucuba japonica (*below*)   z 7
A shade-loving evergreen shrub that
makes a dense, rounded bush, 6ft
(1.8m) tall, with large, laurel-like, glossy
leaves. Female plants bear red berries.
'Crotonifolia' has golden speckled
leaves, 'Variegata' (spotted laurel) has
gold blotches. For berries, grow the
narrow-leaved, all-green female
'Salicifolia', with its sea green stems.
Variegated forms retain their colour best
on an open site, but all thrive in sunless
positions in most soils.

Juniperus × media 'Pfitzeriana'   z 5
Pfitzer juniper
Ideal for growing as a lawn specimen or
to break up the outline of a bed or
border, this evergreen shrub is also
useful as a tall ground cover. It reaches
10ft (3m) and spreads 10-15ft (3-4.5m);
arm-like branches are set at an acute
angle with drooping shoot tips. It has
glaucous, scale-like juvenile leaves.
'Pfitzeriana Aurea' has golden-yellow
young shoot tips and foliage; the latter
turns yellowish-green in winter. Very
versatile; good for alkaline soils.

Lonicera fragrantissima   z 5
The flowers of this semi-evergreen
shrubby honeysuckle give off a strong
scent during the coldest winter months.
The small cream blossoms appear on
part-naked branches from winter to
spring, followed occasionally by red
berries. Liven up the dull summer
phase with a fast-growing clematis or
other climber; this will scramble over
the bush which can reach 6ft (1.8m).
The deciduous *L. standishii* is similar
and *L. × purpusii* is more vigorous.
Prune out old wood in spring.

Mahonia aquifolium (*above*)   z 5
Oregon grape
This vigorous, spreading, suckering
evergreen shrub reaches 2ft (60cm) in
height and makes good ground cover. In
spring, dense terminal clusters of
fragrant yellow flowers appear, followed
by black, bloomy berries that give the
plant a bluish sheen. The spiny, glossy,
leathery leaves can turn orange-red in
winter and are up to 1ft (30cm) long.
'Atropurpurea' has rich reddish-purple
winter and early spring foliage. 'Moseri'
has bronze-red young leaves which turn
apple green and then dark green in
summer. Needs well-drained soil.

Philadelphus coronarius 'Aureus'   z 4
(*above*)
Golden mock orange
The leaves of this deciduous plant are
bright yellow in spring, ageing to
greenish-yellow. It makes a dense bush
6ft (1.8m) high, covered in scented,
creamy-white flowers from early
summer. Use in a mixed border,
masking the lower stems with
herbaceous plants such as *Euphorbia
griffithii* 'Fireglow', which has orange-
red flowers. Cut back the flowered
stems immediately after the blooms
have faded. Tolerates dry soils. Direct
sun may bleach the leaves.

Pieris japonica (*below*)   z 6
This evergreen shrub can reach 4ft
(1.2m) and has a compact, bushy habit.
The young leaves are coppery-pink in
spring, turning a darker, glossy green.
Flower buds are decorative in winter,
the long-lived waxy flowers opening in
drooping panicles in spring. 'Daisen'
has pink flowers, deeper when in bud;
the leaves of 'Bert Chandler' turn from
salmon pink to cream, white and then
green. Needs moist acid soil; protect
from cold winds and early frost.

Lawn specimens

Prunus lusitanica (*below*)   z 6
Portugal laurel
This can make an excellent specimen tree of 20ft (6m), doing particularly well on thin alkaline soil. The evergreen leaves are dark glossy green with red stalks. Small flowers appear in long, thin racemes in summer and have a sweet fragrance. Mature plants often fruit following a hot summer, the red fruits turning deep purple as they ripen. The less vigorous 'Variegata' has white-splashed leaves, flushed pink in winter; *P. l. azorica* has larger, brighter green leaves which are red as they unfold; *P. laurocerasus*, the cherry laurel, is less hardy and often used in hedging.

Rhododendron **'Blue Peter'**   z 5
This hybrid can grow to 6ft (1.8m), with a vigorous, upright habit and dark, glossy evergreen foliage. The large cobalt-violet and white flowers are funnel-shaped with frilled margins and are held in conical trusses. Each flower has an eye of deep purple spots. All rhododendrons need moisture-retentive, humus-rich, acid soil so suit a shady, woodland garden. Mulch in spring; no regular pruning is necessary.

Viburnum rhytidophyllum   z 5
A large rhododendron-like evergreen that grows in the dappled shade of trees. The drooping, long leaves are dark glossy green above with a thick grey tomentum underneath. Shoots are felty grey-brown. Upright clusters of white spring flowers are followed by small oval fruits which turn from red to black. Two or more specimens must be planted together to ensure fruiting. Plants can reach 6ft (1.8m) or more. 'Roseum' has rose-tinted flowers. Gives structure to a mixed border; ideal for alkaline soils.

Acer cappadocicum (*above*)   z 6
Notable for its brilliant autumn colour, this elegant maple makes a fine specimen, up to 70ft (21m) high, with a rounded crown. The broad leaves are bright green, five- to seven-lobed, and turn a rich butter yellow in autumn. 'Aureum' has leaves which turn from red to golden-yellow over several weeks. For attractive blood red young foliage grow 'Rubrum'; the leaves turn green in summer and reddish-gold in autumn. Needs fertile, well-drained soil.

Betula ermanii (*below*)   z 6
Grown largely for its stem colour, this Asian birch also has attractive yellow autumn leaves. A tree can reach 70ft (21m) when fully grown, but it is just as useful as a young garden specimen. The small glossy leaves have deep, parallel veins. The trunk has pinkish-white peeling bark while the branches are an orange-brown. On old trees the bark hangs from the branches. Plant with some thought as the beautiful bark colours are easily lost if not set against a dark backcloth such as evergreen shrubs. Grows well on most soils except shallow, calcareous types.

Cedrus atlantica **'Glauca'**   z 6
The blue-grey form of the atlas cedar is pyramid-shaped when young, with ascending tips to its branches, and reaches 110ft (33m) when fully mature. The silvery-blue, needle-like leaves are held in rosettes on plentiful short lateral shoots. The pale brown cones are up to 3in (7.5cm) long and sit topside of the branches. *C. deodara*, the deodar, has drooping tips, while the cedar of lebanon, *C. libani*, has level branches: both have grey-green foliage. All three trees develop a flatter habit when mature. Grows in most fertile soils.

Cornus controversa **'Variegata'**   z 5
This spectacular deciduous dogwood is ideal for a lawn where its horizontal, tiered branches can spread fully, giving it an architectural quality. The leaves have silver variegations, enhanced by clusters of creamy-white flowers in summer. In autumn the foliage turns purple-red and small black fruits may form. This species grows in most fertile soils, and benefits from shelter and sun. It can reach 15ft (4.5m) or more in height, and can spread to 10ft (3m), making this one of the most impressive of all foliage plants.

Davidia involucrata (*above*)   z 6
Pocket-handkerchief, dove or ghost tree
The extraordinary inflorescences of this tree are its chief glory. Each small flower is protected by two paper-thin white bracts which hang below the branches in summer. These bracts are between 4in (10cm) and 8in (20cm) long. The deciduous leaves are fresh green, heart-shaped and felted beneath. Green fruits litter the ground in autumn and winter. Plants can reach 30ft (9m), need rich, moisture-retentive soil and prefer a sunny, sheltered position.

Fragrance

Ginkgo biloba (*below*) z 5
Maidenhair tree
This deciduous conifer is slow to
establish but can reach 80ft (24m) with
an open habit. The leaves are fan-
shaped and two-lobed, pale green in
summer, yellow in autumn. Plants are
single-sex: male trees produce small
catkins, females bear tiny flowers. The
hard, yellow fruits smell of rancid
butter when ripe. The nut-like seeds are
edible. 'Pendula' has spreading,
weeping branches. Resistant to
atmospheric pollution.

Laburnum × *watereri* 'Vossii' z 6
In late spring and early summer the
golden chain tree is massed with
hanging racemes of golden-yellow, pea-
like flowers. This cultivar reaches 25ft
(7.5m) and has extra-long racemes at 2ft
(60cm). The deciduous leaves have
three leaflets. It does not produce seed
pods, which are poisonous in other
laburnums, as are all the genus' parts.
Train a late summer-flowering clematis,
such as 'Ernest Markham', through its
branches. Laburnums can be trained to
form tunnels. Grows in most soils.

Magnolia stellata z 5
Star magnolia
A fine shrubby magnolia that is covered
with fragrant white blooms in spring
which burst from silky, grey buds.
Slow-growing to 10ft (3m), it has a
rounded, compact habit. 'Rosea' and
'Rubra' have pink flowers. Plant in a
sheltered position in rich, well-drained
soil that receives plenty of moisture.
Mulch regularly with organic matter.
Avoid disturbing the roots and only
prune if essential. Underplant with
dwarf bulbs such as *Narcissus
bulbocodium*. Tolerates alkaline soil and
atmospheric pollution.

Metasequoia glyptostroboides z 5
Dawn redwood
This deciduous conifer was known only
as a fossil until it was rediscovered in
1941. It grows in a pyramid-shape,
reaching 36ft (11m) in 25 years and
ultimately 100ft (30m). The tapering
trunk bears a light, airy canopy of
feathery foliage, carried in opposite
rows on short branches. The leaves are
bright green in spring, turning golden-
yellow in autumn. The shaggy,
cinnamon-brown bark is attractive
during winter. This tree grows well in
moist soil and is resistant to pollution.

Salix caprea 'Weeping Sally' z 4
Rarely growing to more than 6ft (1.8m),
this small weeping willow is a female
form of the larger goat willow,
S. caprea, grafted on to a straight-
species rootstock. It grows slowly into a
graceful umbrella-shaped tree, the
branches growing down to the ground,
and bears soft silvery-white catkins in
spring. The deciduous leaves are glossy
green with woolly undersides and form
a dense mass in summer, allowing little
to grow under the tree other than
spring-flowering bulbs.

Viburnum plicatum 'Mariesii' z 4
(*below*)
This form of the Japanese snowball tree
is best grown as a specimen shrub.
Horizontally tiered branches make it a
fine architectural plant reaching 6ft
(1.8m) in height and spread. The
flowers are made conspicuous by white,
sterile, ray florets which form heads
2-3in (5-7.5cm) across. These are held
above the branches in early summer and
persist for many weeks. In autumn the
leaves turn a rich burgundy-red. Grows
in most soils including those over chalk;
needs no regular pruning.

Cercidiphyllum japonicum (*above*) z 5
Katsura tree
As the leaves of this tree take on their
greyish-pink, vermilion and yellow
autumn tints they release a delicious
caramel-like fragrance. They begin
coral-pink in late spring, turning sea-
green above and bluish beneath. Small
flowers appear before the leaves. In
cultivation this large tree normally
forms a small- to medium-sized
specimen. *Helleborus orientalis* makes a
good underplanting. Grow in a sunny,
sheltered position, in any moist soil,
preferably against dark evergreens.

Clethra alnifolia 'Paniculata' (*above*) z 4
The sweet pepper bush grows to 6ft
(1.8m) and is prized for its late-summer
flowers which fill the air with a sweet
fragrance. 'Paniculata' is a superior
form with the near-white flowers held in
terminal panicles. Its deciduous foliage
is attractive year-round and turns a
bright yellow-orange in autumn. 'Rosea'
has flowers flushed pink. In warm areas
black, peppercorn-like seeds follow the
flowers. Succeeding in damp, acid soils,
this plant is useful for woodland
gardens. Good at the back of a border.

Daphne odora 'Aureomarginata' z 8
This is one of the most scented and hardiest of the early-spring flowering daphnes. Plants form a rounded bush, 4ft (1.2m) high with a 5ft (1.5m) spread. The tight clusters of purplish-red flowers, which fade with age, are complemented by the evergreen, gold-rimmed leathery leaves. 'Alba' has white flowers. Some protection is beneficial, especially from strong, cold winds, but the plants will stand some frost. Grow this species in moist, free-draining loam, in a situation where its fragrance can be savoured to the full.

Fothergilla monticola z 5
This deciduous shrub makes a rounded plant of 5 × 5ft (1.5 × 1.5m) in ten years. Small, bottlebrush flowers appear in spring, creamy-white and sweetly scented. The coarse, dark green leaves are up to 4in (10cm) long and turn orange and yellow in autumn, blending with the scarlet autumn hues of *Acer palmatum*. The leaves of *F. major* begin golden-orange then deepen to crimson-reds. Grow in moist, acid soil, in sun or partial shade, among heathers or evergreen azaleas. No regular pruning is necessary to maintain this plant.

Oemleria cerasiformis (*above*) z 6
Oso berry
A suckering deciduous shrub which bears male and female flowers on different plants. The small, bell-shaped, fragrant white flowers appear in very early spring, carried in pendulous racemes on erect stems some 8ft (2.4m) tall. The sea green leaves emerge on vigorous young shoots. Of little real interest during the summer, plant towards the back of a border. Fruits are plum-like, turning from brown to purple as they ripen.

Philadelphus 'Virginal' (*above*) z 5
In early summer the plentiful double flowers of this vigorous mock orange fill the air with their rich fragrance. It produces upright shoots 10ft (3m) tall and has deciduous leaves, 4in (10cm) long. The compact 'Belle Etoile' reaches 6ft (1.8m). It has 2in (5cm)-wide scented flowers with a reddish-purple blotch in the centre. This patch can be picked out in the mixed border with mauve-flowered herbaceous plants such as hardy geraniums. Easily grown, even on poor dry soils, it should be pruned straight after flowering.

Sarcococca hookeriana z 8
Christmas box
This spreading, shade-tolerant, evergreen shrub has erect stems that reach 3ft (1m). In late winter the small, pink-tinged white male flowers release a distinctive scent which is strongest on moist, mild days. Leaves are lance-shaped. The insignificant female flowers are followed by shiny black berries in early spring. *S. h. digyna* has narrower leaves and reddish-tinged stems. This species grows in any fertile soil, including that over chalk.

Styrax japonica z 5
This graceful plant makes a small tree which may reach up to 25ft (8m) and has slender drooping branches. It requires protection from cold spring winds and late frosts that damage the opening buds. The fragrant white flowers are pendulous and open in early summer. The roundish to oval deciduous leaves are dark shiny green. In cooler climates it is best grown in full sun, but some shade is necessary in sunny areas. Can be slow to establish but thrives in deep moisture-retentive soil with plenty of organic matter.

Syringa vulgaris (*below*) z 3
Hundreds of forms of the common lilac exist in cultivation as shrubs or small trees. They reach 5-10ft (1.5-3m) and have a tendency to sucker. The large, spring flowers, held in dense pyramidal panicles, have a delicious scent and can be white, pink, cream, purple or mauve, single or double. The heart-shaped deciduous leaves are fresh green in spring. Plant in any fertile soil in a sunny position, preferably towards the back of a border as it tends to become bare at the base. Deadhead, but avoid hard pruning which encourages growth.

Viburnum carlesii (*below*) z 4
The heavy daphne-like scent of this popular viburnum permeates the air in spring. Clusters of pink buds make pure white flowers, followed by jet black autumn fruits. The leaves are dull green above, grey below, and often take on orange-red autumn hues. A rounded shrub, 4ft (1.2m) high, it makes a fine specimen plant. 'Diana' and 'Aurora' have red flowers which turn pink; 'Charis' has red flowers which turn pink then white. Cut out suckers sent up by grafted plants. Easily grown in most soils, it requires little pruning.

Winter colour

BARK

Acer griseum (*above*)   z 6
Paperbark maple
This slow-growing, lime-tolerant tree grows to 40ft (12m) with an open, rounded crown. The polished, orange-brown peeling bark is fully developed on wood three or more years old. In spring the trifoliate leaves emerge buff yellow. They turn dark green, reaching 2-4in (5-10cm) across, and become deep scarlet-orange in autumn. Greenish-yellow flowers appear in early summer. Needs a moist soil. Grouped plants should be well-spaced.

Betula papyrifera (*above*)   z 4
Paper bark or canoe birch
During its first five years this deciduous tree develops a smooth, white bark which then peels away in sheets. This peeling continues throughout the tree's life, revealing new glistening bark beneath. It grows to 60ft (18m) but the canopy casts only partial shade, allowing other plants to grow at the base. The irregularly toothed leaves turn a rich yellow in autumn. *B. jaquemontii* is similar but has brown peeling bark. Grows in most soils.

Cornus alba 'Sibirica' (*below*)   z 2
The bright red, glossy, upright stems of this winter dogwood form a thicket some 6ft (1.8m) high; they are stronger in moisture-rich soils. The leaves are up to 5in (13cm) long and turn shades of plum-red in autumn before falling. For deep purple, almost black stems, grow 'Kesselringii', striking if combined with red- and yellow-stemmed forms. Plant in groups for the best effect, avoiding shaded positions. Cut the stems very hard back in early spring to encourage fresh growth; flowers and fruits will be sacrificed as a consequence.

Cornus stolonifera 'Flaviramea'   z 2
(*below*)
This dogwood is grown for its bright yellow and olive green stems which can grow to 6ft (1.8m) if cut hard back in early spring. The growth is vigorous and suckering, forming a dense thicket if left unpruned. The light green deciduous leaves are up to 5in (13cm) long and turn yellow in autumn. Choose a site where the stems can be illuminated by the winter sun. It will tolerate waterlogged conditions. Grow with the red-stemmed dogwoods for beautiful winter colour.

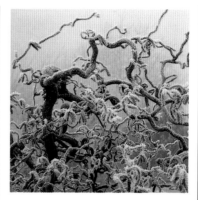

Corylus avellana 'Contorta' (*above*)   z 5
Corkscrew hazel or Harry Lauder's walking stick
The branches and the thread-like twigs of this deciduous bush are twisted and looped in a knotted mass. Reaching 10ft (3m), the plant is covered in spring with yellow male catkins and tiny, red, tufted female flowers. The leaves are up to 4in (10cm) long and more crinkly than the ordinary hazel; they turn yellow in autumn. Grows in most soils. Cut out vigorous suckers from the base. Plants look striking when seen against snow or covered in frost.

Leycesteria formosa   z 7
Himalayan honeysuckle or pheasant berry
This deciduous shrub has bright sea green stems which are hollow, upright and reach 6ft (1.8m) in a season. The young stems are covered with a glaucous bloom. Olive green pointed leaves are 2-7in (5-18cm) long; they turn yellow in autumn. In summer the white flowers emerge from purple-red bracts and hang in heavy racemes. These are followed by purple-brown fruits which smell of caramel. Grow in moist, fertile soil. Cut back to ground level in spring.

Parrotia persica   z 6
Persian ironwood
Grown mostly for its vivid red, orange and yellow autumn leaf colour, this plant also has beautiful flaking grey bark on its older stems. It grows as a spreading large shrub or small tree and can reach 25ft (7.5m) with a similar spread, the stiff, horizontal tiers of branches making an excellent winter silhouette. The flowers appear in late winter, conspicuous for their bright red stamens and lack of petals. Grows in most soils apart from highly alkaline.

Pinus bungeana z 5
Lace-bark pine
An unusual evergreen conifer, this
slowly forms a low-branching specimen
shrub or tree up to 40ft (12m) tall. The
grey-green bark flakes away, leaving a
beautiful jigsaw-like pattern of white,
olive green, yellow, brown and purple.
The colours change as more flaking
occurs. The yellow-green, needle-like
leaves are about 3in (8cm) long. *P.
gerardiana*, Gerard's pine, has pinkish-
grey bark that flakes to reveal brown,
green and yellow wood. Grow both in
full sun, avoiding shallow alkaline soils.

Prunus serrula (*above*) z 6
Tibetan cherry
The smooth bark of this tree resembles
polished mahogany. It peels horizontally
between large, pale brown lenticels
which ring the trunk and stems. A tree
is at its best after ten years when it is
15ft (4.5m) tall. Ideal for a lawn,
underplanted with *Narcissus* 'February
Gold' or similar. It grows in all soil
types including alkaline. Plant in full
winter sunlight, removing lower
branches to gain trunk length. Polish
the bark with a soft cloth to enhance the
beautiful sheen.

Rhododendron barbatum z 8
Dense heads of crimson red flowers
appear in spring on this evergreen
rhododendron. It has deep purple,
peeling bark, large leaves with sunken
veins, and bristly young branches and
petioles. It forms a very large shrub or a
tree 30ft (9m) high. *R. thomsonii* has
cinnamon-coloured bark and blood red
flowers. Plant in semi-shade in moist,
acid soil, mulching with leaf mould.
This species is ideal for woodland.
Water well until established. No regular
pruning needed.

Rubus cockburnianus (*above*) z 5
Whitewashed bramble
A whitish bloom covers the arching,
purple stems of this deciduous rubus.
The lower surfaces of the pinnate, fern-
like leaves are also bloomy. Small
flowers are sometimes followed by black
fruits. All shoots should be cut to within
1in (2.5cm) of the ground in spring to
encourage new growth; this can reach
6ft (1.8m) on established plants. Will
grow in shade or sun in most soils. Plant
against a dark background in full winter
sun, with *Eranthis hyemalis* beneath.

Salix alba 'Chermesina' z 2
Scarlet willow
Similar to the winter dogwoods in habit,
the young shoots of this shrub are
bright orange-red. Deciduous, pale
green leaves open in summer. Prune
hard back at least twice in spring to
encourage fresh growth. Plants will
reach 6ft (1.8m) in two seasons,
considerably more if left unpruned. *S.
alba* 'Vitellina', the golden willow, has
bright yellow shoots. For contrast, plant
with dogwoods such as the dark purple-
stemmed *Cornus alba* 'Kesselringii'.
Best in moist soil, especially near water.

Salix matsudana 'Tortuosa' z 4
Corkscrew willow
The twisted shoots and branches of this
willow are dramatic against the winter
sky. It makes a narrow, pyramidal tree
and, once settled, grows to 20ft (6m) in
ten years. The olive green twisted stems
carry narrow, contorted, bright green
deciduous leaves in spring, as well as
small yellow-green catkins. Train
Clematis 'Bill Mackenzie' through it for
yellow flowers and fluffy seed heads.
Quickly regrows if cut hard back.
Prefers moisture-rich soil, near water.

FLOWERS AND BERRIES

Camellia 'Salutation' z 7
This hybrid evergreen shrub grows to
6 × 6ft (1.8 × 1.8m) in ten years. The
silvery-pink flowers are semi-double,
5in (13cm) across, and appear in late
winter and spring. The leaves are matt
green. Grow camellias in humus-rich,
acid soil and mulch regularly with
organic matter. Choose a sheltered spot,
out of strong winds and protected from
the early morning sun which can
damage the flowers after frosts: a
woodland garden is ideal. Water in the
summer, especially until established.

Corylopsis pauciflora z 6
Winterhazel
The arching stems of this deciduous
shrub can reach 6 × 6ft (1.8 × 1.8m).
The leaves emerge pink and open a dull
green, with good autumn colour.
Drooping racemes of scented, bell-
shaped yellow flowers are carried in
early spring. *C. spicata* is larger, with
yellow flowers and purple anthers; *C.
willmottiae* 'Spring Purple' has purple-
red winter shoots. Plant in deep, lime-
free, humus-rich soil in some shade.
Underplant with *Narcissus cyclamineus*.

Cotoneaster lacteus (*above*) z 7
This plant bears large clusters of small
red fruits which last throughout the
winter if they survive the attention of
birds. Evergreen, leathery, oval leaves
have deep-set veins and felted grey
undersides. Creamy-white flowers
appear in summer. It can be pruned to
make a short, single-stemmed tree, but
is more usually a free-growing shrub up
to 12ft (3.6m) tall, with similar spread.
The mauve flowers of *Clematis viticella*
'Abundance' will give interest in late
summer. Grows in most soils.

Hamamelis mollis (*above*)　　z 5
Chinese witch hazel
One of the first winter-flowering shrubs, this has sweet-scented, golden yellow flowers with hardy strap-like petals, borne on bare, upward-growing branches. The light, open canopy reaches 10ft (3m). Hazel-like deciduous leaves are up to 5in (13cm) across, turning deep yellow in autumn. 'Pallida' has larger, sulphur-yellow flowers; *H. × intermedia* 'Diane' has rich copper-red flowers and good autumn colour. Slow-growing; do not prune. Plant in humus-rich acid soil in full sun.

Ilex verticillata　　z 3
Winterberry
This holly is quite unlike all others because of its deciduous nature. It forms a rounded shrub reaching 13ft (4m) in ten years. In winter the bare green-purple stems are clothed with long-lasting, bright red berries. An unusual shrub, also noted for its purple-tinged 1⅔in (4cm)-long leaves, which are particularly well-coloured in spring, turning yellow in autumn. The female form 'Christmas Cheer' has many persistent fruits. Needs acid soil.

Malus 'Red Sentinel'　　z 5
With fruits lasting into mid- and late winter, this crab apple is a valuable small- to medium-sized tree. The deep red fruits hang in large clusters from bare branches. They are preceded in summer by groups of white flowers. The deciduous leaves are 2in (5cm) long. It forms a round-headed tree 20 × 10ft (6 × 3m) after ten years. 'Golden Hornet' carries bright yellow fruits and is a useful pollinator for dessert apples. Thrives in most soils except those which are waterlogged; needs little pruning.

Pernettya mucronata　　z 7
Small, cup-shaped, white flowers appear in summer on this evergreen shrub, followed by dense clusters of shiny, marble-like fruits. 'Mulberry Wine' has large magenta berries, 'Pink Pearl' lilac-pink, and 'Alba' white. They grow to 2ft (75cm), making a rounded mass of wiry stems. The small evergreen leaves are held close to the red stems. Grow in acid soil, in sun or semi-shade; good in peat beds and for growing with heathers and callunas. Plant in groups, ensuring one plant is a male. Prune back straggly shoots. Makes useful ground cover.

Prunus × subhirtella 'Autumnalis'　　z 6
(*above*)
Autumn or winter flowering cherry
This tree grows to 16ft (5m) in ten years. Small, white, semi-double flowers appear throughout the autumn, winter and spring on bare branches; the blooms may be damaged by severe weather conditions. The 2in (5cm)-long leaves have yellow-bronze autumn colours. 'Autumnalis Rosea' has rose pink flowers. Plant in fertile, moist soil, avoiding frost pockets or very exposed positions. Can also be grown as a multi-stemmed shrub. Slow to establish.

Rhododendron 'Praecox'　　z 5
This rhododendron bears funnel-shaped flowers in late winter and early spring. Two or three crimson-purple buds form at the tips of each shoot and open rose-purple. The flowers are held well above the glossy dark green leaves which are aromatic when crushed. Plants are sometimes part-deciduous. Makes a compact rounded bush only 3ft (90cm) high. The purplish-pink, crimson-spotted flowers of 'Tessa' open slightly later than 'Praecox'. Grow plants in acid, humus-rich soil; mulch regularly.

Sorbus cashmiriana　　z 2
Kashmir mountain ash
From autumn onwards pearl white fruits are borne in dense clusters on the bare branches of this ash. They are ⅖in (1cm) across, have reddish stalks and last well into winter. The pinnate leaves are 9in (23cm) long with numerous grey-green leaflets that turn yellow in autumn. Soft pink flowers appear in spring. Makes a small rounded tree or large shrub, reaching 10ft (3m) in ten years. *S. hupehensis* (z 5) has smaller fruits tipped pink. Does not need pruning. Suitable for most soils.

Symplocos paniculata　　z 5
Sapphire berry
The ultramarine, jewel-like fruits of this plant are dazzling. Carried in dense clusters, they follow the fragrant, white spring flowers. Small leaves turn yellow in autumn. It forms a dense, twiggy shrub or small tree up to 10ft (3m) tall in ten years. Plants need cross-pollination and only fruit fully after several seasons. Grow in rich, deep, non-alkaline soil, in a sheltered spot in sun or shade. Fruiting is most prolific after a hot, dry summer.

Viburnum × bodnantense 'Dawn'　　z 6
(*above*)
This deciduous viburnum has a strong, upright habit and grows to 8ft (2.4m). Clusters of sweetly scented, tubular, pink flowers appear from early winter through to spring. In 'Deben' the flowers are pink in bud opening white. Leaves are bronze-tinted in spring, maturing to green and turning reddish in autumn. The purple-green stems darken as they age. Thin out some of the oldest flowering stems each spring when fully established. Suitable for any soil; reasonably frost-tolerant.

19

Spring colour

FLOWERS

Berberis darwinii (*above*)   z 7
Clusters of double, cup-shaped, orange
flowers are borne by this evergreen
barberry from early spring onwards.
The dark green, spiny leaves have
silvery undersides. In autumn dark
purple, bloomy fruits appear and some
older leaves turn fiery orange and fall.
Grows to 6 × 6ft (1.8 × 1.8m) in ten
years. Underplant with the bright blue-
flowered *Brunnera macrophylla*. Grow in
sun or shade; avoid dry soils. Use at the
back of a border or as a hedge.

Cercis siliquastrum (*below*)   z 6
Judas tree
In spring the branches and trunk of this
plant are covered with clusters of pea-
like, pink flowers. These are followed
by kidney-shaped glaucous leaves,
which turn yellow in autumn. Purple-
tinged seedpods appear in late summer.
Makes a small tree but gives more
flowers as a multi-stemmed shrub,
reaching 8 × 7ft (2.4 × 2.1m) in ten
years. Grow in full sun and well-drained
soil. Plants need little pruning until they
are five years old. *C. canadensis* is
hardier (z 4).

Chaenomeles × superba   z 5
Japanese quince or japonica
Forms of this vigorous, small- to
medium-sized thorny shrub include
'Knap Hill Scarlet', with orange-scarlet
flowers, and 'Pink Lady', rose-pink.
Loose-petalled flowers appear in mild
winters, but the main flush is in spring.
Dark green deciduous leaves follow.
The fragrant, yellow fruits can be used
to make jelly. Grow freestanding or as a
wall shrub in sun or shade; avoid
alkaline soils which cause chlorosis.
Prune back the previous season's
growth after flowering.

Cornus florida   z 5
Flowering dogwood
This deciduous plant makes a beautiful
specimen shrub or small tree. It is
covered in blooms in spring, each
"flower" actually consisting of four,
slightly twisted, petal-like bracts that
surround the insignificant true flowers.
The oval leaves take on rich autumn
colours. It reaches 13ft (4m) in ten years
and needs acid or neutral soil and
shelter from cold winds and frost. No
pruning required.

Cytisus × praecox (*above*)   z 5
Warminster broom
The spindly, green stems of this shrub
form a mass that makes 4 × 4ft (1.2 ×
1.2m) in eight years. In spring the stems
are weighed down by pea-like, light
yellow flowers. 'Allgold' has long-lasting
yellow flowers, 'Albus' pure white and
'Buttercup' golden-yellow flowers. The
small deciduous leaves drop early in the
season. Grows in full sun in most soils.
Plants tend to be short-lived; they have
weak root systems and need staking in
exposed sites. Prune if necessary after
flowering, removing one-year-old wood:
never remove mature wood.

Erica arborea 'Alpina'   z 7
During spring this form of the
evergreen tree heath is awash with
frothy white flowers which complement
the feathery foliage. The blooms have a
strong honey-like fragrance. Making 6ft
(1.8m) in ten years, it is a fine specimen
shrub and gives height to a heather
garden. Works well with a basal
planting of *Erica carnea* or *Calluna
vulgaris* in their various forms.
'Riverslea' has purple flowers but is less
hardy. Needs acid soil and full sun or
very slight shade. Prone to damage by
high winds or snow: only prune to
remove damaged growth.

Exochorda × macrantha 'The Bride' z 5
(*above*)
The graceful stems of this deciduous
shrub are covered with racemes of
small, white saucer-shaped flowers in
spring. Each flower has five petals. The
light green, lanceolate leaves are 3in
(8cm) long and turn yellow in autumn.
Plants grow upright for the first few
years and then develop arching shoots,
making a rounded bush, some 6ft
(1.8m) high and often wider. Grow in a
sunny position, avoiding alkaline soils.
Remove a third of the old wood after
flowering to encourage new growth.

Forsythia × intermedia   z 5
Forsythia carries masses of early spring,
yellow flowers before the leaves emerge.
This vigorous hybrid will grow to 12ft
(3.6m) in ten years, but can be kept
smaller with regular pruning. Plants
have an upright habit when young but
form a rounded shrub when mature.
'Spectabilis' is the most floriferous
form. Cut back one third of the oldest
wood immediately after flowering to
encourage new shoots. Easy to grow, it
succeeds in sun in all soils.

Magnolia × soulangiana (*above*)   z 6
Tulip magnolia
Large, loose-petalled, sweetly scented flowers appear on bare branches in spring, the white petals shaded pink with purple bases. Oval leaves open later. A small tree or a multi-stemmed shrub, it reaches 16ft (5m) in 20 years. 'Brozzonii' has huge white flowers, 'Rustica Rubra' reddish-purple, goblet-shaped flowers and 'Lennei' has rose-purple flowers with white insides; it may have a second flush in early autumn. Needs shelter and a heavy soil, enriched with compost. A superb specimen plant.

Prunus 'Okame'   z 7
This cherry is renowned for its display of clear pink flowers, which are carried in profusion in early spring. The flower buds are equally attractive. Trees bloom over a period of 2–3 weeks, and in autumn the leaves turn attractive shades of reddish-orange. In winter there is the added attraction of brownish-red bark. Plants grow to 25ft (8m) and have an upright oval shape. Quick growing in most soils in a sunny position.

Rhododendron luteum   z 5
Also known as *Azalea pontica*, this deciduous shrub can grow to 5 × 5ft (1.5 × 1.5m) in ten years. It tolerates poorer and drier conditions than most deciduous azaleas but still requires acid soil. The winter buds and young shoots are characteristically sticky. Funnel-shaped, yellow flowers appear in round heads, in advance of the leaves; they have a very strong fragrance. The leaves are oblong, 4in (10cm) long, and turn rich shades of orange-crimson in autumn. Growth tends to slow with age. Pruning is usually unnecessary.

Stachyurus praecox (*below*)   z 6
From early spring onwards this deciduous shrub bears plentiful frost-hardy, pale yellow flowers in small rigid racemes. Long, oval leaves with dark veins open later and turn yellow in autumn. Stems are purple-green. It makes a domed bush 6 × 6ft (1.8 × 1.8m) in five years. Underplant with *Helleborus orientalis* and *H. niger* or use it at the rear of a border. *S. chinensis* has smaller, more numerous flowers. Plant in sun or semi-shade in fertile soil. Once established, prune out a third of the older wood every few years.

Viburnum × carlcephalum (*below*)   z 5
This deciduous viburnum carries large heads of scented, white, tubular flowers, pink in bud. The grey-green leaves often take on orange-red colours in autumn. A rounded bush of compact habit, reaching 5 × 5ft (1.5 × 1.5m) in ten years, it makes a good specimen, or can be grown in a border or large tub. Grows well in most soils, but avoid extremes of dryness or wetness, which damage the surface root system. Plants need sun or partial shade to thrive. Remove any suckering growths that appear at the base.

FOLIAGE

Acer pseudoplatanus   z 5
'Brilliantissimum' (*above*)
This sycamore is a slow-growing, small deciduous tree, reaching 12ft (3.6m) in ten years. The spring foliage emerges bright shrimp pink, turns pale yellow-green and then green during the summer. Autumn leaves are usually yellow. It has an architectural quality, forming a rounded, mop-headed shape after three or four seasons. Succeeds in most soils, in full sun. Remove wood affected by coral spot disease.

Aesculus neglecta 'Erythroblastos'   z 5
Sunrise horse chestnut
A beautiful, slow-growing, medium-sized tree with spectacular spring foliage. The leaves are composed of five leaflets, each up to 6in (15cm) long. They unfold bright pink in spring, then fade over a period of weeks to a pale yellowish-green and finally turn yellow-orange in autumn. Pale yellow flowers appear in summer. It can reach 25ft (7.5m). Grow in any good soil; choose an open position in spring sun, with some protection from larger trees.

Cryptomeria japonica 'Elegans'   z 7
This cultivar of the evergreen Japanese cedar has small, drooping, awl-shaped leaves that make a dense head. In spring the foliage turns blue-green, also the colour of new growth. It assumes brown-bronze tints in winter; the change is sometimes so dramatic the plant appears to be dead. A rounded coniferous bush or small tree, it grows to 8 × 8ft (2.4 × 2.4m). The reddish, peeling bark is only really noticeable on older plants. 'Elegans Aurea' turns green-gold in winter. Grows best in moist soils.

Larix decidua (below)   z 3
European larch

This deciduous conifer is beautiful in spring as the leaves emerge; light green and needle-like, they are held in rosettes along the shoots and are set off by the yellowish-brown bark. In autumn they turn golden-yellow. Mature trees produce pink-purple female cones, along with smaller yellowish male cones. Quickly forms a large cone-shaped tree, reaching 60ft (18m); the branches droop with age. Avoid wet soils.

Photinia × fraseri 'Red Robin'   z 7
(below)

This evergreen shrub makes its boldest statement in spring. Red leaves appear in autumn, the colour intensifying during winter, so that by spring the plant is covered with flaming foliage. Leaves continue to appear until mid-summer, when they turn bronze and then green with age. White flowers may open in spring. Plants can grow to 6ft (1.8m) in height in ten years, with a rounded habit. Mature specimens are a good support for a summer-flowering clematis. Plant in full sun, and add plenty of compost to the soil. Prune hard every few years.

Pieris formosa forrestii   z 7
'Forest Flame'

An acid-loving evergreen shrub, ideal for a woodland garden. Fiery red foliage opens at the shoot tips in spring. The small lanceolate leaves change to shrimp pink, then white, and finally to dark green as summer progresses. Sprays of slightly fragrant, white, lily-of-the-valley-like flowers appear in late spring. Plants can reach up to 6ft (1.8m) in height when mature, and need little pruning. Avoid full sun and alkaline soils; add leaf mould at planting. Protect from cold winds.

Spiraea japonica 'Goldflame'   z 5

An easily grown, deciduous shrub that reaches only 2ft (60cm) in height after ten years, this plant is a useful addition to the shrub or mixed border. In spring the brownish-red stems are adorned with new apricot-orange leaves; these turn orange-red and then golden-yellow as the season progresses. Reddish-pink flowers appear in summer. Grow as a specimen or in groups, avoiding strong sun (which can scorch the leaves) and dry and alkaline soils. Prune plants to ground level in spring to encourage healthy re-growth.

Viburnum opulus 'Aureum' (above)   z 3

This yellow-leaved form of the guelder rose is useful in moist soil and for wilder parts of the garden. The deciduous leaves are 2-5in (5-13cm) long with five lobes. New spring growth is bright yellow, ageing to greenish-yellow during summer. It reaches 6ft (1.8m) in ten years and can be left unpruned; alternatively, a third of the oldest shoots can be cut to ground level every two or three years once the plant is established. Protect from strong, direct sun which scorches the leaves.

FLOWERS

Aesculus × carnea 'Briottii'   z 4

This compact form of the red horse chestnut will reach 20ft (6m) in ten years, forming an oval-canopied tree. It has upright, 10in (25cm)-long panicles of deep reddish-pink flowers in early summer. The dark deciduous leaves are digitate and up to 1ft (30cm) across; they turn deep orange-yellow in autumn. The "conkers" (fruits) are smooth-coated. Plant in moist soil, avoiding high alkalinity, in full sun. Casts deep, unfruitful shade so best-suited to the larger garden.

Buddleja davidii (above)   z 5
Butterfly bush

Fragrant, tubular flowers, held in large racemes, appear on this arching shrub from summer to early autumn. Deciduous lanceolate leaves are 4-12in (10-30cm) long and are light green with silvery-grey undersides. Forms include: 'Black Knight' (velvety-purple flowers) and 'Peace' (white with orange eyes). Grows to 10ft (3m) in five years in the poorest soils. Spreads by seed; can become a weed. Prune hard back in early spring to 4in (10cm) from the base.

Calycanthus floridus   z 4
Carolina allspice

During summer this shrub bears red-brown, star-like, scented flowers on wood that is more than two seasons old. These are set off by the light green, deciduous leaves, which have downy undersides and are aromatic if crushed. In autumn the foliage turns yellow. It reaches 6 × 6ft (1.8 × 1.8m) in ten years, with a rounded habit. Grow in deep, rich, alkaline-free soil, in diffused shade, as found under a light tree canopy. Pruning is not necessary.

Crataegus laevigata 'Crimson Cloud' z 4
(*above*)
Also listed as *C. oxycantha*, this
hawthorn is a deciduous, spiny tree that
reaches 20ft (6m) with a rounded
crown. The small leaves are lobed, grey-
green, and often have attractive yellow
tints in autumn. However, the flowers
are the greatest asset. Held in dense
clusters, they are deep red with a white
patch at the base of each petal. 'Paul's
Scarlet' has double flowers. Bunches of
shiny red berries follow in autumn and
persist for at least six weeks. Prune only
to remove suckers. Avoid over-dry soils.

Deutzia* × *elegantissima 'Rosealind' z 5
(*below*)
The arching stems of this shrub are
covered with dense corymbs of pink,
five-petalled, fragrant flowers from late
spring to early summer. The oval,
deciduous leaves are slightly rough.
Plants reach 6ft (1.8m) and should have
a third of the oldest wood removed after
flowering. Train a large-flowered
clematis through the branches. Plants
need moist fertile soil and regular
watering during periods of drought.
Select a sheltered spot.

Enkianthus campanulatus z 4
A member of the heather family, this
deciduous shrub flowers in early
summer, producing clusters of waxy,
bell-like blooms, creamy-yellow with
red stripes. Growth is bushy and
upright, reaching about 13ft (4m) with a
spread of 8ft (2.4m); the base of mature
plants is open. The glossy green leaves
turn shades of orange, red and scarlet in
autumn. 'Red Bells' has more
prominent stripes. Cut back one or two
shoots each season. Plants need lime-
free soil and grow best in partial shade
in moist, deep, acid soil. They are
excellent for a woodland garden.

Halesia carolina z 5
Snowdrop tree or Carolina silverbell
This spreading deciduous shrub grows
12ft (3.6m) tall in ten years. Clusters of
nodding, pure white flowers cover the
branches in early summer. Four-winged
fruits follow as the flowers fade. The
deciduous oval leaves are pale green,
yellow in autumn. *H. monticola vestita*
has larger flowers that can be tinged
pink. Grows well in moist, acid soil,
high in organic matter in a protected
site. Takes two or three seasons to
establish; needs no pruning.

Kalmia latifolia (*above*) z 5
Calico bush or mountain laurel
This rhododendron-like evergreen
shrub is one of the most beautiful
summer-flowering plants for an acid
soil!. In early summer the striking buds
open into clusters of pink flowers.
These last for several weeks, framed by
the narrow, glossy, mid-green leaves. It
makes a rounded bush, 10 × 10ft (3 ×
3m). Full sun is needed for maximum
flowering. Soil should be deep and
moist. Only prune for shaping when
young. This plant is poisonous.

Koelreuteria paniculata z 6
**Golden rain tree, Chinese rain tree or
Pride of India**
This excellent tree reaches upwards of
20ft (6m) in 20 years. Upright terminal
panicles, 1ft (30cm) long, hold small,
yellow flowers in mid- to late summer.
These are followed by three-lobed,
bladder-like fruits which are pale green
with a reddish tint, turning yellow-
brown in autumn. The light brownish-
green bark is also attractive. Needs full
sun and a well-drained soil; tolerant of
heat and drought, alkaline soil and
atmospheric pollution.

Kolkwitzia amabilis (*above*) z 4
Beauty bush
A hardy shrub with slender, drooping
branches, clothed in bell-shaped, pink,
yellow-throated flowers in summer. The
calyxes and flower stalks are hairy. It
forms a vase-shaped bush of 6ft (1.8m)
in ten years, and is suited to the rear of
a border. The small, deciduous leaves
are tooth-edged. Peeling, silvery-brown
bark gives winter interest. 'Pink Cloud'
has larger flowers. Grows in most soils,
needing full sun. Cut a third of the old
wood to ground level after flowering.

Paulownia tomentosa z 6
Princess or foxglove tree
Panicles of brown buds form in autumn
on plants that are at least five years old;
these open the following spring as blue-
mauve, foxglove-like flowers. Lobed,
deciduous leaves, up to 10in (25cm)
long, appear after the flowers. Reaches
16ft (5m) in 20 years. If only foliage is
required, cut stems hard back in spring
to produce vigorous shoots with
enormous leaves, 2ft (60cm) across.
Some damage to buds is likely in severe
weather, even in a shelterd site. Needs
deep, rich, soil and full sun.

Rubus × tridel 'Benenden' (*above*)   z 5
This vigorous, shrubby rubus has
arching, thornless, reddish canes and
grows to 10ft (3m). The blackberry-like,
deciduous leaves are lobed and turn
yellow in autumn. In summer it carries
2in (5cm)-wide white flowers with
clusters of yellow stamens. Good on
most soils and happy in some shade.
Prune a third of the oldest shoots out
after flowering; new growth will reach
6ft (1.8m) in a year. This form has
larger flowers than the type. Old shoots
have peeling bark.

Syringa meyeri 'Palibin'   z 3
Korean lilac
This smaller-growing relative of
S. vulgaris is suitable for planting in a
container as well as in the open garden.
It grows slowly, forming a low, neat
shrub 4ft (1.2m) high. During summer
it is covered with small trusses of pale
lilac-pink, fragrant flowers; this is
particularly true of younger plants. The
deciduous leaves are rounded, up to 3in
(8cm) long, with a velvety texture; they
turn yellow in autumn. Succeeds in any
fertile soil and flowers best in partial
shade. Pruning unnecessary.

Viburnum opulus 'Roseum'   z 3
Snowball shrub
Also classified as *V. opulus* 'Sterile', this
form of the guelder rose has creamy-
white, snowball-like heads of sterile
flowers which weigh down the spreading
branches in summer. The light green
deciduous leaves often turn attractive
shades in autumn. Quickly reaching 12ft
(3.6m), it can be left to form a mound;
alternatively, a third of the oldest shoots
can be pruned back in spring. Grows in
all soils, even with extremes of dryness
or wetness. Non-fruiting.

FOLIAGE

Berberis × ottawensis 'Purpurea'   z 5
A vigorous, deciduous barberry which
reaches 12ft (3.6m), it carries large,
purple, ovate leaves along the upright,
thorny shoots. Racemes of golden-
yellow flowers form in spring, hanging
clusters of red berries in autumn. Useful
as an informal hedge or planted with
white or gold variegated shrubs such as
Rhamnus alaternus 'Argenteovariegata'.
B. thunbergii 'Rose Glow' is smaller,
with pinky-white leaves. Grow in full
sun; avoid over-dry soils. Prune out a
few old stems occasionally.

Cotinus coggygria 'Royal Purple'   z 4
(*above*)
Smoke tree or bush
The leaves of this deciduous shrub open
a deep wine red, changing through the
growing season to a velvety maroon.
They are rounded and turn shades of
orange, scarlet and red in autumn.
Plume-like panicles of pink blossom are
at their best in late summer. The plant
reaches 10ft (3m) if left unpruned, or it
can be cut back each spring to produce
vigorous 6ft (1.8m) shoots with large
leaves but no flowers. Plant in rich,
deep soil, in a sunny position.

Gleditsia triacanthos 'Sunburst'   z 5
Golden honey locust
Vibrant, golden-yellow, late spring
foliage characterizes this plant. The
leaves are pinnate or bipinnate. It makes
an elegantly branching tree, 13ft (4m)
tall after five years; on older plants the
bark is deeply fissured. It does not bear
the vicious spines of the species. An
ideal host for *Clematis macropetala*.
Needs rich, well-drained soil, full sun
and protection from winds as branches
are brittle. Prune for shape when young.

Pyrus salicifolia 'Pendula' (*above*)   z 5
Weeping silver pear
Few small trees are as graceful as this
specimen plant. In spring the small,
lanceolate leaves open with a silvery
down and are followed by small clusters
of creamy-white flowers. Reaching its
full height of about 15ft (4.5m) in 15
years, its pendulous branches sweep to
the ground. Mature plants have a mop-
headed appearance. In summer the
foliage is a cool greenish-grey. Spring-
flowering blue or purple clematis make
excellent companions. Grows in most
soils and needs full sun.

Rhododendron yakushimanum   z 6
This dome-shaped evergreen
rhododendron has unusual young leaves
that resemble silvery shuttlecocks. They
appear from a collar of older, dark
green, leathery leaves which are 2in
(5cm) long and have brown, felted
undersides. The silver hairs disappear as
the leaves mature. Trusses of flowers
open earlier, apple-blossom pink, fading
to white. Very slow-growing, reaching
3-4ft (90-120cm) in ten years, it needs a
well-drained, acid soil in some shade
but no pruning.

Robinia pseudoacacia 'Frisia'   z 4
Golden false acacia
Similar to, if more slender than *Gleditsia
triacanthos* 'Sunburst', this tree has 6in
(15cm)-long pinnate leaves that open
bright yellow-green in late spring, turn
green during summer and butter yellow
in autumn. The petioles are orange.
Mature trees bear clusters of pea-like
white flowers in mid-summer. It grows
rapidly, achieving 20ft (6m) in 20 years.
Container-grown specimens establish
themselves best. Needs moist, well-
drained loam and shelter from winds.

Autumn colour

Sambucus racemosa 'Plumosa Aurea'
(*below*)   z 4
This form of the red-berried elder is one
of the finest deciduous shrubs for
golden-yellow foliage. The fern-like,
dissected, pinnate leaves are 3-6in (8-
15cm) long and wide. The largest leaves
are produced by plants that are pruned
hard back each spring: unpruned plants
bear large panicles of white flowers,
followed by translucent red berries. It
can reach 6ft (1.8m) but annual pruning
will reduce height and spread. Most
soils are suitable; some shade is good, to
protect the leaves from sun-scorch.

Sorbus aria   z 5
Whitebeam
In spring leaves emerge greyish-white
on this tree and turn bright green
above, with dense silvery-grey hairs
beneath. Autumn leaves are brownish-
yellow. In early summer 4in (10cm)-
wide panicles of white flowers appear,
followed by bunches of scarlet fruits. It
reaches 20ft (6m) in ten years with a
rounded crown. The leaves of
'Lutescens' have creamy-white hairs. A
fine specimen tree, it can also be trained
over a wall, archway or pillar. Most soils
are suitable; tolerates alkalinity.

Weigela florida 'Foliis Purpureis'   z 5
The leaves of this deciduous shrub are
flushed purple in spring and darken
during summer. Foxglove-like purple-
pink flowers appear in late spring along
the arching branches. 'Variegata' has
leaves with creamy-white margins and
pink flowers, while 'Looymansii Aurea'
has golden foliage and pale pink flowers.
Plants grow in all types of soil, reaching
2 × 2ft (60 × 60cm). To maintain good
leaf colour on established plants, prune
out a third of the old wood in early
summer after flowering.

FOLIAGE

Acer japonicum (*above*)   z 5
Japanese maple
The large, lobed, red-veined leaves of
this tree turn red in autumn. 'Aureum'
has golden-yellow summer foliage and
darker autumn colour; 'Vitifolium' has
fan-shaped leaves that turn plum-
purple; 'Aconitifolium' has dissected
leaves with orange-red autumn tints.
Groups of reddish-purple flowers form
from early spring. The spreading open
habit reaches 10ft (3m). Needs slightly
acid, moist soil; best in partial shade.

Amelanchier lamarckii (*below*)   z 4
Snowy mespilus or juneberry
Crimson, orange and red autumn foliage
adorns this plant. The small leaves open
coppery-pink. Plentiful sprays of star-
shaped, white spring flowers become
scarlet fruits in summer; these turn
black in autumn. 'Ballerina' has more
abundant pink-tinged flowers but less
striking autumn foliage. Makes a small
cone-shaped tree or multi-stemmed
shrub of 20ft (6m) in 20 years. Use
against a dark background or as a lawn
specimen. Plants need moist soil and
little pruning.

Euonymus sachalinensis (*below*)   z 5
This shrub has large leaves which turn
orange-red in autumn, enhanced by red
fruits with deep pink seeds. The leaves
open dark green and have a reddish
tinge in summer. Makes 13 × 13ft (4 ×
4m) in ten years. *E. europaeus*
'Atropurpureus' has purple summer
foliage and red autumn colour; *E. e.*
'Aucubifolius' has yellow and white
mottled leaves, tinted pink in autumn.
E. alatus 'Compacta' is the dwarf form
of 'Burning Bush' and has scarlet
autumn foliage and red fruits. Needs
sun; will grow on alkaline soil.

Fraxinus oxycarpa 'Raywood'   z 6
Raywood ash
This ash is beautiful in autumn when its
10in (25cm)-long pinnate leaves turn
reddish-purple. Clusters of creamy-
white, petalless, fragrant flowers appear
in late spring, developing into small,
orange-brown, key-like fruits. The
canopy broadens with age and makes it
a fine specimen tree, reaching 35ft
(10.5m) in 20 years. It casts only slight
shade, useful for underplanting. 'Flame'
has brilliant red autumn leaves. Grow in
any soil, in full sun.

Hydrangea quercifolia   z 5
Oak-leaf hydrangea
The large, deciduous, oak-shaped leaves
of this shrubby hydrangea turn bright
reddish-orange to purple in autumn.
From late summer the plant carries
conical panicles of white flowers which
fade to pink as they age and turn brown
in winter. Growth is slow, making a
rounded bush of 4 × 4ft (1.2 × 1.2m)
after ten years. Shoots tend to be brittle.
Thrives in sun or shade and grows in
most fertile, moist soils. Can be wall
trained. Pruning is unnecessary, but
plants will re-grow if cut back.

Liquidambar styraciflua (*below*)   z 5
Sweet gum
Similar to the maple, this tree differs in
having alternate lobed leaves which
release a distinctive aromatic fragrance
when crushed; they turn red with hints
of yellow, orange and purple in autumn.
Slow to establish, it can reach 20ft (6m)
in 20 years with a regular, conical
canopy. Older trees have fissured bark.
'Worplesdon' and 'Lane Roberts' have
more upright-growing branches and
deep crimson-purple autumn foliage.
Grow in full sun in rich, moist soil.

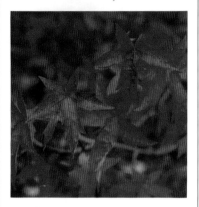

Malus tschonoskii (*below*)   z 6
Of all the crab apples, this species has
the most spectacular autumn colours,
the leaves turning yellow, then shades of
red, crimson and orange. Clusters of
rose-pink spring flowers are followed by
yellow-brown fruits. This species has an
upright habit, growing up to 25ft (7.5m)
in height in 20 years, with a spread of
5-10ft (1.5-3m). Enliven the grey-green
summer foliage with the climbers
Clematis macropetala or *C.* 'Bill
Mackenzie', which have bluish-mauve
macropetals and yellow flowers
respectively. Grow plants in sun in
moist, rich soil.

Prunus sargentii (*above*)   z 5
Sargent's cherry
One of the first trees to colour-up in
autumn, this has brilliant orange and
crimson foliage. In spring the abundant
pale pink flowers are followed by the
leaves which open bronzy-red and turn
dark green with strong veins. Chestnut-
brown bark is a feature of older trees. It
can reach 20 × 16ft (6 × 5m) in ten
years. Grow singly or in a small group;
underplant with spring bulbs such as
Narcissus triandrus 'Thalia'. Best in full
sun; needs moist, rich soil.

Quercus coccinea   z 4
Scarlet oak
During autumn the foliage of this tree
turns scarlet; branch by branch, before
falling; some leaves often persist until
mid-winter. The leaves are up to 6in
(15cm) long, deeply-lobed with bristly
tips; they are light green in summer.
Slow to establish, the tree reaches 23ft
(7m) in ten years and ultimately 70ft
(21m), with an open, broad crown. The
red oak, *Q. rubra*, is over 100ft (30m)
tall when mature, with 10in (25cm)-long
matt leaves. Best in full sun, on acid
soil. Tolerates pollution.

Spiraea prunifolia   z 4
Bridal wreath spiraea
The arching branches of this dense-
growing shrub are ablaze with colour in
autumn when the finely toothed leaves
turn bright orangey-red. The branches
can reach 6ft (1.8m) and are clothed in
spring with button-like, double, white
flowers. The leaves are mid-green in
summer. Stands out against dark plants
and works well with an underplanting of
low-growing bamboos. Grows in
moderate shade or full sun; avoid
alkaline soils. Prune out a third of the
older wood after flowering.

BERRIES AND FRUIT

Callicarpa bodinieri giraldii (*below*)   z 6
Clusters of lilac-purple fruits form on
this deciduous shrub in autumn and can
last for several months. The dull green,
lanceolate leaves turn purplish at the
same time. Small, mauve flowers appear
in late summer. The upright stems
reach 6ft (1.8m) after ten years.
'Profusion' is a particularly reliable form
with larger fruits. Plant in acid soil with
added leaf mould; may suffer in hot,
dry summers on thin soil. Grow more
than one plant to guarantee berries.

Clerodendrum trichotomum fargesii
(*below*)   z 6
This shrub is a remarkable sight when
mature. In late summer the delicate
buds open into fragrant, star-like, white
flowers, set in maroon calyxes. Electric
blue fruits follow, held in the now deep
red calyxes. The large, deciduous leaves
have a fetid smell if crushed; they take
on purple tints in autumn. It makes 8 ×
8ft (2.4 × 2.4m) in ten years. Grow in
some shade, in moist, non-alkaline soil.
Prune out winter damage. The fruits
glow in sunlight. Prone to whitefly,
mealy bug and red spider mite.

Cotoneaster × watereri 'Cornubia' z 6
(*above*)
This semi-evergreen vigorous shrub is one of the finest tall cotoneasters. In autumn its branches are weighed down by bunches of bright red berries. These are preceded in early summer by clusters of white flowers. The small dark green leaves are lanceolate. Graceful with spreading branches, it makes 10 × 10ft (3 × 3m) in ten years. 'Rothschildianus' has clusters of yellow fruits and can make a small, single-stemmed tree. *C. × watereri* has large crops of orange-red berries. Grow in full sun or part shade in moist, fertile soil.

Malus 'John Downie' z 5
Probably the finest fruiting crab apple, this forms a medium-sized tree some 26ft (8m) tall when mature. The white, spring flowers are followed by small fruits which turn bright orange-scarlet in late summer and autumn. They are edible and used for jelly. 'Professor Sprenger' has amber fruits which persist into winter, 'Dartmouth' has large, reddish-purple fruits. Grow in full sun on moist, fertile soil. Prune to allow light in to ripen the fruit.

Pyracantha 'Mohave' z 6
This stiff-growing, evergreen shrub makes a 6ft (1.8m) vase-shaped specimen in ten years. Abundant small, white summer flowers are followed by orange-red berries that persist into winter, birds permitting. Leaves are dark green and shiny. It is good for windy areas and resistant to fireblight and scab. 'Orange Glow' has dark stems and large clusters of orange fruits. 'Shawnee' has orange-yellow berries that colour early. Full sun gives the best berries, on moist, rich soil.

Sorbus commixta (*below*)　　　z 5
Scarlet rowan
This tree not only has clusters of large, bright red berries in autumn but also dramatic foliage colour. The large pinnate leaves emerge coppery in spring, turn glossy green in summer, then purple and finally flaming scarlet during autumn. It has a columnar habit when young, broadening with age, and reaches 16ft (5m) in ten years. *S. aucuparia* 'Beissneri' has shiny coppery-orange stems. Needs full sun and grows on most soils, including alkaline.

Viburnum opulus 'Fructuluteo'　　z 3
(*below*)
This form of the guelder rose carries bunches of translucent, lemon yellow, pink-tinged fruits in autumn. They are preceded by corymbs of white flowers. Large, lobed, light green leaves take on warm shades in autumn. For larger flowers and golden-yellow fruits which darken as they ripen, grow the cultivar 'Xanthocarpum'; 'Notcutt's Variety' has red fruits. The spreading habit reaches 8ft (2.4m) in ten years. Plants are tolerant of most soils, dry or wet. Prune out one-third of old wood annually, or leave to grow freely.

FLOWERS

Abelia × grandiflora (*above*)　　z 6
This semi-evergreen shrub carries pale pink, slightly scented flowers on its arching branches from late summer into autumn. It grows to 5 × 5ft (1.5 × 1.5m) in ten years, rarely any taller. Olive green ovate leaves are up to 2in (6cm) long. 'Francis Mason' has gold-variegated leaves. A good companion for autumn-flowering bulbs such as *Schizostylis coccinea*. Prune out a third of the old shoots in early spring; take care as the branches are brittle. Grow in moist soil, in full sun.

Ceanothus 'Autumnal Blue' z 8
One of the hardiest evergreen forms of the Californian lilac, this densely-growing, bushy shrub carries panicles of fluffy, dark blue flowers from late summer onwards. Green stems bear leaves that are shiny green above, grey below. Reaches 10ft (3m) in ten years. Use at the back of a border or as a host for a spring-flowering scrambling climber such as *Clematis* 'Marie Boisselot'. Can be wall-trained. Needs full sun and deep, rich soil. If damaged in winter cut hard back.

Hydrangea paniculata 'Grandiflora' z 4
Flowering from late summer into autumn, this makes a spectacular specimen plant. The huge panicles of white, sterile florets fade to pink before turning brown. Each panicle can be 18 × 12in (45 × 30cm). The broad leaves turn yellow in autumn. For the best flowers, cut back all shoots in spring to within two buds of the base: regrowth will be 10 × 10ft (3 × 3m) in ten years. Protect from strong winds if grown as a standard as the stems are brittle. Needs slight shade and deep, rich, moist soil.

27

CLIMBERS AND WALL SHRUBS

Garden walls present the best opportunities for growing climbers and shrubs that benefit from the support and protection offered, whether it be from the cold, the wind or the sun. Trellis, screens, fences, pergolas, arcades, arbours, arches and summer houses also provide good support for climbing plants and have an immediate impact on the garden while introducing a valuable vertical element.

Certain plants are better suited to specific structures according to their vigour and means of attachment. Reasonably vigorous twining climbers that provide adequate cover without swamping the structure are suited to pergolas and arbours. Either a single species, like wisteria, can be used for spectacular display at one time of the year or a collection of plants, including *Clematis armandii* and *Vitis vinifera* 'Purpurea', can be used to provide a succession of flowering and foliage interest.

Slow-growing scramblers, such as roses and *Jasminum nudiflorum*, that require careful tying in because they do not actually attach themselves to the structure, work well on small trellis screens; while self-clinging climbers such as ivies, *Schizophragma* and *Hydrangea petiolaris*, are best suited to walls which provide a suitable surface for their aerial roots or suckers to adhere to. The habit of a plant may also make it suitable for growing against a wall. *Kerria japonica*, *Pyracantha coccinea*, *Chaenomeles* species,

Right: Parthenocissus tricuspidata, the Boston ivy, is a vigorous climber that turns crimson-purple in the autumn. It attaches itself to walls by means of sticky tendrils and is tolerant of shady conditions.

Left: Pyracantha coccinea is a vigorous, evergreen shrub of stiff, erect habit suitable for training against a shady wall. In late spring or early summer it is covered with small, white flowers, which are followed by a plentiful crop of orange berries. These specimens, trained to great effect like espalier fruit trees, should be trimmed in early autumn.

Forsythia suspensa and *Robinia hispida* all have fairly stiff, upright stems that grow close to the wall and can be pruned and trained to fill the available space.

Climbers that hook their stems onto the support with the help of coiling tendrils need wires to wrap themselves around, or alternatively are well adapted to threading their way through other plants as they do in their wild state. When choosing a host plant the climber's vigour should be taken into account.

Many other factors will govern the choice of plants. The style of the garden dictates whether the plants should be slow-growing and neatly tied in to give a controlled form or whether they should be given a fairly free rein to grow at will. For example, the relaxed effect that is achieved by allowing honeysuckle to cascade over a structure with its scent mingling with that of other vigorous climbers, such as rambling roses and summer jasmine, is perfect for a cottage, romantic or wild garden. In contrast, a strictly pruned and flat-trained *Magnolia grandiflora* with its large, smooth, architectural leaves and single, stiff, waxy-white summer flowers, would be a fitting focal point in an enclosed courtyard.

It may be that a fast-growing climber is required to camouflage an ugly building or cover a trellis screen placed in front of an eyesore: *Persicaria aubertii* (the mile-a-minute or Russian vine), *Parthenocissus quinquefolia*, Virginia creeper, and the related species

P. tricuspidata (the Boston ivy), *Vitis coignetiae* (the crimson glory vine), *Celastrus orbiculatus* (the Oriental bittersweet), *Akebia quinata* and *Clematis montana* are all suitable for this. However, these plants need a lot of space and require constant pruning or have to be replaced in order to prevent them from swamping all other nearby plants, lifting tiles or blocking gutters. Their speed of growth, which can be their greatest asset, has also earned them a bad reputation.

In fact most climbers are fast growers which need pruning and tying in to keep them under control. Some need near constant attention, others can be attended to once a year, either in the winter or in early spring or after flowering, depending on the requirements of the plant. It is always advisable to ensure that the structure is sound before the plant starts to cover it and that it is large enough to accommodate the plant when mature.

The aspect of the wall is an important consideration when choosing suitable plants to clothe it. A protected wall that receives the sun for most of the day is likely to be several degrees warmer than one that receives little direct sunlight. Marginally hardy plants can survive when grown against such south-facing, warm walls. For example, in areas where *Clematis montana* is perfectly hardy, *C. armandii* will require a southern aspect. Many Californian and Central American species such as the attractive *Ceanothus* and

Below: Climbers are particularly useful in the garden to create quick screens and an instant vertical element. Here, a large-leaved evergreen ivy, *Hedera colchica* 'Dentata Variegata', mingles with the autumnal foliage of *Parthenocissus quinquefolia*, the Virginia creeper, to create a "volcanic" effect. On the left is the herbaceous golden hop, *Humulus lupulus* 'Aureus'.

Right: Wisterias are fast-growing climbers with flowers that are generally violet-blue to mauve. There are also white- and pink-flowered forms of the commonly grown species which are attractive alternatives, as can be seen from this salmon pink variety.

Fremontodendron californicum will flourish in temperate climates when grown against a wall. *Magnolia grandiflora* makes a large freestanding tree in Mediterranean climates but will also survive and flower in areas where the summer rainfall is higher and season shorter when placed against a wall. The way in which a wall absorbs and then releases heat produces not only additional winter warmth and hotter summers but also extends the season, allowing the wood to ripen well and survive the winter cold.

In contrast, there are many plants that prefer shady situations – including *Jasminum nudiflorum*, *Kerria japonica*, *Garrya elliptica*, *Berberidopsis corallina* and *Lapageria rosea* – but this does not necessarily mean that they are frost-hardy; many shade-loving climbers are still tender. There are also a number of plants that tolerate the poorest conditions and are able to clothe seemingly inhospitable walls. These include ivies as well as the climbing *Euonymus radicans*, *Parthenocissus* species and *Hydrangea petiolaris*.

Camellias, winter sweet (*Chimonanthus praecox*) and *Jasminum nudiflorum* which blossom early in spring, when there is still a risk of frost, benefit from growing against a wall that does not receive direct morning sun, because this would defrost the blooms too quickly and damage them.

A notable way of extending the season of certain plants and adding a new dimension to a design is to grow climbers through other plants. The most vigorous climbers such as *Vitis coignetiae*, *Celastrus orbiculatus* and *Wisteria sinensis* are successful only in tall trees, but there are a number of other species that grow happily through shrubs without swamping them. Clematis are the most frequently used in this instance. Herbaceous climbers such as *Codonopsis convolvulacea*, *Tropaeolum speciosum* and *Lathyrus grandiflorus* are also well suited.

Left: Clematis 'Perle d'Azur' is an outstanding large-flowered cultivar, which is covered in blossom in late summer.

Below: Wisteria has traditionally adorned the warm, sunny face of many country houses. The scented, pea-like flowers are produced abundantly if specimens are pruned in summer, after flowering, and again, more severely, in winter, when plants are dormant.

Quick-growing

FLOWERS

Clematis × jackmanii (above)   z 5
A succession of large, velvety, purple
blooms cover this clematis from early to
mid-summer or even into autumn.
Cultivars include 'Gypsy Queen' (violet-
purple), 'Perle d'Azur (pale blue) and
'Comtesse de Bouchaud' (pink). Grow
through *Pyrus salicifolia* 'Pendula', with
its silver-grey foliage, and underplant
with *Allium christophii* and *Geranium
endressii*. Reaches 10 × 3ft (3m × 90cm)
in moisture-rich soil; prune hard in late
winter or early spring to within 3ft
(90cm) of the ground.

Clematis montana (above)   z 5
In late spring this plant is covered with
four-petalled, vanilla-scented, creamy-
white flowers. Use it to brighten a
north-facing wall or grow it through a
deciduous tree for early colour. Reaches
20ft (6m) in ten years. 'Elizabeth' has
soft pink flowers, 'Picton's Variety'
deep pink and 'Grandiflora' pure white.
C. montana rubens has pink flowers with
golden stamens and bronze foliage.
Plant with the roots in shade in moist,
rich soil. Prune immediately after
flowering to prevent rampancy.

Lonicera japonica 'Halliana'   z 4
The flowers of this honeysuckle open
white and change to orangey-yellow as
they age. They are produced throughout
the summer and have a strong
fragrance. Small, shiny, black berries
follow the flowers. The foliage is bright
green. It quickly covers a pergola or
garden structure, and can also be used
as ground cover. Grows in most soils, in
sun or shade. Prune hard back in early
spring to prevent growth developing
into a knotted mass.

Wisteria sinensis (above)   z 5
Chinese wisteria
Racemes of mauve or white scented
flowers appear in early summer, before
the long compound leaves. 'Black
Dragon' has dark purple blooms, 'Alba'
white. It achieves 30ft (9m) if grown in
full sun on a wall or pergola, and up to
100ft (30m) in a tree. Twines
anticlockwise; the hardier Japanese
wisteria, *W. floribunda*, spirals
clockwise. Cut back in late winter and
reduce shoots in late summer. In cold
areas protect from early frosts. Plant
containerized specimens year-round.

FOLIAGE

Aristolochia macrophylla   z 4
Dutchman's pipe
With heart-shaped, bright green leaves
some 12in (30cm) long, this climber has
a tropical look. It reaches 20ft (6m) in
ten years on a wall, fence, over a tree
stump or in a tree. Pairs of small
tubular flowers open in mid- to late
summer in the leaf axils; they are
greenish-yellow and purplish-brown.
A. tomentosa is less vigorous, growing to
10ft (3m), with smaller dark, evergreen
leaves. Needs a good fertile soil. Prune
lightly in late summer or early spring.

Hedera colchica 'Dentata Variegata'   z 5
This Persian ivy has the largest leaves of
the genus and is an ideal evergreen
backcloth to autumn-fruiting climbers
and wall shrubs. The large, leathery
leaves are creamy-yellow with irregular,
rolled margins; when crushed they give
off a spicy smell. It climbs to over 12ft
(3.6m) over a wall or pergola. Virginia
creeper, *Parthenocissus quinquefolia*, is a
good partner, with its crimson autumn
foliage. Grows in sun or deep shade in
any good soil. Trim back frost-bitten
growth in spring.

Holboellia coriacea   z 9
A vigorous twiner, reaching 20ft (6m),
with glossy, evergreen leaves composed
of three leaflets. The spring flowers have
a sweet, strong scent. Cylindrical,
bloomy, purple pods follow in long hot
summers if the plant is in sun. Grow
through a tree with an open habit, or on
a sunny wall with other sun-loving
climbers such as the double, yellow-
flowered *Rosa banksiae* 'Lutea'. Plant in
fertile, well-drained soil and only prune
to keep the plant within bounds.

AUTUMN COLOUR

Akebia quinata (above)   z 4
After a mild spring and hot summer,
this vigorous twining shrub produces
dark purple, sausage-shaped fruits
which split to reveal black seeds bedded
in white flesh. The leaves comprise five
notched leaflets. Reddish-purple,
fragrant flowers appear from spring
onwards. It is evergreen in mild areas,
deciduous in cold. Reaching 33ft (10m),
it can be trained over a tree, hedge, wall
or pergola. Suits most soils; needs sun
to fruit. Prune after flowering, leaving
some branches if fruiting is likely.

Ampelopsis brevipedunculata z 4
(*below*)

Grown for its attractive fruits, this climber can reach 8ft (2.4m). It has three- or five-lobed leaves, dark green above and paler and hairy underneath. The flowers appear in late summer, followed by masses of small fruits which turn from white to china blue to deep purple after a long hot summer. Grow in fertile soil, in sun. Plants need to be supported and trained, and are useful for covering walls and growing into trees. Fruiting and winter-hardiness is encouraged by restricting the roots.

Persicaria aubertii z 4
Russian vine

The tightly twining, hairy stems of this climber reach 25ft (7.5m) in ten years. It is one of the best plants for clothing old stumps, bare banks, garden structures, and unsightly fencing. The leaves are heart-shaped. Frothy, creamy-white panicles of flowers appear in summer, followed by rust-coloured seed heads. Cut some vines back to ground level in spring to prevent the plant becoming a tangled mass. Grows in almost any soil, in sun or partial shade.

Pyracantha coccinea z 6

This firethorn quickly makes a freestanding wall shrub 10ft (3m) tall. Evergreen, with sharp woody spines, the branches are covered with hawthorn-like masses of flowers in summer, followed by dense clusters of orange-red fruits. In a mild winter, fruits last until the following spring. The dark green leaves are oval and finely-toothed. Cut back long growths after flowering. Grow with other summer-flowering climbers. Grows happily on north- or east-facing walls, in any fertile soil; tolerates pollution.

Vitis 'Brant' (*above*) z 6

Also listed as *V. vinifera* 'Brant', this popular, hardy, fruiting vine is capable of growing to 30ft (10m) on suitable supports. It produces sweet, edible aromatic bunches of grapes, which are blackish-purple when ripe, covered in a beautiful waxy bloom. The leaves take on a range of deep reddish-purple tints in autumn before they eventually fall. Best grown against a wall, although it will also succeed on a pergola or arbour. Grows in most fertile soils and should only be pruned back if plants are getting out of control.

Vitis vinifera 'Purpurea' (*above*) z 6
Teinturier

The foliage of this remarkable cultivar opens grey-white in spring, turning red in the summer, darkening to deep purple in autumn. Like all grape vines, it climbs by means of tendrils and can reach 12ft (3.6m) in a single season. Prune during the dormant season, and in mid-summer to curb excessive growth – but never in spring and early summer as this causes profuse bleeding (an excessive flow of sap). Fruits are carried on one-year-old stems.

Shade tolerant

FLOWERS

Camellia japonica z 7

All cultivars of this shrub have glossy, evergreen leaves. 'Contessa Lavinia Maggi' has pale pink flowers with rose stripes; 'Adolphe Audusson' has blood red flowers; 'Alba Simplex' has white flowers with gold stamens. Plants reach 30 × 30ft (9 × 9m) and do best in moist, acid or neutral, peaty soil; mulch to prevent drying out which causes bud-drop. Good in a shaded, sheltered spot such as a north- or west-facing wall; complements ivies and spring-flowering bulbs. Deadhead and prune in spring.

Clematis 'Lasurstern' (*above*) z 5

This vigorous clematis can reach 10ft (3m). Blue flowers, up to 7in (18cm) across, cover the plant in early summer; a second flush of fewer, smaller blooms follows in early autumn. Eight broad, pointed sepals surround cream stamens. Grow in humus-rich soil with plenty of moisture, shading the roots with an underplanting of low-growing shrubs. In early spring cut out dead wood and shorten stems to a pair of healthy buds; in shade, reduce some shoots to 12in (30cm). Sun can bleach the flowers.

Clematis 'Nelly Moser' z 6

The flat flowers of this clematis are up to 7in (18cm) wide and are composed of eight pale mauve-pink sepals, each with a central purple bar which bleaches in sunlight. The plant either has two flushes of flowers in summer and autumn, or a slightly larger, early autumn crop, effected by hard pruning in early spring. Grow through another climber or wall shrub. Needs humus-rich, moist soil and shade for the roots. Prune as for *Clematis* 'Lasurstern'. Ideal for a shady spot.

Forsythia suspensa z 5

Bell-shaped yellow flowers cover this shrub in early spring. It can reach 25ft (7.5m) when trained on a wall, where the slender branches hang freely. Flowers are carried on the previous season's wood; prune immediately after flowering to promote new growth. The leaves emerge after the blooms and are a fresh green throughout summer. *F. s. atrocaulis* has purple-black young stems. Grow with clematis or other climbers for summer interest. Useful for a north- or east-facing wall and most fertile soils.

Hydrangea petiolaris (*above*) z 4

Also listed as *H. anomala petiolaris*, this climbing hydrangea clings with small aerial roots. Slow to establish, it reaches 10ft (3m) in ten years but eventually can make 50ft (15m). Flowers appear from early summer in large, flat clusters comprising off-white fertile heads surrounded by white sterile heads. In autumn the leaves often turn a rich yellow before falling. Peeling rusty-brown bark provides winter interest. Grows in most fertile soils and is very tolerant of pollution. Support and train until established; prune only to keep within bounds.

Kerria japonica 'Pleniflora' z 4

A deciduous suckering shrub with stiff upright growth that sits well against a wall. This is the vigorous double form reaching 10ft (3m) high, with deep golden-yellow flowers. 'Variegata' is more compact. The less common single form (*K. japonica*) has flowers that resemble large buttercups and a more graceful habit. The green stems set off winter-flowering plants such as *Viburnum × bodnantense*. Grow in moist, fertile soil. Suckers and older stems should be thinned after flowering.

Lapageria rosea (*above*) z 8

A sheltered, shaded or semi-shaded wall is essential to grow this tender evergreen climber. It will not stand strong sunlight and needs a cool, moist, acid soil, rich in organic matter, to grow well. Fleshy, bell-shaped pink flowers hang in clusters from the leaf axils in summer and autumn, set off by the leathery, heart-shaped foliage. The tough, wire-like, twining stems can reach 12ft (3.6m) with support. *L. r. albiflora* has glistening white flowers; 'Nash Court' has pink bells. Prune to keep in check or to remove dead wood.

Lathyrus latifolius (*above*) z 5
Everlasting pea

This perennial climbs to 6ft (1.8m) every year. The bluish-green leaves have tendrils which support the flattened winged stems. Purple flowers are held in dense racemes throughout the summer. Cultivars include the white 'Albus' and 'White Pearl', pink 'Splendens' and the dark purple and red 'Pink Beauty'. Useful for masking the bare lower parts of other climbers. Grows well in most soils. Takes several seasons to settle, dislikes being transplanted.

Lonicera periclymenum 'Belgica' z 4
(*below*)

The highly scented flowers of the "early Dutch" honeysuckle are cream, ageing to golden yellow with rose tints. They appear in spring and again in late summer. The "late Dutch", 'Serotina', has darker flowers which appear from mid-summer to autumn. Shiny red berries follow. Plants can reach 15ft (4.5m), the twining stems growing through other shrubs or trees. Plant in deep, shaded, moisture-retentive soil. Prune lightly after flowering.

Schizophragma integrifolium z 7

Related to the hydrangea, this plant climbs to 40ft (12m) by means of aerial roots. Lateral branches bear 1ft (30cm)-wide inflorescences of creamy-white flowers and marginal sepals that are white with dark veins. The heart-shaped, deciduous leaves are up to 7in (18cm) long. It is suitable for a wall, tree or tree stump. *S. hydrangeoides* is smaller and hardier (z 5) with reddish young stems. Grow in good soil and support the stems until aerial roots are established. Prune in winter if needed.

Tropaeolum speciosum z 7
Scottish flame flower

The deep-rooted, creeping rhizomes of this hardy herbaceous perennial produce long strand-like stems that reach 10ft (3m), climbing by means of leaf stalks. The deep crimson flowers appear from mid-summer until early autumn, followed by bright blue fruits set in persistent red calyces. The lobed leaves are pale green. Train on a wall through trellis or netting, or through a dark-leaved evergreen such as box or yew. Plant in cool, moist, humus-rich soil. Thrives in cool conditions: ideal for north- or east-facing positions.

FOLIAGE

Euonymus fortunei radicans   z 5
This leathery-leaved evergreen climber
uses aerial roots to reach 12ft (3.6m)
with a broad spread. It has a juvenile
phase which ends when it stops
climbing, at which point it produces
larger leaves and flowers and fruit.
'Variegatus' has white-edged leaves,
often tinged pink; 'Silver Gem' has
white variegations; the foliage of
'Coloratus' turns reddish-purple in
winter, especially on poor soil; 'Vegetus'
bears deep orange fruits in autumn.
Grows well in most soils, including
alkaline. A good substitute for ivy, it
needs no regular pruning.

Hedera helix 'Tricolor'   z 5
The evergreen common English ivy
climbs to 30 × 15ft (9 × 4.5m) by
means of aerial roots. The leaves of
'Tricolor' have broad, creamy-white
margins, tinged rose red in winter.
'Goldheart' has yellow-centred leaves;
the dark green leaves of 'Atropurpurea'
turn deep purple in winter; 'Digitata'
has deeply lobed leaves, 'Buttercup' rich
yellow leaves that turn pale green with
age. Grow up a tree or over a wall or
fence. Tolerates shade and pollution.
Cut out shoots reverting to green.

Humulus lupulus 'Aureus' (*above*)   z 3
Golden hop
This herbaceous perennial grows to 20ft
(6m) in a single season, forming a mat
of twining stems across a fence or over a
pergola. The yellow palmate leaves are
up to 6in (15cm) long, with three to five
lobes. Small flowers appear in autumn,
followed by cone-like spikes of aromatic
(if rubbed) fruits. Needs moist, fertile
soil. Cut back old growth in spring. Dry
fruits can be used in arrangements.

Parthenocissus henryana (*above*)   z 7
The leaves of this deciduous, self-
clinging vine have three to five dark
green or bronze ovate leaflets with
silvery-white veins. The foliage turns
red in autumn, highlighting the dark
blue fruits. The tendrils are tipped by
sucker-pads which cling to walls or
trees, reaching 30ft (9m). Needs some
shelter in cold areas and moist fertile
soil; leaf colour is strongest in half-
shade. Growth can be rampant.

AUTUMN AND WINTER EFFECT

Azara microphylla   z 9
In late winter and very early spring the
vanilla-like fragrance of this tender
shrub fills the air. The yellow flowers
have no petals but prominent stamens,
and are held on the underside of the
spray-like twigs in small clusters. Each
dark green, evergreen leaf has a large
leaf-like stipule at its base. Grows up to
22ft (7m), but even mature plants can
be killed in a severe winter. Needs a
moist loamy soil, and shelter from cold,
drying winds. Prune in spring to
remove dead or unwanted growth.

Berberidopsis corallina   z 8
Coral plant
The globular, berberis-like flowers of
this evergreen climbing shrub are deep
crimson and hang in clusters in late
summer and early autumn. The
leathery, oval or heart-shaped leaves are
edged with spiny teeth. Plants can reach
15ft (4.5m) or more on a shaded wall.
Does best in a lime-free, moist sandy
loam, with protection from buffeting
winds. Mulch after planting; prune to
remove dead or unwanted growth.

Chaenomeles speciosa (*below*)   z 5
In mild weather flowers appear on the
bare stems of this spiny shrub from
mid-winter into spring. The species has
scarlet or blood red flowers but there are
many cultivars, including the pink,
semi-double 'Phylis Moore', white
'Nivalis' and salmon pink 'Umbilicata'.
Leaves are a glossy dark green. It
reaches 8 × 15ft (2.4 × 4.5m) on a wall
in fertile soil; best in partial shade.
Prune all stems after flowering to within
two or three buds of the base. This
prevents breastwood developing.

Cotoneaster horizontalis   z 5
This deciduous shrub has stiff branches
that grow closely against a wall or fence
in a herringbone pattern. In spring they
are smothered with small, scented, pink
flowers (which attract masses of early
bees), followed by red fruits that last
well into winter. Tiny, glossy, dark
green leaves turn orange-red in autumn.
'Variegatus' has cream-variegated
leaves, suffused with red in autumn. It
reaches 4 × 5ft (1.2 × 1.5m) and suits a
dry, shady site, such as a north- or east-
facing wall; succeeds in alkaline soil.
Prune out old branches.

Garrya elliptica   z 7
Silk-tassel bush
Male plants have 6in (15cm)-long grey-
green catkins which appear from mid-
winter into spring. Female plants have
shorter catkins but produce clusters of
silky purple-brown fruits. Both have
leathery evergreen leaves. Grows to 20ft
(6m) in well-drained soil. 'James Roof'
has larger leaves and longer catkins. An
excellent host for the summer-flowering
Clematis viticella which is pruned back
in early winter. Tolerates pollution and
salt; protect from cold, drying, east and
north winds. Prune back long shoots.

Sun-loving

Jasminum nudiflorum   z 5
Winter jasmine
Pale yellow, trumpet-shaped flowers appear on this plant's bare green stems from late autumn to spring, followed by glossy, dark green foliage. The strong, angular stems reach 15ft (4.5m) if trained on a wall; they can then be left to weep. Grow with other climbers such as the scrambling *Clematis* × *jackmanii*. Ideal for a north-facing wall, out of the morning sun (which scorches frosted blooms). Hardiest of the jasmines, it grows in most well-drained soils. Cut out old or dead shoots after flowering.

Parthenocissus tricuspidata (*above*) z 4
Boston ivy
This vigorous, self-clinging climber forms a dense covering on a wall and can reach 65ft (19.5m). The toothed, three-lobed leaves turn crimson in autumn before dropping. 'Veitchii' is a smaller form with purple young foliage and, after a hot summer, bloomy, dark blue fruits. Growing in most positions and soils, this rampant climber may require severe pruning of roots and, in summer, shoots to prevent it clogging gutters and covering windows.

Parthenocissus quinquefolia   z 3
Virginia creeper
Growing to 50ft (15m) or more, this climber is ideal for high walls and trees. The leaves have five leaflets, dull green above, glaucous below which turn to bright scarlet, orange and crimson in autumn. Blue-black fruits are sometimes seen. Plant in any soil, avoiding deep shade, and support young shoots until the sucker-pads have taken hold. Grow with the evergreen, yellow-variegated *Hedera colchica* 'Sulphur Heart' for good effect. Cut plants back hard in summer or winter.

FLOWERS

Abelia floribunda   z 8
This evergreen shrub grows to 10ft (3m) on a warm west- or south-facing wall. Young shoots are downy and red while the flowers are cherry red and appear in drooping clusters of two or three in mid-summer. The conspicuous calyces persist after the 2in (5cm)-long tube of petals has fallen. The leaves are rounded and glossy. Remove old and dead growth immediately after flowering, cutting shoots well back. Grow in moist, loamy soil and mulch heavily to prevent drying out in summer.

Bougainvillea glabra (*below*)   z 9
Massed purple, papery floral bracts cover this rampant evergreen climber in summer. In 'Snow White' the bracts are white with green veins; in 'Magnifica' they are reddish-purple. 'Variegata' has creamy-white margins to its leaves. The coarse stems bear vicious backward-pointing barbs which hook over other plants; tie it in to any other support. It grows to 16ft (5m) in a sheltered, frost-free spot and rich, well-drained soil. Protect your eyes from the sharp barbs when pruning.

Campsis radicans   z 4
Trumpet vine
Exotic trumpet-shaped orange and scarlet flowers appear in late summer on this deciduous self-clinging climber. They are borne at the tips of new shoots and are sometimes followed by spindle-shaped fruits. It can reach 35ft (10.5m) and will grow on a wall or tree stump or will clamber over a roof. 'Flava' has yellow flowers. Plant in any fertile soil, kept moist all summer, and support until the aerial roots are established. Prune back after frosts in early spring.

Ceanothus arboreus 'Trewithen Blue'
(*below*)   z 9
A large-growing Californian lilac with 5in (13cm)-long panicles of deep blue, scented flowers. It can reach 28ft (8.4m) and has flaking bark, downy younger shoots and broad, dark evergreen leaves. *C. sorediatus* 'A.T.Johnson' has bright blue flowers, while 'Autumnal Blue' is hardier with deep blue flowers. They will tolerate all but the thinnest alkaline soils and most are ideal for protected, coastal gardens. Prune only to restrict growth, after flowering (but prune deciduous forms in spring).

Cestrum parqui   z 10
This tender wall shrub is deciduous except in very mild, sheltered areas. The narrow, lance-shaped leaves are 5in (13cm) long and have a pungent, spicy smell when crushed. Greenish-yellow flowers appear in mid- to late summer; they release a powerful fragrance at night. Shiny black berries follow. Plant near a door or window, or at the base of a bare-stemmed climber such as clematis. Grows to 7ft (2m) in most well-drained soils in a warm, sunny position. Prune in spring, removing some of the old growth.

Chimonanthus praecox   z 7
Established plants begin to flower in the coldest winter months, filling the air with a sweet fragrance. The waxy, straw yellow blooms have purple centres and are borne on bare twigs. It reaches 7ft (2m) and can carry a climber such as *Clematis* 'Royalty' which will mask the large, coarse, deciduous foliage during summer. Grow in moist, well-drained soil in a sheltered, sunny spot. Useful on alkaline soils. Prune after flowering, taking out weak shoots. 'Grandiflorus' has deeper yellow flowers.

Clematis armandii (*above*)   z 7
An evergreen clematis which is strong-growing on a warm sheltered wall, where it can reach 15ft (4.5m). Each leaf is composed of three, long, dark green, leathery leaflets that make an excellent background to the creamy-white flowers. These are 3in (8cm) across, vanilla-scented and are carried in clusters from early spring onwards. 'Snowdrift' has pure white flowers, 'Apple Blossom' pink flushed sepals and bronze young leaves. Plant in shaded soil, enriched with organic matter. Prune hard and train after flowering.

***Clematis* 'Ernest Markham'** (*above*)   z 5
Often considered the best of the red-flowered clematis, this reliable cultivar will produce velvety, petunia-red flowers for four months during summer and autumn, if pruned annually. Flowers are 5in (13cm) across, with six broad, rounded sepals. It reaches 8ft (2.4m). Grow through winter fruiting and flowering shrubs such as *Pyracantha* 'Mohave' or *Viburnum* × *bodnantense* 'Deben'. Also looks effective growing through silver-foliaged trees and shrubs. The roots need shaded, rich fertile soil.

Clianthus puniceus   z 9
Glory pea, parrot's bill or lobster claw
This evergreen or semi-evergreen wall shrub can reach 10ft (3m) with some training. It tends to be short-lived but is well worth the effort. Brilliant red, claw-like, 2in (5cm)-long flowers hang in clusters. 'Albus' has white blooms but is less free-flowering. The attractive pinnate leaves are 6in (15cm) long and have pale undersides. Needs a hot, sunny, west- or south-facing wall and very well drained soil. Pinch out growing tips to encourage bushiness. Prune in spring to remove dead wood.

Cobaea scandens (*above*)   z 10
Cup and saucer plant
This tender, tropical perennial will not stand frost and is raised annually from seed. The bell-shaped flowers are held on 10in (25cm) stalks. They are 2in (5cm) long, greenish-white when they open, turning mauve as they age. 'Alba' has white flowers. It rapidly grows to 10ft (3m), climbing by means of leaf tendrils. A fine gap-filler for pergolas or walls. Sow in spring after the last frosts in rich moist soil. Pinch out to get bushy plants with plenty of flowers.

Fremontodendron californicum   z 8
The large butter yellow flowers of this striking evergreen shrub appear from spring into early autumn. The three-lobed leaves are green above, with brown indumentum beneath. On a warm, sunny wall it quickly grows to 15ft (4.5m). 'Californian Glory' has larger, lemon yellow flowers, with a slight flush of red on the outside. Happy in poor sandy soil. Prune in spring to reduce growth; the leaf hairs can cause irritation to the throat and skin. Plants dislike being moved and are prone to dying suddenly.

Ipomea tricolor (*above*)   z 5
Morning glory
Large trumpet-shaped flowers open china blue in the morning and close by midday. They are up to 4in (10cm) long. 'Heavenly Blue' has clear metallic blue flowers. A short-lived, tender, twining perennial, it is usually grown annually from seed and is good on trellis, walls and pillars. Grow in soil enriched with manure or compost, in a warm, sunny position, and water well throughout summer. Dislikes root disturbance. Support with twigs to start climbing.

Jasminum officinale   z 7
Summer jasmine
This quick-growing climber will reach 25ft (7.5m) if trained. Night-scented white flowers are held in terminal clusters from summer to early autumn, set-off by glossy, pinnate leaves. Excellent for a wall or pergola near a house or sitting area, or it can be trained around a window or doorway. Combines well with other fragrant plants such as *Nicotiana alata*. In cold areas grow in a sheltered, sunny position, in any fertile, fairly moist soil. Avoid severe pruning; thin the green stems in spring.

Lathyrus odoratus   z 3
Sweet pea
The winged stems of this annual climber can reach 6ft (1.8m). Often grown up canes for cutting, it works equally well on walls or pergolas. Flowers come in a range of colours and are often highly fragrant. Picking the blooms encourages further flowering. Before sowing, chip the hard seed coats and soak for 24 hours. Grow in moist, loamy soil with plenty of compost. Remove seed pods immediately. Support young plants with hazel twigs.

Lonicera hildebrandiana (*below*) z 7
Giant Burmese honeysuckle
This strong-growing but tender climber
can reach 70ft (21m). It has the largest
leaves, flowers and fruits of all
honeysuckles but is a shy flowerer when
young. The flowers are up to 6in (:m)
long, fragrant, creamy-white, chan ng
to rich yellow, and appear in termii l
leaf axils during summer. The roun ed
leaves are dark green. Spectacular on a
pergola, trellis, wall or fence. Grow in
moist, rich soil with the roots in shade,
watering and mulching during summer.
Prune lightly after flowering.

Passiflora caerulea z 8
Blue passion flower
The hardiest of the passifloras, this can
grow to 15ft (4.5m) in a good season,
climbing by means of twining tendrils,
and is evergreen in mild areas. The
flowers are likened to the instruments of
Christ's Passion: the corona (crown of
thorns) is striped purple, white and
blue, against greenish-white tepals (the
apostles); the stigmas (the three nails)
are creamy-white. Flowers remain
closed on dull days. Orange, egg-shaped
fruits follow a hot summer. Grow in
rich, well-drained soil and cover the
roots with peat or grit in winter. Prune
out winter-damaged shoots in spring.

Rhodochiton atrosanguineum z 9
The flowers of this perennial climber
make an unusual addition to the garden,
where it is grown as a tender annual.
They are long and pendulous with large,
bell-shaped calyces and 2in (5cm)-wide
tubular corollas of a deep blackish-
purple. Climbs by its twining leaf-stalks
to reach 10ft (3m) in a season. It needs
support and training. Plant after frosts,
in a sunny spot in moist fertile soil. It
may be short-lived.

Solanum crispum 'Glasnevin' z 9
(*above*)
A spectacular climber for a sheltered,
frost-free wall in full sun. It grows to
15ft (4.5m) in well-drained, alkaline
soil. Clusters of small violet-blue flowers
open from mid-summer, continuing into
autumn. Cream-coloured berries appear
in autumn. It is semi-evergreen. Plant
Lavatera 'Barnsley', with its pinky-
white flowers, at the base, or grow it
with the yellow climbing rose 'Golden
Showers'. Prune in spring after frost,
wearing gloves against the sap which is
an irritant.

Sollya heterophylla z 9
Bluebell creeper
An extremely beautiful evergreen
twiner, bearing clusters of nodding
bluebell-like, sky-blue flowers in
summer and autumn. Plants can reach
6ft (1.8m) and are effective if trained on
a low wall or allowed to scramble
through other shrubs. The leaves are
insignificant. Grow in humus-rich, well-
drained soil; where frost is likely,
provide some winter protection.

Trachelospermum jasminoides z 9
Star jasmine
Hardy against a wall in frost-free areas,
the stems of this self-clinging climber
can reach 25ft (7.5m) on older plants.
The sweetly fragrant flowers are 1in
(2.5cm) across, white, turning cream
with age. The evergreen leaves are
glossy, thick and leathery. 'Variegata'
has leaves splashed creamy-white;
'Wilsonii' has bronze leaves that turn
deep red in autumn. Flowers appear on
old wood, so prune immediately after
flowering to remove dead wood or
unwanted shoots. Grow in moist, rich
soil for the best results.

Wisteria floribunda (*below*) z 4
Japanese wisteria
This wisteria grows to 30ft (9m), with
10in (25cm)-long racemes of strongly
fragrant, bluish-purple flowers. After
hot summers, velvety, bean-like
pendulous seed pods may form. 'Alba'
has white, lilac-tinged flowers in 2ft
(60cm)-long racemes, while those of
'Macrobotrys' are up to 3ft (90cm) long.
It is ideal for pergolas, arches or
doorways. Plant in full sun, in fertile
loamy soil. Train the shoots to prevent
tangled growth. Prune in summer and
winter to encourage flowering.

FOLIAGE

Actinidia kolomikta z 4
The leaves of this hardy deciduous plant
are up to 6in (15cm) long and
tricoloured, with green, white and pink
variegations. It can reach 14ft (4.2m),
with a twining habit that needs support.
Young plants can be damaged because
of their strange attractiveness to cats.
Small, slightly fragrant white flowers
appear in summer, sometimes followed
by yellow fruits. Plant male and female
forms for fruit-setting, in full sun for
maximum leaf colour. Prune in winter
to achieve a strong framework.

Magnolia grandiflora z 5
This magnificent evergreen wall shrub
grows to 25ft (7.5m) in a warm position.
The large, glossy leaves are dark green
above, covered with fine, rusty-brown
hairs beneath. Highly fragrant, creamy-
white flowers appear in summer and
early autumn. 'Goliath' has very large
flowers. Underplant with *Choisya ternata*
(z 7), which carries white flowers in the
spring. Tie in stems to stop wind
damage, pruning lightly in summer.
Tolerates pollution.

Climbers for trees

Pittosporum tenuifolium z 9

This tender evergreen shrub thrives in coastal gardens, in mild areas. It has brownish-purple flowers which are honey-scented, and is noted for its pale, shiny, oval leaves, 2in (5cm) long, which have wavy margins. 'Purpureum' has mauve leaves, while those of 'Garnettii' have white margins. The mature foliage of 'Warnham Gold' is golden yellow. *P. tobira* has creamy-white, strongly fragrant flowers, similar to orange blossom. Grow in well-drained soil where plants can reach 30ft (9m). Prune only to keep within bounds.

Robinia hispida 'Rosea' (*above*) z 5

This form of the rose acacia has pinnate leaves with many small, dainty leaflets, carried on bristly stems. It bears racemes of rose-pink pea-like flowers in late summer, and will grow to 10ft (3m). Train with *Wisteria sinensis*, which has pink and lavender flowers, or grow with *Ceanothus* 'Gloire de Versailles', which has china blue flowers. The best specimens are those grafted onto *R. pseudoacacia*. Useful in all soils, it is suitable for a dry spot and tolerates pollution. The stems need shelter.

Vitis vinifera 'Incana' z 6
Dusty miller grape

This cultivar of the deciduous grape vine is excellent for decorative use in the garden. Plants can reach 12ft (3.6m) in a single season, climbing by means of tendrils. They are useful on walls, pergolas, bridges and fences. The grey-green leaves are covered in a cobweb-like down, which goes well with purple-foliaged shrubs, such as *Cotinus* 'Notcutt's Variety'. Grow in moist, rich soil. Prune back long shoots in summer and again in late winter to just above a pair of stout buds.

FLOWERS

Clematis macropetala (*above*) z 5

Growing to 10ft (3m), this early-flowering clematis has small, nodding, double violet-blue flowers from mid- to late spring. The silky, fluffy seedheads give a good show in autumn. The delicate leaves comprise three leaflets, each subdivided into three. 'Markham's Pink' has dark pink flowers, which are effective against the silver foliage of *Pyrus salicifolia* 'Pendula'. Grow with the roots in shade, in moist fertile soil. Cut back in autumn, leaving some shoots intact to enjoy the seedheads.

Clematis tangutica (*above*) z 5

The deep yellow, lantern-like flowers of this dense-growing climber look splendid bursting from the crown of a good-sized tree. Globes of silky feathery-tipped seedheads appear in autumn; flowers and seedheads are seen together for a while. Sea-green, finely dissected leaves provide the perfect foil. Grown on a wall or over a fence or hedge, it can reach 20ft (6m). Plant roots in shade and prune lightly in late winter if necessary, but not too hard. Raise named forms from cuttings.

Lonicera × americana z 5

This vigorous deciduous honeysuckle provides a spectacular display in summer. The fragrant, yellow-flushed, reddish-purple, tubular flowers are held in whorls at the tips of the shoots. It can grow to 30ft (10m) in a good-sized tree. The roots should be shaded and planted in moist, fertile soil. Prune lightly after flowering, removing weak and dead growth; cut a few stems to ground level to promote growth at the base which otherwise tends to become bare.

AUTUMN COLOUR

Celastrus orbiculatus z 4
Staff vine or climbing bittersweet

A strong-growing climber, its twining stems are armed with pairs of fierce spines at each bud. Choose a stout host tree such as a maple, birch, pine, larch, alder or lime, at least 20ft (6m) tall: it can reach 40ft (12m). The dense coat of rounded, deciduous leaves turn a rich golden-yellow in autumn. Brownish-yellow fruits split open in autumn to reveal bright red seeds set in a yellow lining, which persist all winter. Grows in most soils. Plant the self-pollinating hermaphrodite form to ensure fruiting.

Vitis coignetiae (*below*) z 5
Japanese crimson glory vine

Perhaps the most spectacular of all vines to grow in a large tree, it can reach up to 90ft (27m). The huge, broadly heart-shaped, deciduous leaves emerge dull-green in spring, with a rich felt of rusty hairs on the undersides. They turn brilliant scarlet, orange and crimson in autumn. Grow with *Clematis tangutica* for a stunning autumn effect. Needs a moist, rich soil to support the vigorous growth, and a sunny position. Prune in early spring to a plump healthy bud.

ROSES

Roses have always been an essential element in the garden, valued highly for the colour and scent of their flowers. Their hardiness varies widely depending on which part of the world they originated from. A few species are native to northern Europe; others came from an area stretching from southern France to the Middle East; while many roses introduced to cultivation in the late eighteenth and throughout the nineteenth century come from China.

In cold climates roses need to be chosen with care to ensure that they survive the winter; varieties bred from *Rosa rugosa* and *R. wichuraiana* are among those most tolerant of the extreme cold found in Canada, the northeastern United States and parts of continental Europe. Although roses require plenty of summer heat to ripen, their flowers tend to bleach and burn under intense sun.

Today, there are an enormous number of cultivars available to the gardener which often makes it difficult to know which to choose. However, broadly speaking there are three main groups – shrub, bush and climbing – each adapted to a different use.

Right: Many modern repeat-flowering roses make effective bedding plants. Here they are planted up in large blocks of a single cultivar but the same treatment can be used on a much more intimate scale. The impressive, mature trees at the back of the display provide a useful element of height.

Left: The sweet and powerful scent of many roses adds greatly to their garden value. The scented dimension of the garden can be enhanced by growing roses with excellent fragrant climbers such as honeysuckles and other richly perfumed summer flowers.

Below: 'Wedding Day', like other vigorous climbing and rambling roses, creates a wonderfully romantic effect when in full flower. Sturdy trelliswork, pergolas and old trees make suitable supports; think ahead and make sure the host structure or plant will be able to hold the mature rose.

Shrub roses include both the old-fashioned varieties bred mostly in the nineteenth century (such as 'Madame Hardy' and 'Cécile Brunner') and the modern shrub roses (for example, 'Marguerite Hilling', 'Frühlingsgold' and 'Fritz Nobis'), including the new English roses ('Graham Thomas', 'Gertrude Jekyll' and 'Mary Rose'), bred by David Austin and first marketed in the early 1980s. Shrub roses make large plants to 6ft (1.8m) high or a little more, which require little or no pruning and need space to look their best. Some give a single massive display early in the summer and nothing else for the rest of the season; others flower again later on, if less profusely; yet another group make a good display of hips in the autumn. All look good in a shrubbery or large mixed border, where the cultivars that flower only once can be part of a continuous display or a large-flowered hybrid clematis can be trained through them to extend the season of interest. In addition, some shrub roses are suitable for making hedges.

Most bush roses were created in the twentieth century. They are often planted en masse in rose gardens and require annual pruning in the late winter or early spring. They include the wonderful Hybrid

Left: Roses are available in such a wide range of colours that it is not difficult to select one that matches a particular scheme. Oranges and yellows suit old, mellow brick walls, while red stands out against the cream of many sandstones. Vibrant pinks are shown off by the subdued grey of this handsome lead tank.

Teas which are characterized by elegant but robust flowers and flower freely and continuously throughout the summer; (for example, 'Peace', 'Mister Lincoln' and 'Just Joey'); the Floribundas, which have multiflowered stems producing an abundance of colour for the whole summer (and are sometimes referred to as bedding roses); and the Grandifloras (such as 'Queen Elizabeth'), American hybrids with characteristics between Hybrid Teas and Floribundas. Grandifloras, as their name suggests, are taller (up to 10ft/3m) and have larger flowers than the Teas (3-5ft/1-1.5m) or Floribundas (2-4ft/60cm-1.2m).

Climbing roses combine the best qualities of other climbing plants with those of roses. In the wild they extend long vigorous stems towards the light through the branches of other plants, using their thorns to attach themselves. The most vigorous climbing roses are the ramblers (for example, 'Félicité et Perpétue', 'American Pillar' and 'Albéric Barbier') which send out long new shoots each summer. In the following year these shoots are covered with clusters of flowers along their entire length and should then be pruned away. Ramblers are best for clothing a large pergola, long wall or tall, sturdy tree. Less vigorous climbers (such as 'Climbing Etoile de Hollande', 'Maigold' and 'Handel') grow thick stems which flower over several years and sometimes reach a considerable height. They can be used for covering pergolas, trellis structures and smaller buildings. There are also some shrub roses (including 'Madame Isaac Pereire' and 'Zéphirine Drouhin') that can be trained against walls, where they will grow twice as high as normal, or up a freestanding pillar or the uprights of a pergola.

There are a number of slightly tender cultivars ('La Follette', 'Desprez à Fleur Jaune' and 'Hume's Blush' among them) that in cool climates benefit from the protection of a sunny wall. In contrast, other cultivars flower abundantly against walls that receive little direct sunshine ('Albertine', 'Climbing Iceberg' and 'Madame Alfred Carrière' are excellent examples).

Roses are very versatile, rewarding plants. Their popularity never fails, reflected in the ever growing number of varieties available to the gardener. Choosing the correct plant for a particular site and design can be a daunting prospect. There is a lot to be said for opting for tried and tested varieties that have proved their worth in neighbours' gardens. However, at the risk of disappointment, you could gamble on a new plant that might be the making of your garden, adding a beautiful note or a delightful fragrance to a bed.

There are countless ways to use roses, not least being the formal rose garden which has enjoyed something of a revival in recent years, used as much in modern designs as traditional Victorian-style settings. Ranks of healthy, well maintained roses are a delight to behold, whatever the scale of the planting. Contrast with this the freedom of a cottage garden, and the versatility of the rose becomes clear.

For fragrance

CLIMBING

'Albertine' (*above*)   z 4

This vigorous, prickly, large flowered rambler will grow to a height of 20ft (6m) and is ideal for training along a hedge or low wall; it will also grow well into trees. The strongly scented flowers, which are a warm salmon or coppery pink, appear in one spectacular display in early summer. At the peak of flowering, well-grown plants have so many flowers that little foliage is visible. Prune back to younger stems after flowering to encourage new growth. The deep green leaves are prone to mildew.

'Climbing Etoile de Hollande'   z 4

A climbing sport of the hybrid tea 'Etoile de Hollande', this recurrent-flowering climber has clear crimson blooms with a very good scent. It flowers freely throughout summer, the blooms decreasing in number as the season draws on. Plants are fairly vigorous, growing to 25ft (7.5m) . One of the drawbacks of this rose in the hybrid tea form is that it has weak flower stalks, but this is an advantage in the climber where the drooping heads are brought more into view. It is also useful as a pillar rose.

'Madame Alfred Carrière'   z 6

Although of a mainly upright habit, this vigorous climber can be trained along a wall, reaching 20ft (6m) if pruned. The stems have few thorns and produce light green shoots; leaves are light green. The large, double flowers open white from pink buds, are hybrid tea-shaped and strongly fragrant. The display begins in early summer, peaks in mid-summer and continues to the end of the season. Good for a north-facing wall, a large pergola or to grow over a mature tree.

'Maigold'   z 4

This climber bears large, semi-double bronzy-yellow flowers with bosses of golden stamens in autumn. The flowers are reddish in bud, open quite early in the season and are highly scented. 'Maigold' is suitable for a wall, fence or pillar, or for growing as a loose open shrub in borders. It grows vigorously to 20ft (6m) and bears many thorny branches with glossy green foliage. Plants look effective against sand-coloured brick or stonework, or on wood. If deadheaded, they will produce a second flush of flowers.

'Zéphirine Drouhin' (*below*)   z 4

This bourbon rose can achieve 10ft (3m) in height, if trained as a climber, and is very popular because of its freedom of flowering and almost thornless habit. It produces sweetly scented, semi-double, carmine pink flowers continuously from summer to autumn. Flowering is improved by regular deadheading. Young growths are bronze-coloured. A vigorous grower, this cultivar can be used as a bush or a hedge as it is tolerant of heavy pruning. It is slightly prone to mildew and blackspot.

SHRUB

'Buff Beauty'   z 4

A very floriferous, vigorous hybrid musk which makes a shrub 6ft (1.8m) high with an equal spread. The flowers are carried in large clusters. They are varying shades of apricot and buff-yellow, semi-double or double, medium-sized and deliciously scented. The petals become paler at the edges as the blooms age. Plants begin flowering in summer and continue until autumn. The foliage is a rich brown-bronze when young, turning dark green as it matures.

'Frühlingsgold' (*below*)   z 4

Also listed as 'Spring Gold', this modern shrub rose will thrive in all soil conditions. Its branches quickly reach 7ft (2.1m) and then arch outwards. They are clothed with heavily fragrant, creamy-yellow flowers which reach up to 5in (13cm) across, each one bearing a cluster of golden yellow stamens. The flowers fade in hot sun. The main flush is in early summer with occasionally another show later in the year. The grey-green leaves complement the blooms. Plants are generally strong and disease-resistant.

'Madame Isaac Pereire' (*below*)   z 4

A very vigorous bourbon rose with large, double, strongly scented, deep pink flowers. These appear in clusters throughout the summer months, the best blooms often being produced late in the season. Earlier flowers frequently appear in the centre of the plant, later ones on the outside. The strong thorny shoots can reach 6ft (1.8m) in a single season, and mature plants grow to 10ft (3m) in height. This cultivar can also be trained as a pillar rose or pegged down: maintenance must be considered if the plant is pegged.

R. rugosa 'Blanche Double de Coubert'
(*above*) z 2
This large, spreading shrub can reach
5ft (1.5m) high, with a similar spread,
and has a loose-growing habit. Large,
semi-double, fragrant white flowers first
appear in early summer and recur
throughout the season. The petals are
silky and slightly pleated. Hips, which
are large and reddish-orange, form less
readily than on the similar 'Alba'. Like
most derivatives of *R. rugosa*, stems are
prickly and the leaves have deep veins.

'William Lobb' z 4
A damask moss rose which grows
quickly to 6ft (1.8m) or more, this is the
most vigorous member of this sweetly
scented group. Large clusters of flowers
are produced in mid-summer. These are
semi-double, crimson in bud, opening
purple and fading to grey-mauve with a
lighter-coloured base. The flower buds
and stalks are covered with green
"moss", typical of the group. The tall,
rather lank habit make it suitable for
growing up pillars and pergolas. Small
reddish thorns clothe the young shoots.

BUSH

'Betty Prior' z 4
An outstanding floribunda which
combines health and vigour with a
wealth of long-lasting blooms. The deep
pink buds open as delicate, single pink
flowers, reminiscent of the wild dog rose
but held in large trusses. Blooms appear
from late spring into the autumn; they
become darker as the temperature falls
and the light intensity diminishes.
Flowers produce a spicy scent that
spreads generously. It forms a compact
sturdy mound 3-4ft (90-120cm) high,
making plants suitable for hedging.

'Fragrant Cloud' z 4
Also listed as 'Duftwolke' and 'Nuage
Parfumé', this hybrid tea is a vigorous,
upright grower with large, exhibition-
quality geranium-red blooms. Flowers
are produced freely, mostly in summer
and again in autumn, with some
between the two flushes. They fade to
reddish-purple in hot weather and need
regular deadheading. Their scent is very
strong all season. The glossy dark green
leaves are resistant to disease, but may
need protection from blackspot in some
areas. Plants grow to 3ft (90cm) and can
be raised as standards.

'Mister Lincoln' z 4
Cherry red flowers appear singly during
the summer following deep maroon
buds. They are large and very full and
have an exceptional fragrance. The
long-lasting blooms tend to flatten out
as they open, making a dramatic splash
of colour. They are carried at the top of
long stems, making them favourites for
showing and cutting. The glossy foliage
is medium to light green in colour and
makes an excellent foil for the flowers.
A tall plant reaching 6ft (1.8m) in
height, this hybrid tea is considered to
be one of the best red roses available.

'Peace' z 4
If lightly pruned, this vigorous hybrid
tea will form a tall branching shrub,
upwards of 4ft (1.2m) in height with
large, full yellow flowers flushed with
pink, which become paler with age. The
colouring tends to vary from season to
season. The main flushes are in summer
and autumn, with a few blooms
bridging the gap. The flowers are
weather resistant and the strong-
growing, deep green, glossy leaves are
little troubled by disease. Excellent as a
cut flower, 'Peace' is much prized as an
exhibition rose.

'Saratoga' z 4
The white flowers of this floribunda are
carried on the upright, vigorous bushy-
growing plant. The large flowers are
produced freely in irregular clusters and
are strongly scented. The foliage is dark
glossy green. The plant can achieve a
height of 3ft (90cm) or more. A more
compact white-flowered floribunda is
'Irene of Denmark', which grows 3ft
(90cm) at most, and produces flowers
freely which are tinted pink in bud and
open white, large and double.

Borders

SHRUB

'Cécile Brunner' (*below*) z 4
Rarely growing more than 4ft (1.2m)
high, this shrubby rose is characterized
by its small neat leaves and delicate,
perfectly formed blooms. The small
flowers are blushed pink with deeper
centres, pointed when in bud and sweet-
scented. Plants flower recurrently
throughout the summer. Only
moderately vigorous, this cultivar
should not be hard-pruned: remove
weak growth and occasionally one or
two older branches. Valued for its neat
habit and useful for cutting.

'Ferdinand Pichard' (*below*) z 4
Sometimes classed as a bourbon rose,
this hybrid perpetual shrub is recurrent
and free-flowering, producing semi-
double pink flowers with petals streaked
and splashed crimson, which tends to
deepen as the flowers age. The flowers
carry a good scent and appear in tight
clusters from mid-summer through to
autumn. They are particularly abundant
if the faded blooms are removed
regularly. Plants grow to a height of 8ft
(2.4m) and have a rather spreading,
bushy habit. The leaves are light green.

'Fritz Nobis' (*above*)   z 4
This is one of the most beautiful of the
modern shrub roses available. It grows
to 6ft (1.8m) high and gives one
spectacular display of flowers in early
summer. The pale salmon-pink flowers
are medium-sized, semi-double and
open out flat like many of the old roses.
In the centre of the flowers lie clusters
of yellowish-brown stamens. 'Fritz
Nobis' has a good scent and in the
autumn bears dark red rounded hips
which last into winter. Vigorous, it soon
forms a finely shaped bush.

'Graham Thomas'   z 4
Also listed as 'Ausmas', this English
rose was raised in 1983 and named after
the most influential of all the old rose
enthusiasts, Graham Stuart Thomas.
The flowers are tea-scented and appear
throughout the season. They are double
and of a glistening yellow, carried on
slightly arching branches. Each flower is
4in (10cm) across and cup-shaped.
Plants grow vigorously with a bushy lax
habit. They achieve a height and spread
of 4ft (1.2m). Other English roses raised
in the 1980s with similar outstanding
qualities include the pink 'Gertrude
Jekyll' and crimson 'Mary Rose'.

'Madame Hardy'   z 4
A vigorous damask rose growing to 6ft
(1.8m) tall with clear green foliage,
forming a strong bush. Cup-shaped
when opening, the flowers expand to
reveal a green eye surrounded by
incurving petals which start off creamy
pink-white before becoming pure white.
They are of a medium size, double,
carried in clusters and appear in a single
flush in summer. The scent is delicious
and fresh with a hint of lemon. A
favourite among the old white roses.

'Marguerite Hilling' (*below*)   z 4
A sport of 'Nevada' also sometimes
listed as 'Pink Nevada', this modern
shrub rose has great vigour and is a
prolific flowerer for which it is very
popular. It grows up to 8ft (2.4m) tall.
The flowers appear in summer and are
light pink with some deeper shading.
They are slightly recurrent with odd
flowers appearing throughout the rest of
the season. Each flower is 3in (7cm)
across and semi-double. Grow this
cultivar towards the back of a border
due to its large size. The leaves are
small and dull and prone to blackspot.

'Nevada' (*below*)   z 4
Spectacular when in full flower, this
vigorous modern shrub is covered in
blooms during summer, carried on long
arching shoots. Most of the flowers
appear in one main flush. They are
scentless, semi-double, and open a
creamy-white, becoming pink-tinged in
hot weather, and fading white in duller
conditions. The centre of the flower is a
cluster of yellow stamens. As the
blooms mature they become rather loose
and untidy. Plants can grow to 11ft
(3.3m) high with equal spread and are
sometimes prone to blackspot.

***Rosa × alba* 'Maxima'** (*above*)   z 2
White rose of York or Jacobite rose
Adopted as an emblem by the Yorkists,
the origins of this historic *alba* rose are
still undecided. It is characterized by its
erect, thorny, dense growth and
glaucous foliage. The flat ivory flowers
are flushed with cream, scented and
semi-double. 'Maxima' flowers in mid-
summer and is tolerant of a wide range
of conditions except shade. The flowers
are not usually recurrent. In autumn
there are oblong red fruits. Plants can
grow to 8ft (2.4m).

Rosa glauca (*above*)   z 2
Also listed as *R. rubrifolia*, this species
rose is a tall-growing shrub which can
reach 12ft (3.6m) with support, but is
more normally seen growing freely to
7ft (2.1m) with arching branches.
Distinguished by its beautiful blue-grey
foliage, it has few thorns and deep pink
flowers with white centres in summer.
The flowers have long wispy sepals and
are carried either singly or in small
clusters. In autumn the leaves turn
reddish and are accompanied by bright
red, globular hips all along the arching,
elegant branches.

Rosa moyesii 'Geranium'　z 4

One of the finest forms of this species rose, 'Geranium' is grown for its large, bright crimson-red fruits in late summer and autumn. The flowers appear in early summer and are bright red and single with overlapping petals. Plants form open-centred bushes, each with a few stout stems when mature. Some of the older shoots can be removed after flowering on established plants. The vigorous arching shoots are armed with sharp thorns and carry the light green foliage. Slightly more compact than the species and valuable for autumn colour.

Rosa rugosa 'Roseraie de l'Haÿ'　z 2

Named after the rose garden of the same name to the south of Paris established by Jules Gravereaux, this richly-scented rugosa flowers throughout the season and is best planted in small groups. The vigorous growth can reach 8ft (2.4m), with an equal spread, carrying very large, semi-double loose flowers of deep crimson-purple with a velvety sheen and a strong scent. Each bloom is 4in (10cm) across carried among luxuriant, typical rugosa foliage. This form stands out among the rugosa group because of its distinctive wine-coloured flowers.

Rosa virginiana (*above*)　z 4

Grown for its autumn leaf colours and brightly coloured hips, the young leaves of this species rose emerge bronzed, then turn glossy-green during summer and finally to fiery reddish-orange and yellow shades in autumn. They are accompanied at the end of the season by persistent, rounded, bright red hips. The stems are reddish-brown. The rather late flowers are pink with pale centres. Plants form dense rounded bushes with many shoots growing from the base to a height of 6ft (1.8m).

BUSH

'Allgold'　z 4

Unsurpassed for the stability of its flower colour and for its numerous long-lasting flowers, 'Allgold' is a neat, compact, moderately vigorous grower which reaches to just over 2ft (60cm) high. The flowers of this floribunda open in early summer and last until late in the season. They are semi-double and of a deep golden yellow that never fades, even in hot sunny weather. The leaves are dark glossy green and resistant to disease. Plants resists rainy weather well, the flowers remaining unblemished by the water.

'Europeana'　z 4

This vigorous growing floribunda may well need its flowers supporting if heavy rain threatens. This can be overcome by close planting so the plants give each other mutual support. Although this cultivar is susceptible to mildew in some areas, it is well worth growing for its striking, deep crimson flowers which are rosette shaped and carried in heavy trusses. Plants grow to 3ft (90cm) and have glossy, bronze-green foliage, which is coppery when young.

'Just Joey' (*below*)　z 4

Unique for its coppery-orange flowers with lighter and deeper flushes, this hybrid tea is very free flowering and has an open spreading habit. The petals are often veined red, paling toward the edges which are wavy. The flowers appear singly or in clusters on plants growing up to 3ft (90cm) high and have some scent. Each one is fully double and can be up to 5in (13cm) across. The leaves are leathery and dark green. Flowers stand up well to rain and are excellent for cutting in the bud stage.

'Queen Elizabeth'　z 4

One of the commonest pink floribundas with a tendency to produce a few blind shoots in the early part of the season, which eventually revert to flowering normally. It is a vigorous grower reaching 5ft (1.5m) or more in height with almost thornless stems and dark green glossy leaves. The flowers are very weather resistant and open a clear pink, fading as they age. They appear throughout the summer and autumn, carried either singly or in trusses, and are useful for cutting. Plants make an effective informal hedge.

'Starina' (*above*)　z 4

A miniature rose achieving only 10in (25cm) in height, this plant is a vigorous grower with glossy green foliage and fully double, scarlet-orange flowers. This rose should be positioned carefully in a border so as not to allow it to become swamped by other plants. It is suitable for use as a pot plant, for bedding or as a miniature standard. As with all miniatures, 'Starina' resents root disturbance. The flowers are well-formed and last for a long time when used as cut flowers.

'Whisky Mac'　z 4

The shapely blooms of this hybrid tea are gold with tints of bronze and orange; they are freely produced throughout summer. The flowers are quite fragrant, which is unusual among roses of this colour. Plants grow vigorously to 3ft (90cm) and carry holly-like, dark green glossy leaves which are tinted bronze as they unfold in spring. It is susceptible to mildew and damage by frost; this should be borne in mind when choosing a suitable position for planting, a protected, warm site producing the best results.

"Landscape" roses

GROUND COVER

'Nozomi' (*above*) z 4

This miniature climbing rose will form excellent ground cover if left unsupported and planted 2ft (60cm) apart, as well as scrambling effectively along the top of a low wall. Its low arching habit means that it rarely achieves more than 18in (45cm) in height, but when supported it can reach 4ft (1.2m). Small, pale pink, single flowers appear in massed trusses. The leaves are glossy. Plants will also grow as weeping standards.

Rosa × paulii (*above*) z 2

A hybrid between *R. arvensis* and *R. rugosa* that is excellent for smothering weeds because of its sprawling habit. A vigorous trailing rose, it will form a 3ft (90cm)-high shrub if hard-pruned. The long shoots are very thorny, carrying in mid-summer the single white or pink flowers with wedge-shaped petals, each one being 3in (8cm) across, with a central mass of golden stamens. The flowers are produced freely and have a slight scent of cloves. 'Rosea' has deep pink flowers with white centres.

'Max Graf' (*below*) z 2

A hybrid between *R. rugosa* and *R. wichuraiana*, the long growths of this rugosa shrub lie prostrate along the ground unless trained. The dense foliage is effective at smothering weeds, but it can be difficult to weed among the prickly shoots before the leaves emerge. The scented flowers are single, pink, fading to white at the base of the petals, with yellow stamens. They are the size of large dog roses and appear once, but over a long season. Flowers sometimes appear in the autumn. The leaves are a glossy bright green.

'Snow Carpet' (*below*) z 5

Also known as 'Maccarpe', this prostrate, creeping miniature bush rose was introduced to cultivation in 1980. It grows to a height of only 6in (15cm) with a spread of 20in (50cm), making it ideal for low ground cover. It carries fully double, pompom-like white flowers which are 1 ¼in (3cm) across. They appear in clusters, mainly during summer with some into autumn. The small glossy leaves are plentiful, adding to the usefulness of 'Snow Carpet' as ground cover as they smother weeds very successfully.

'The Fairy' z 5

A weather-resistant and vigorous spreading plant which attains a height of 3ft (90cm). It is ideal as tall ground cover or as a low informal hedge and can also be grown as a standard. The small box-like leaves are deep green and shiny with a very healthy sheen. Large trusses of double soft-pink flowers appear later than most floribundas, and fade if the weather is hot. This is one of the few polyanthas available.

HEDGING

'Coupe d'Hébé' (*below*) z 4

This vigorous shrub rose, which can grow to 7ft (2.1m), is usually described as a bourbon but is actually of mixed parentage; this gives it a rather loose growth pattern which makes it suitable for an informal hedge. Copious fresh glossy leaves form a dense barrier. The medium-sized double flowers are pink inside, almost white outside and fragrant, appearing quite late in the summer. The weak flower stalks cause the heads to hang downwards. Although this plant was introduced as long ago as 1840, its shapely outline is reminiscent of more modern cultivars.

Rosa eglanteria z 2
Sweet briar or eglantine

Also listed as *R. rubiginosa*, this species rose has small leaflets which give the whole plant a spicy aromatic scent during damp weather. Plants grow with vigour to a height of 8ft (2.4m) and are excellent as dense informal hedges or as boundary plantings. The single pink flowers appear in clusters. Hips are bright red. 'Amy Robsart' has semi-double pink flowers and gold stamens; 'Lady Penzance' has fragrant leaves when wet and salmon-pink flowers.

Climbing roses

***Rosa pimpinellifolia* 'Hispida'** z 2
Scotch rose or burnet rose
A moderately fast growing form which suckers freely but grows little over 4ft (1.2m) high. The stems are bristly, but not very prickly. Freely-produced white or creamy-white single flowers appear in late spring or early summer in one flush. The rather delicate foliage is bluish-green and much toothed around the leaf margins. The rounded hips are a deep shining purple during autumn. A row of plants will make a good informal hedge. Cut out dead and damaged stems in winter for the best effect.

***Rosa rugosa* 'Fru Dagmar Hastrup' z 2**
(*above*)
Sometimes seen as 'Frau Dagmar Hartopp', this rugosa shrub rose is more compact than other rugosas, making it suitable for hedging with the added attraction of bright red hips throughout summer and autumn, the size and colour of small tomatoes. The leaves are fresh apple green with impressed veins. Plants respond well to winter clipping. They flower over a long period, beginning in mid-summer. Each bloom is up to 3in (8cm) across, single, pink with golden stamens, cup-shaped then saucer-shaped when fully open. In autumn the leaves take on attractive golden-yellow shades.

'Tip Top' z 4
Growing to less than 2ft (60cm), this vigorous, bushy spreading floribunda has large, double, warm salmon-pink flowers in large clusters, appearing continuously over a long season. Plants are rather prone to attack by blackspot. Their low growth makes them well-suited for use as edging plants or in small beds. The leaves are dark glossy green, complementing the flowers.

FOR GARDEN STRUCTURES

'Aloha' (*above*) z 4
This moderately vigorous climbing or shrub rose reaches 5ft (1.5m) if grown as a shrub or up to 10ft (3m) if grown on a pillar. Plants grown as large shrubs need regular pruning. The scented flowers are like those of hybrid teas. They are large and double, pink with darker centres changing to a salmon-pink as they age. The flowers are produced freely, appearing throughout the season. This cultivar derives its free-flowering habit from 'New Dawn' which is one of its parents. The stiff stems perfectly suit its climbing habit.

'American Pillar' (*above*) z 4
A vigorous rambler, it should be pruned by cutting the flowering shoots hard, down to ground level, in late summer: the new shoots are then tied in. Each quite large, pinkish-blue single flower has a white eye and is produced in a large cluster. The flowers are unscented. Plants bloom once in the summer but are very floriferous; they are susceptible to mildew. They reach a height of 15ft (4.5m) and may be trained up arches and pergolas as well as pillars.

'Blaze Improved' z 4
This American climber, introduced in 1932, is one of the most commonly grown in the United States because of its unfailing reliability. The large bright scarlet flowers are 2-3in (5-8cm) across and cover the plant in early summer and again in early autumn with a spattering in between. It grows quickly to 12-15ft (3.6-4.5m), making it ideal for trelliswork and pergolas. The dark glossy green foliage complements the flowers. Tolerant of most soils and shade, it is an excellent, versatile garden plant that well merits its popularity.

'Bobbie James' (*above*) z 2
One of the best ramblers, this vigorous plant reaches 25ft (7.5m). It is related to *R. multiflora* and was named in 1960 after the Hon. Robert James who cultivated a beautiful garden in Yorkshire. The fragrant flowers are cream in bud, opening white with gold stamens. Huge clusters are freely produced in one flush in mid-summer. The sturdy stems bear abundant glossy green foliage. Ideal for a pergola or for growing through a tree.

'Constance Spry' z 4
The large and extremely fragrant flowers are produced in a single display in mid-summer, to spectacular effect. With its open, arching growth, this plant is suited to growing either as a 6ft (1.8m) shrub or as a climber, reaching 15ft (4.5m) with a 6ft (1.8m) spread. The flowers are a glowing pink in the centre, tending to be paler on the outside. They are fully double, 4in (10cm) across and held in groups of three or four. The foliage is deep green. Plants tend to throw up long vigorous growths which need support. Effective against a grey brick wall or on a pillar.

'Félicité et Perpétue' (*above*)   z 4
To maximize flowering on this semi-evergreen rambler, leave the prickly overlapping growths unpruned, cutting out only dead, diseased or damaged wood. The long strong-growing shoots can reach 18ft (5.4m) in length, making it ideal for pergolas or for training into an old tree. The fragrant, small creamy-white flowers with a hint of pink are double and globular, held in large clusters. They appear from mid to late summer. Grows well even in light shade and has small, dark, shiny green leaves.

***Rosa filipes* 'Kiftsgate'**   z 2
A vigorous Himalaya rambler clone, this plant was bred in the garden of the same name in Gloucestershire. It needs a large and robust pergola for support as it can reach 50ft (15m) and is capable of covering buildings and trees. In mid-summer the plant is spectacular, covered in sweetly scented, small, creamy white single flowers which cascade in corymbs over the grey-green foliage. Few roses can rival the huge cascades of flowers.

'Golden Showers'   z 4
A very popular yellow rose which flowers continuously from early to late summer and is tolerant of wind, rain and some shade. This floribunda climber is ideal for trelliswork. It can reach 10ft (3m) in height with its stiff upright growth, carrying rich lemon-coloured flowers which are large, double, with a lemony fragrance and pointed when in bud. They fade in strong sunlight and should be regularly deadheaded. In winter cut out one older stem to ground level to promote new growth, as well as removing dead or diseased wood.

'Joseph's Coat' (*below*)   z 4
Considered by different authorities to be either a tall floribunda or a large-flowered climber, this plant can be effectively trained as a pillar rose. Its growths reach 8ft (2.4m) high and it is repeat-flowering. The semi-double flowers are bright yellow with red and orange flushes, especially at the petal edges, and are produced in large trusses. They appear over a long period and well into autumn. The leaves are dark glossy green. Equally at home grown as a shrub or, with hard-pruning, as a bedding rose.

'Lawrence Johnston'   z 4
A large-flowered climber growing to 10ft (3m), it produces bright yellow blooms in mid-summer, followed by a succession of smaller displays. The semi-double flowers are strongly scented and the leaves are a glossy rich green. The first specimen was bought by Major Lawrence Johnston and planted at Hidcote Manor in England. It was originally named 'Hidcote Yellow', although this name is no longer valid. Can also be grown as a shrub.

'Mermaid'   z 4
Rarely happy in cold situations, where it may die back in severe winters, this modern climber is a vigorous grower which thrives in sun or in a north-facing position in a warm area. Growths reach up to 30ft (9m) and carry clusters of single sulphur-yellow blooms with amber stamens, the latter remaining for a few days after the petals have fallen. The flowers appear repeatedly through the summer, are slightly scented and do not require deadheading. Plants resent root disturbance and should be pruned only to remove dead, diseased or damaged wood.

'Souvenir de la Malmaison' (*above*) z 4
Named in memory of the Empress Josephine's private garden just to the south of Paris, this bourbon rose is suitable for growing on a pillar or as a shrub. It has vigorous shoots which can reach 10ft (3m) in length. The large flowers are pink fading to white, double, cup-shaped when opening, flattening as they mature. Each bloom is up to 5in (13cm) across and strongly scented. The flowers have two flushes, one in mid-summer and a second in late summer. They dislike wet weather, the rain spoiling the petals.

'Swan Lake' (*above*)   z 4
This cultivar was introduced in 1968 and is also listed as 'Schwanensee'. It is one of the best white climbers available and is very resilient in poor weather, which is unusual for a white rose. 'Swan Lake' forms a strong free-growing plant which is well-suited to trelliswork, but can also be grown on pillars and arches. The large flowers are double, white with pinkish centres. They have little scent and appear throughout the season. The leaves are mid-green and are prone to the blemishes of blackspot.

FOR WALLS

Rosa banksiae banksiae z 7
Plant this vigorous climbing species rose on a south-facing wall where it can grow to 30ft (9m). Several forms of the banksian rose exist, all being early and free-flowering with almost thornless stems. Young plants should be allowed to reach their desired height before any pruning starts. The white or pale yellow flowers appear in the second or third year on the older shoots, which tend to trail. Prune to ripen the wood. The leaves have a yellow tint.

'Climbing Iceberg' (*above*) z 4
Discovered by B.R. Cant in 1968, this is a climbing sport of 'Iceberg' or 'Climbing Schneewittchen' (as it is also known) and is a spectacular sight when well trained. It will reach 12ft (3.6m) on a wall and carries a profusion of white flowers early in the season, with more flowers appearing throughout the season on mature plants. The flowers are lightly scented, opening flat to reveal a cluster of brownish stamens. Plants grow well in shade, but are prone to mild attacks of mildew and blackspot.

'Danse du Feu' z 4
Also known as 'Spectacular' and well suited to both its names, this strong climber which will reach 10ft (3m) in rich, well-drained fertile soil which contains plenty of humus. In early summer this cultivar is massed with bright scarlet, slightly scented, semi-double flowers, with a few blooms appearing through the rest of the season. Young foliage is bronzed, ageing to dark glossy green. Suitable for a north-facing aspect, it will grow on a wall, pillar or pergola; benefits from light shade. Deadhead regularly.

'Desprez à Fleur Jaune' z 6
Also known as 'Jaune Desprez', this cultivar was raised by Desprez in 1830 and is probably the earliest yellow climbing rose. Choose a high wall for this plant. Growths can reach up to 15ft (4.5m) and have few prickles. The flowers are held singly or in small clusters, and are beautifully fragrant, appearing from mid-summer through to autumn. They are double, rather flat, pale yellow with peach shades. Plants need some shelter and thrive in sun. Prune in late winter, removing old, weak or diseased wood.

'Dortmund' (*below*) z 4
The bright flowers of this climbing *kordesii* hybrid are reddish-crimson with a white eye surrounding the central golden stamens. The single flowers appear in large clusters and will keep being produced with deadheading; this restricts the production of the large number of striking but energy-consuming hips. Good for the shaded wall, but also valuable for pillars and as a large shrub. The abundant foliage is a healthy, glossy, dark green. This is a very hardy rose with little scent.

'François Juranville' z 4
When young the foliage of this vigorous rambler is bronzed, turning to a rich glossy green as it ages. The strong growths can reach 25ft (7.5m) and are ideal for a large shaded wall. Plants have a rather weeping habit. They flower only once with some later blooms after the main flush. The strongly scented flowers are salmon-pink, double, opening large and flat, with deeper-coloured centres, and are held singly or in clusters. They are paler in dry summers and on dryer soils. Also useful for a large pergola or tree.

'Gloire de Dijon' (*below*) z 6
The double flowers of this hardy climber are up to 4in (10cm) across, of an apricot-orange colour with some darker and lighter petals, and strongly fragrant, especially in hot still weather. This cultivar is very popular and is often seen growing to 15ft (4.5m). It likes sun, but will also grow on north-facing walls and can be grown as a pillar. The bottom half of older plants tend to become bare and needs obscuring with other plants. Blooms appear continually from mid-summer onwards in great numbers.

'Handel' z 4
The unusually coloured flowers of this climber make it popular: each flower is composed of petals which are creamy edged with pink, making an attractive combination, and are beautifully shaped. The flowers are carried on vigorous shoots capable of growing to 20ft (6m) in a hot sunny summer, about half this in cooler seasons, and are weather-resistant. They are only slightly scented and tend to fade in hot weather. The dark green leaves have coppery shades; they are prone to mildew. Blooms appear throughout the season.

'Hume's Blush' z 6
This clone of the vigorous hybrid climber R. × *odorata* originated in China and was introduced to England from the East Indies by Sir A. Hume in 1809. It flowers on wood grown in the previous season so should only be pruned lightly. The flowers are a blushing pink, very strongly scented, large and double, and open from mid-summer onwards. It needs a sunny position to thrive. R. × *odorata* is an important cross in rose history, with R. *chinensis* and R. *gigantea* for parents.

'La Follette' z 4

Raised by Busby at Cannes around 1910, this half-hardy but vigorous climber is often grown into trees on the Italian and French Rivieras where it flowers early. It requires a sheltered wall (or in colder areas the protection of a cold greenhouse) and sun to achieve 20ft (6m). The huge, double, loose flowers appear in early summer in one main burst and are rose pink with shades of salmon and cream, especially towards the outside of the petals. The flower buds are long and pointed.

'Leverkusen' z 4

A useful plant which can be used either as a climber for a wall or pillar or grown as a shrub. Plants grow to 10ft (3m) in height and are very hardy with moderate vigour. The semi-double, pale creamy-yellow flowers with darker centres have their main display in mid-summer, followed by fewer recurrent blooms during the rest of the season. The smallish leaflets are a deep glossy green. An extremely useful rose for its abundant flowers.

'Madame Grégoire Staechelin' z 4
(*below*)

Thriving on shaded walls, this very vigorous climber can grow to 20ft (6m) in a sunny position. The thorny shoots need careful pruning to prevent flowers forming only at the top of the plant: cut some of the most vigorous shoots to the base in the winter after planting, and when mature remove one or two of the old woody stems completely each season. The pink flowers appear early in the season and are slightly pendent which is an advantage on taller plants. They have a fragrance not unlike sweet peas. In autumn the hips turn light orange, adding to the plant's interest.

'Maréchal Neil' (*above*) z 7

Popular in Victorian conservatories, this rather tender climber will grow better under glass in cold areas, with the roots planted outside the greenhouse. Elsewhere, train it against a warm sheltered wall in a sunny spot, where it can grow to 15ft (4.5m). Large tea-scented flowers are produced during summer. They are golden yellow and are held on weak flower stalks which give the plant a nodding habit. In Britain, this cultivar is only sufficiently hardy to be grown in the open in southern England.

'New Dawn' (*above*) z 4

This disease-resistant hardy rose is useful for shady pergolas, walls and fences. A vigorous lateral grower, given space the stems can exceed 15ft (4.5m). The medium-sized flowers are profuse during early summer, of apple-blossom pink with deeper pink centres and a very strong fragrance. A second flush of flowers appears in late summer. The flowers tend to fade to white during hot weather. The foliage is shiny light green. It also grows well into small open-canopied trees.

'Royal Gold' (*below*) z 7

Also suited to growing as a pillar, this climber is rather tender and will only succeed on a sheltered sunny wall in warmer areas. Die-back is common after a severe winter in colder regions: any dead shoots should be pruned out in the following spring. Deep yellow flowers appear from mid-summer onwards; they are large and double, scented and held singly or in clusters. Only moderately vigorous, this cultivar will give poor results unless planted on rich and fertile soil, where it can grow to 10ft (3m). The flowers resemble those of a hybrid tea.

'Veilchenblau' (*below*) z 4

A distinctive plant among ramblers because of its blue-purple flowers and sometimes listed as 'Violet Blue'. It is virtually thornless and has small semi-double flowers which open purplish, with white centres, maturing to dark blue-violet and finally greyish-mauve. They produce a scent of apples. The flowers appear in large clusters in mid- to late summer; there is no repeat flowering. Often called the "blue" rose due to the colour of its blooms, this plant is best grown in shade as the petals fade in direct sun.

HEDGES AND WINDBREAKS

The way in which a hedge is intended to be used in the garden, whether it be for its aesthetic qualities or for purely practical reasons or a combination of the two, influences the species chosen to make the hedge.

Aesthetically, hedges compartmentalize a garden creating a number of distinct areas that can each be given an individual style and character with a feeling of intimacy and seclusion from other parts of the garden. However, with a clever use of openings, either "windows" or "doors", an element of surprise and invitation is introduced which gives the illusion that the whole garden is larger than it really is. In addition, hedges form a valuable backdrop against which any

composition of other plants stands out and in a relatively short period of time they give the garden a satisfying air of maturity.

As windbreaks, hedges generate a precious microclimate which enables a wider range of plants to be grown. Often in an exposed new site it is necessary to use the fastest growing species. If there is the space, it may be a good idea to choose trees, such as poplars, alders or scots pines, that do not require any pruning and maintenance as this can make for heavy and time-consumming work. In the last 25 years or so the Leyland cypress has been used in many small gardens to create quick screens, but is invariably left to grow too

Right: Rhododendron ponticum is an evergreen that grows vigorously in cool shady conditions. It makes a tall, windproof, informal hedge that is a blaze of colour in late spring and early summer.

Left: A tightly clipped cypress hedge makes a fast-growing backdrop to a traditional herbaceous border, giving good protection from wind. Yew would be slower growing, requiring only one clip a year. Even when this border is dormant, the hedge remains interesting because of the way the top has been shaped.

Below: Privet is a semi-evergreen that is commonly used as a fast-growing hedge. To the right of the golden form shown here is a tiered topiary specimen of holly and, behind this, a formally trained beech hedge.

big before it is pruned severely and left looking like a skeleton. In many cases a good solid hedge of yew, for example, requiring only one cut a year, would have been achieved in less than eight years and is exceedingly long lived. If there is any risk of livestock eating any part of the hedge then use thuja instead of yew.

Yew and thuja make dense evergreen screens that are usually kept tightly trimmed, both responding to this treatment by generating plenty of new shoots after being cut back. The structural quality of a tightly clipped hedge gives a garden a strong form, whatever the season, and is best used in formal designs. A variety of textures and colours are available to the gardener through the choice of species. For example, a beech or hornbeam hedge offers a soft green colour which turns to russety brown in the autumn lasting through the winter and into spring, in contrast to the evergreen broadleaves of the Portugal laurel, *Prunus lusitanica*, or the English holly, *Ilex aquifolium*, which make a strong, glistening, dark green hedge all year round. For those who live in very cold climates, the choice of evergreens may be limited to the hardiest conifer, the western hemlock, *Tsuga heterophylla*, or a number of deciduous plants such as *Ilex verticillata* (z 3), which has rounded leaves that are smaller and less prickly than those of the English holly or sea buckthorn, *Hippophae rhamnoides*.

Left: The frost-hardy *Fuchsia magellanica* is deciduous but makes a good informal hedge, flowering over a long season in summer and autumn. The pendulous flowers are followed by black fruits. Pruning in early spring will help to keep plants strong and compact.

Below: Several spiraeas are good shrubs for informal hedges, the arching stems being wreathed in glorious white flowers in late spring or early summer.

Some plants that respond well to tight clipping, such as lime and hornbeam, can be used for pleaching, creating what is sometimes referred to as a hedge on stilts. This is a useful technique for making a boundary without reducing the sense of space. Others, such as the small-leaved box 'Suffruticosa' and wall germander (*Teucrium*), are small enough to use for edging and parterres. Box and yew are the best choice for topiary. They are slow-growing, with small, dense leaves, and respond well to very specific, intricate cutting. Patience is vital with topiary, and dedication to maintaining the chosen forms. It is important to select shapes and designs well within your capabilities.

A hedge can also be used informally, such as in a cottage or landscape garden, where it introduces a free-flowing line to the design. For example, *Rhododendron ponticum* makes a tall, windproof evergreen hedge, that is covered with purple blossoms in spring. Where space is at a premium compact forms need to be chosen. In most cases informal hedges are made of flowering and, in some instances, fruiting species giving them seasonal interest. Some, like the laurustinus, *Viburnum tinus*, combine glossy evergreen foliage with pink winter flowers that are followed by blue-black fruit. There are a number of flowering plants that flower on old wood, such as forsythia and *Cornus mas*, that can be lightly pruned to make an informal hedge. They can also be clipped hard back to make a formal hedge, although flowers will be lost.

Quick-growing

Alnus cordata z 4
Italian alder
An extremely useful plant for wet conditions, this quickly forms a barrier against the wind and reaches 40ft (12m) in twenty years with a narrowly conical habit. In spring the crown is hung with clusters of yellow, male catkins. The tiny female flowers form small, round, woody fruits which persist throughout winter. The deciduous leaves are a shiny dark green above, paler beneath and up to 3in (8cm) long. Thrives in all moist soils, acid or alkaline; dislikes dry conditions. Needs sun or partial shade.

Chamaecyparis lawsoniana (*above*) z 4
Lawson cypress
One of the fastest-growing evergreen conifers used in gardens, this can be free-grown, reaching 60ft (18m), or clipped for formal use. Drooping, deep green leaves with greyish undersides set off small pinkish-red male cones in spring, then (on mature plants) woody cones. Forms have blue, grey, green or yellow foliage: 'Green Hedger' is ideal for screens. Excellent for exposed, windy sites and heavy soils; succeeds in shade. Plant 2ft (60cm) apart. Trim in late summer if used formally.

Crataegus monogyna z 4
Common hawthorn
This deciduous shrub has extremely spiny stems which act as a deterrent to unwanted animals. If free-growing it reaches 20ft (6m) in ten years and produces large clusters of single white flowers followed by red berries. For a formal hedge, plant 1ft (30cm) apart and clip monthly from late spring to late summer. The small, lobed leaves turn yellow in autumn. Useful for coastal sites and all exposed, windy gardens; excellent for heavy clay soils.

Cupressus macrocarpa z 7
Monterey cypress
One of the best evergreen conifers to grow for shelter in coastal areas, this species has bright green foliage that grows in upright, dense sprays. The leaves smell of lemons when crushed. Left unclipped, the Monterey cypress makes a tree 25ft (7.5m) high in about ten years. The conical habit broadens with age. Yellow-foliaged forms such as 'Goldcrest' must be planted in full sun or they fade to green. Older plants carry clusters of small, shiny brown cones. Plant 2ft (60cm) apart.

Elaeagnus × ebbingei (*below*) z 6
A fast-growing evergreen that reaches 6ft (1.8m) in ten years. The large, oval leaves are dark green above with round, silvery scales beneath. Yellowish-silver, fragrant flowers appear in autumn, followed by orange, silver-specked fruits in spring. 'Gilt Edge' has gold-margined leaves that need protection from cold winds. Plants dislike their roots being disturbed, which leads to the sudden death of entire limbs. Cut back long shoots by two-thirds in spring to promote bushiness.

Escallonia macrantha z 8
Plant specimens of this evergreen shrub 2ft (60cm) apart for a semi-formal, 6ft (1.8m)-tall hedge in five years. The small, scented, sticky leaves have indented margins. In summer it is covered with masses of rose red flowers. It thrives in most soils, resists drought and tolerates alkalinity: a good choice for exposed coastal gardens in warmer regions. Cut out a third of the oldest wood after flowering and trim back long shoots. Overgrown plants can be cut back to the ground and will take two to three seasons to regrow.

Hippophae rhamnoides (*above*) z 3
Sea buckthorn
This shrub is the perfect choice for a coastal windbreak. The silvery, narrow leaves are 2in (7cm) long and give good yellow autumn colour. Male and female plants must be grown together to ensure fruiting; the orange-yellow berries last into winter. Reaches 10ft (3m) in ten years, spreading rapidly by seed and suckers if well-established. Grow in full sun and, ideally, in light, sandy soil. Pruning is unnecessary but the plant will regenerate if cut hard back to ground level. It can become invasive.

Ligustrum ovalifolium (*below*) z 5
Privet
This species grows quickly, is evergreen or semi-evergreen, ideal for exposed sites, and will tolerate alkaline soils as well as atmospheric pollution. It reaches 8ft (2.4m) in eight years but is prone to sudden die-back in patches. The roots may deprive neighbouring plants of nutrients and water. For a bright yellow hedge grow 'Aureum'. Plant 1ft (30cm) apart. Clip at least monthly from mid-spring to late summer for a pleasing formal appearance.

Formal

Populus alba '**Richardii**' (*below*)   z 4

This form of the white poplar makes 33ft (10m) in ten years if free-growing. It has bright, golden yellow lobed leaves with white undersides and wavy margins. Trees make excellent windbreaks if pollarded; alternatively, grow the plants as large shrubs, cutting them back every two to three years. Valuable for exposed sites and for coastal areas, it tolerates some waterlogging but fails in dry soils. Grow in full sun to keep foliage colour. Plant well away from buildings and drains.

Thuja occidentalis (*below*)   z 3
American arborvitae

An evergreen conifer with a broad, conical habit and reddish-brown peeling bark, this species makes 10ft (3m) in ten years. The smaller 'Rheingold' has coppery-gold foliage that darkens to orange by winter. *T. plicata* 'Atrovirens' (z 5) has flat sprays of shiny foliage, and will tolerate shade and thin alkaline soil. The Chinese arborvitae, *T. orientalis*, has a formal habit, producing its foliage in vertical sprays. Plant 2ft (60cm) apart and trim during late summer. The foliage of the American arborvitae releases a fruity aroma when crushed.

Buxus sempervirens (*above*)   z 7
Common box

This slow-growing evergreen shrub makes only 4ft (1.2m) in ten years. It has small leaves and is able to withstand severe pruning, making it an ideal subject for a formal hedge; it is also used extensively for topiary. Mature, free-growing plants make small trees or large shrubs 8ft (2.4m) high. For a low edging along a path or for a knot garden or parterre, choose the dwarf form 'Suffruticosa'. Grows in most types of well-drained soil.

Carpinus betulus (*above*)   z 4
Common hornbeam

On heavy, damp soils, unsuitable for beech (*Fagus sylvatica*), hornbeam makes a good alternative. Bright green summer foliage turns yellow-brown in autumn. It retains its dead leaves during winter, providing an effective wind-filter throughout the year. As the new leaves unfold the old ones fall. Plant 18in (45cm) apart and trim frequently to form a dense hedge 8ft (2.4m) high in ten years. Hornbeam succeeds in sun or shade and makes a fine backcloth for the herbaceous or mixed border.

Fagus sylvatica (*below*)   z 4
Common beech

Beech grows best on well-drained, sandy or chalky soil and is intolerant of damp conditions which are better-suited to *Carpinus betulus*, the common hornbeam. Leaves open bright green but darken. The dead leaves are carried throughout winter. Susceptible to late spring frosts, it will only make 8ft (2.4m) in ten years in a sheltered spot; in the longer term, it is useful for windy sites. Plant 18in (45cm) apart and prune in late summer.

Ilex aquifolium (*below*)   z 4

Reaching only 5ft (1.5m) in ten years, this holly makes an excellent dense hedge with very prickly, dark green leaves. The leaves of 'Golden Queen' have yellow edges, while those of 'Silver Queen' are white-edged (both of these cultivars are male). 'J. C. Van Tol' has spineless leaves. The hardiest hollies are *I. × meserveae*, the blue holly, and the deciduous winterberry, *I. verticillata*. Plant 18in (45cm) apart in fertile soil; useful for heavy soils and coastal gardens. Trim plants in late summer. For berries, female forms need a pollinator to ensure setting.

Lavandula angustifolia (*above*)   z 7
A fine shrub for a low hedge, both the
mauve flowers and the silver-grey,
evergreen leaves are aromatic. 'Hidcote'
is dense with violet flowers. Thrives in
full sun, in well-drained soil and is
useful in coastal areas. Clip the plant
several times during the growing season
for a formal shape; this effectively stops
flowering. Unclipped plants reach 2ft
(60cm) with an equal spread. Discard
leggy plants and replant every five to six
years. Complements blue and grey
borders, rose gardens and stonework.

Lonicera nitida (*above*)   z 7
This evergreen shrubby honeysuckle
needs careful and regular clipping into a
wedge-shape to prevent bare patches
developing, particularly at the base of
the plant. The stiff, twiggy branches are
clothed with tiny, glossy green leaves
which are golden in 'Baggessen's Gold'.
Plants grow quickly to 5ft (1.5m). An
old or neglected hedge can be renovated
by being pruned hard back in early
spring to stimulate fresh growth. Grow
plants 1ft (30cm) apart, in any soil;
prune back to 1ft (30cm) immediately
after planting.

Prunus laurocerasus   z 7
Cherry laurel
This evergreen shrub quickly makes a
dense hedge 20ft (6m) high if free-
growing. It has large, dark-green, glossy
leaves. 'Rotundifolia' has leaves half as
broad as long. Succeeds best in acid soil
with some shelter; tolerates shade and
dripping water from overhanging trees.
Plant 2ft (60cm) apart and trim in
summer with secateurs: shears or hedge
trimmers cut through the leaves which
turn brown at the edges. Useful as a
dark backcloth for a border.

Rosmarinus officinalis (*above*)   z 6
Rosemary
A fast-growing evergreen shrub which
can be clipped into a low, formal hedge
or left as an informal hedge, making
5 × 5ft (1.5 × 1.5m) when mature. The
leaves are deep green, off-white below
and aromatic when rubbed. Flowers are
blue. 'Benenden Blue' is smaller-
growing with dark, very narrow leaves
and bright blue flowers. Plant 18in
(45cm) apart in a sunny, sheltered spot
in well-drained soil. Clip often when
young to induce bushiness. Rosemary is
useful in herb gardens, as an edging, or
in knot gardens.

Taxus baccata   z 6
Yew
This popular plant makes a dense hedge
if regularly clipped. The narrow, glossy,
evergreen leaves are poisonous, as are
the seeds (surrounded by a fleshy red
aril). *T.* × *media* 'Hicksii' is hardier,
with a broadly columnar habit. A fairly
rapid-grower if top-dressed annually
with fertilizer, it reaches 8ft (2.4m) in
ten years. Plant 2ft (60cm) apart:
tolerant of shade, exposed windy sites
and heavy or chalky soils. Trim in late
summer. Much-used for topiary.

Teucrium chamaedrys (*above*)   z 6
Wall germander
This shrub has a dwarf, bushy habit and
grows from a creeping rootstock. It has
dark grey-green, toothed leaves. Useful
for edging and in parterres where, with
regular clipping, a neat low hedge can
be produced. If plants are left
untrimmed they produce whorls of rose
pink flowers from mid-summer
onwards. Grow in sun in well-drained,
fertile soil. Can reach 3ft (90cm) if free-
grown. A good alternative to box, *Buxus
sempervirens*.

Tilia × euchlora (*below*)   z 5
Limes are tolerant of hard pruning and
are often seen as pleached specimens.
While free-growing trees can exceed
50ft (15m) in height, plants can be kept
to the required height with regular
clipping. The 4in (10cm)-long rounded
leaves are a shiny, dark green above and
pale and glaucous below, with brown
tufts between the veins. This form is
not susceptible to attack by aphids.
Grows well in full sun on all but the
poorest soils. Prune in spring before
growth begins. Plants can be trained to
form a tunnel or arbour.

Informal

Acer campestre (*below*)   z 5
Field maple
This deciduous plant is an excellent
choice for a country or cottage garden.
It is moderately fast-growing and
reaches 35ft (10.5m) if left free-growing.
The lobed leaves are green in summer
and turn reddish-yellow in autumn. The
trunk and stems of older plants develop
corky, raised ridges. Plant 18in (45cm)
apart in alkaline soil, in an open, sunny
position, or in some shade. Prune to
restrict growth in winter or, preferably,
in summer.

Arbutus unedo (*below*)   z 8
Strawberry tree
An unusual ericaceous plant in that it is
tolerant of alkaline soils. This species
makes a shrub or small tree some 20 ×
20ft (6 × 6m). It is often gnarled or
twisted when mature, with deep brown,
peeling bark. The evergreen leaves are
narrow, dark and glossy. Panicles of
white, pitcher-shaped flowers and edible
fruits are carried together in autumn
and winter. 'Rubra' has pink-flushed
flowers. The strawberry tree is a good
choice for exposed coastal gardens.
Pruning is necessary only to keep the
plant to the desired height.

Berberis thunbergii (*above*)   z4
This deciduous, spiny barberry reaches
5ft (1.5m) in ten years, 6ft (1.8m) when
mature. It makes a dense hedge of
small, bright green leaves with grey
undersides. Red-tinged, yellow flowers
open in spring, followed by bead-like,
shiny red fruits. The reddish-brown
bark is striking in winter. 'Rose Glow' is
illustrated; *atropurpurea* also has
reddish-purple leaves, which take on
good colours in autumn. Plant 18in
(45cm) apart. Grows in alkaline or clay
soil, in sun or shade: suitable for an
exposed position. Prune in winter.

Camellia × williamsii (*above*)   z 7
Camellias need shelter and are
unsuitable for very cold and exposed
positions; this is one of the best and
hardiest. In winter and early spring
velvet-petalled flowers in shades of
pink, red and white are set off by the
evergreen, dark, glossy leaves. Cultivars
include 'Donation' (dark pink double
flowers) and 'Francis Hanger' (white).
Can grow to 10ft (3m) in ten years in
humus-rich acid soil; will not tolerate a
trace of lime. Plant in partial shade.
Prune out long, leggy shoots.

Cornus mas (*below*)   z 4
Cornelian cherry
Usually seen as a free-growing large
shrub or densely-branched small tree,
this dogwood can be grown as a closely-
pruned hedge if clipped in early
summer. Clusters of small yellow
flowers appear on bare branches in early
spring. The dark green, oval leaves turn
orange-red in autumn. After a warm
summer, small, red, edible fruits form.
Enliven with *Tropaeolum speciosum* or
Clematis 'Perle d' Azur'. Grows in sun
or partial shade in most fertile soils.

Forsythia × intermedia '**Spectabilis**'   z 5
(*below*)
The golden bell bush is covered with
rich yellow flowers in spring. This
vigorous deciduous hybrid is
particularly floriferous. It has stout
growths and can make a wide-spreading
hedge 12ft (3.6m) tall by 10ft (3m) wide
in ten years if left unpruned. The
summer foliage is mid-green and
sharply toothed, unfolding as the
flowers fade. Other notable cultivars are
'Lynwood', 'Beatrix Farrand' and
'Spring Glory'. This bush tolerates most
soils and is suited to exposed sites. Cut
back after flowering if necessary.

Hibiscus syriacus (*above*)   z 5
This shrubby mallow carries large cup-shaped flowers from summer into autumn. The red, pink, purple, blue or white flowers last only a day before fading. Grey-green stems give winter colour; lobed leaves appear in late spring. 'Blue Bird' has dark-eyed, violet-blue flowers; 'Woodbridge' is the best large, single, pinkish-red form. Plants grow to 5 × 5ft (1.5 × 1.5m) in ten years, unless they are pruned in spring to keep them within bounds. Best in rich, well-drained soil in a sheltered, sunny position.

Hypericum 'Hidcote' (*above*)   z 5
One of the most popular flowering shrubs, this hardy, semi-evergreen has slender, low-growing, arching brown stems which can grow to 5 × 5ft (1.5 × 1.5m). The leaves are bright, apple green; the large yellow summer flowers are noted for their prominent golden stamens. This cultivar has the largest flowers. Grows equally well in dry or humus-rich soil, in full sun or semi-shade. Reduce plants if necessary by pruning hard back in late winter or early spring to the desired shape.

Osmanthus delavayi (*below*)   z 6
Grow this evergreen shrub for a wonderful fragrance in spring. The small, sweetly scented flowers are creamy-white and trumpet-shaped; they are held in plentiful clusters. The small, oval, dark green leathery leaves are fringed with minute teeth. It will grow to 5 × 4ft (1.5 × 1.2m) in ten years in well-drained soil, in sun or partial shade, with some shelter from other evergreens. Slower growth can be expected in cold areas. Any trimming should be carried out straight after flowering, using secateurs.

Potentilla fruticosa 'Goldfinger'   z 2
(*below*)
In ten years this shrubby cinquefoil can grow to 5ft (1.5m), forming a rounded bush with twiggy stems. The deciduous pinnate leaves are deep green and hairy. A profusion of large, deep yellow, five-petalled flowers appear from summer into autumn. Other forms include 'Katherine Dykes' (pale yellow flowers), 'Farrer's White' (white with yellow stamens) and 'Red Ace' (vermilion flowers with yellow centres). Plant 18in (45cm) apart in most soils. Prune in early spring to control growth.

Rhododendron ponticum (*above*)   z 6
This very resilient rhododendron will succeed in deep shade and is excellent for hedging. An evergreen shrub with large dark green ovate leaves, it grows to around 6ft (1.8m) in ten years. In late spring and early summer it is covered with tubular, lilac-pink flowers. 'Variegatum' has creamy-white margined leaves and is one of the few variegated rhododendrons. Needs a moist, acid soil and will benefit from a humus-rich mulch in summer. When the desired height has been reached, prune selected shoots after flowering.

Viburnum tinus (*above*)   z 7
Laurustinus
The stems of this adaptable plant carry dark, glossy, evergreen leaves and flat cymes of flowers at the tips. Pink in bud, these open white from late autumn to mid-spring. Shiny blue-black fruits often coincide with some flowers. Plants reach 10 × 10ft (3 × 3m) in ten years. 'Eve Price' is denser and smaller with pale pink flowers. Tolerates most soil conditions, shade, pollution and salt spray. Remove weak growth and prune lightly to maintain the shape.

GROUND COVER

For most people, the aim of ground cover in a garden is to minimize the number of weeds that seed themselves and grow rapidly, marring the appearance of the planting and competing with cultivated plants for moisture, nutrients and, in some cases, light. In the last 40 years or so, as labour has become more expensive, densely leaved low-growing plants have been widely used to accomplish this aim and the term "ground cover plants" has been applied to them.

They are comparatively cheap to buy, easy to plant and available in many different forms: quick or slow to increase; suitable for sun or shade; thriving in freely draining or moisture retentive soils; appropriate to formal or informal schemes, according to species or cultivar. Ground cover plants can be prostrate conifers, shrubs or herbaceous plants, evergreen or deciduous: something to satisfy every need, taste and planting plan.

Ground cover plants quickly colonize sizeable areas and build up a thick thatch of vegetation that suppresses most weeds. The one exception is woody weeds, but these usually appear singly and are easily removed. The perennial quality of most ground cover plants ensures that, with a minimum of pruning and splitting during the winter months, maintenance during the growing season is negligible. Once they are established, there is no longer any necessity to dig and hoe the areas of the garden that are planted with them. The chances of success are maximized if the ground is cleared of perennial weeds before planting. This can be a time-consuming task but it pays dividends.

The art of ground cover lies in spacing the plants correctly to ensure that the ground is covered quickly but without the plants competing for space or losing their characteristic habits from having to spread too far. The estimated spread of a plant can be used as a guide, taking into consideration the means by which it spreads. Those plants that spread by underground or overground runners are, as a rule, the most vigorous. They can be useful when a large area needs to be covered, but the larger plants, in particular, tend to suffocate and choke everything in sight. Clump forming plants are much more containable and there are a number that self-seed as well. These days, when a plant becomes a pest it is possible to eradicate it by painting it out with a glyphosate-based translocated herbicide that is deactivated as soon as it comes into contact with the ground; this should be used sparingly, over limited areas. However, most plants can be kept at bay by digging them up regularly.

The value of leaves cannot be overemphasized when looking at ground cover plants, the different textures and colours being so closely juxtaposed that they create an intricate tapestry. There are greens in every hue, yellow-flushed plants and white-variegated cultivars that prefer shade (for example, *Hosta fortunei* 'Aurea', *Lysimachia nummularia* 'Aurea' and *Lamium maculatum*); while silvery, yellow-variegated, purple and glaucous foliage perform best in sunshine (*Heuchera* 'Palace Purple', *Stachys byzantina*, *Ruta graveolens*). Flowers must be woven into the whole scheme, bringing seasonal interest to the composition (*Geranium endressii* 'Wargrave Pink', *Helleborus orientalis*, *Phlox subulata*).

Ground cover plants can be used in great informal drifts, covering large areas of the garden. A suitable scheme for a moist shady position would include hostas in variety, pulmonarias, hellebores, bergenias, solomon's seal and epimediums; in direct sunlight

catmints, pinks, thrifts, snow-in-summer, jerusalem sage and thymes thrive. A steep bank, where it may be difficult to grow grass, can be successfully clothed in a thick mat of St John's wort (*Hypericum calycinum*) which carries bright yellow flowers throughout the summer, or periwinkle (*Vinca*) that raises starry blue eyes over a dense carpet of green leaves in spring – both require pruning in late winter.

In formal designs, where labour-intensive bedding plants might have been used in the past, it is possible to associate neatly clipped cotton lavenders, coloured leaved sages, blue leaved festuca, ivies and chamomile for a pleasing effect.

Left: A sunny well-drained sloping site is completely clothed with low-growing perennials, including *Convolvulus sabatius*, helianthemums, pinks and thrift. Dense planting suppresses weeds and creates a rich tapestry effect. The conifers introduce a discreet vertical element that emphasizes the flatness of the ground cover. This planting demonstrates the wealth of colour and texture provided by ground cover plants.

Below: Ivy is a thorough and accommodating ground cover in shady, cool conditions, creating a dense and weed-proof carpet.

For flowers

Arabis caucasica   z 3

Often listed as *A. albida*, this useful plant forms loose mats of grey-green oblong leaves with bright white, slightly fragrant flowers carried in lax racemes 8in (20cm) tall in spring. It succeeds in dry situations and combines well with *Aubrieta* hybrids and *Alyssum saxatile*. The best forms are the double 'Flore-Pleno', 'Rosabelle' with its single, deep pink flowers, and the green-and-yellow leaved 'Variegata'. Propagate from cuttings taken in the summer or raise from seed sown during the autumn; plants may also be divided. Deadhead after the flowers have faded.

Asperula odorata   z 4
Sweet woodruff

Also listed as *Galium odoratum*, the whole of this carpeting perennial is aromatic. It bears whorls of star-shaped white flowers during summer and reaches a height of 6in (15cm), with a spread of 12in (30cm). When in ideal conditions – partially shaded and in moist but well-drained soil – sweet woodruff needs to be kept in check as it tends to be invasive. Propagate either by softwood cuttings or raise from seed sown in early summer.

Cerastium tomentosum (*above*)   z 6
Snow-in-summer

This widely-spreading, extremely vigorous perennial is an excellent for dry, sunny banks. It will become straggly if grown in the shade. From late spring the star-shaped white flowers are held above the foliage in a dense bright display. The spreading, prostrate stems are clothed in a mat of very small, grey shiny leaves. Plants reach a height of 6in (15cm) and tend to be rampant when established. Propagate by division or sowing seeds during spring.

Cotoneaster dammeri   z 6

In well-drained soil, this low evergreen cotoneaster makes excellent ground cover, especially beneath other taller shrubs. It reaches 4in (10cm) in height, spreading to 2ft (60cm) or more, and needs hand weeding until a dense canopy is formed. The prostrate stems carry oval alternate leaves which are 1in (2.5cm) long, with small white flowers appearing in late spring and bright sealing-wax-red fruit in autumn. The deciduous *C. horizontalis* reaches 2ft (60cm); it has a variegated form.

Geranium endressii **'Wargrave Pink'**
(*above*)   z 3

Originating from the Pyrenees, this geranium is ideal in a mixed border between large evergreen shrubs. 'Wargrave Pink' is a vigorous plant which produces flowers (bright salmon-pink with pale veins) throughout the summer and into the autumn, if cut back. The stems can reach 2ft (60cm) in height; the deeply divided leaves are 2-3in (5-8cm) across and form neat clumps. Plants will grow in most soils, in sun or light shade, and are useful as a weed-suppressant. Propagate by division in autumn or spring.

Helleborus orientalis   z 3
Lenten rose

Choose a sheltered spot to grow this beautiful, evergreen hardy perennial. The flowers are extremely variable, ranging from creamy-white to deep-purple with yellow stamens, as plants readily cross-pollinate. They open from mid-winter onwards on stems 12-18in (30-45cm) high, above divided, mid-green leathery leaves. Plants self-seed very easily. Combines well with galanthus (snowdrop) and the perennial *Brunnera macrophylla*.

Iberis sempervirens (*above*)   z 4
Candytuft

With its compact, cushion-like growth of dark green, evergreen leaves and dense smothering in late spring of white flowers, this sub-shrub makes ideal ground cover. It is also often grown as edging or in rock gardens. For best results plant in well-drained, slightly alkaline soil. Plants can reach 9in (23cm) in height and spread to 2ft (60cm). 'Snowflake' has larger-petalled, brighter flowers; the smaller 'Little Gem' has more erect growth. Propagate from softwood cuttings in mid-summer.

Hypericum calycinum (*above*)   z 5
Rose of Sharon

The suckering habit of this dwarf evergreen shrub allows it to cover large areas quickly, even on poor and impoverished soils. The solitary flowers appear at the end of shoots up to 20in (50cm) tall. They are 4in (10cm) across and golden-yellow with a central boss of yellow stamens tipped by red anthers. Once established, cut hard back in spring to promote fresh growth, which is vital if plants have been affected by rust disease.

Lamium maculatum (*below*)   z 3
Spotted deadnettle
In deep shade this rampant perennial will establish quickly where other plants might struggle. It has the characteristic "square" stems of the Labiate family, cream-striped, pungent leaves and mauve-pink flowers which appear in early summer. Plants can spread to 3ft (90cm), reaching a height of 8in (20cm). The cultivars tend to be less vigorous: 'Beacon Silver' has green-edged silver leaves and pink flowers; 'Aureum' has pale yellow leaves with pink flowers.

Lysimachia nummularia (*below*)   z 3
Creeping Jenny
In moist, sunny conditions this plant is especially rampant and needs to be checked by regular pulling and thinning of wandering shoots. 'Aurea', which has yellow-green leaves, is less invasive and makes an excellent low-growing perennial ground cover; it is also used in hanging baskets, containers and for edging. The leaves are opposite on the prostrate stems, barely 1in (2.5cm) long and an ideal foil for the bright yellow flowers in summer. Plants reach only 1in (2.5cm) in height but can spread for 3-4ft (60-90cm).

Phlox subulata (*above*)   z 2
Moss phlox
In spring, mats of bright flowers hide the narrow, spiky leaves of this evergreen, mound-forming perennial. Colour variations include the clear blue 'G.F. Wilson' and 'Scarlet Flame' with its deep red flowers. Plants need sun and fertile, well-drained soil. They reach 6in (15cm) in height and spread up to 20in (50cm). In early spring liven the flat mounds with underplantings of dwarf bulbs. Propagate by taking 2in (5cm) cuttings through the summer. 'Marjory' is illustrated.

Polygonum affine 'Donald Lowndes'   z 3
This evergreen perennial is outstanding when planted in bold drifts on large banks. It produces small rose-red flowers in dense spikes in summer which fade and pale as they age. Plants grow to a height of 6in (15cm) and spread up to 6in (15cm). The narrow, pointed green leaves often take on attractive bronze tints in autumn and winter. For a larger plant grow *P. bistorta* 'Superbum' which has 2ft (60cm)-tall pokers of pink flowers in late summer. Grow both in sun or partial shade, where they will succeed in most fertile soils. Divide in autumn or spring.

Saxifraga umbrosa   z 6
London pride
The dark green leaves of this saxifrage cover the ground throughout the year. In summer, small pink flowers are carried in delicate sprays 1ft (30cm) above the evergreen rosettes of leaves. Remove flowering stems as they fade. Plants need a moist soil and partial shade to grow well. Propagate in spring by dividing clumps. 'Variegata' has yellow-splashed leaves.

Vinca minor (*below*)   z 4
A trailing evergreen perennial of use in shady positions and on inaccessible, steep banks. The bright bluey-mauve flowers appear from early spring to autumn, with the main flush in summer, among glossy, dark green, lanceolate leaves. To encourage a second flush, cut back after the main display. Plants need well-drained soil. The arching shoots can reach 8in (20cm) in height, spreading to 2ft (60cm). There are a number of cultivars; 'Variegata' has creamy-white splashed leaves and 'Multiplex' double plum-purple flowers.

Waldsteinia ternata (*below*)   z 4
Also listed as *W. trifolia*, this semi-evergreen creeping perennial is notable for its trifoliate leaves and saucer-shaped, yellow flowers. In autumn, the leaves turn golden which is an added attraction. Plants grow to a height of 4in (10cm) forming loose spreading mats in well-drained soil in sun. Useful on banks where it soon spreads by fast-growing runners. Propagate by division in spring. Similar is *W. fragarioides* which has deeper toothed, strawberry-like leaves. Both are uncommon but well worth growing.

For foliage

Aegopodium podagraria 'Variegata' z 3
(*above*)
Variegated bishop's weed, gout weed or ground elder
A variegated form of the weed ground elder, this perennial has lobed pinnate leaves, with creamy-white variegated margins, which smother the ground. Plants grow to a height of 4in (10cm). In summer insignificant white flowers appear which are best removed. A good plant for a shady position, it will grow equally well in full sun; prefers moist soil. Propagate by division of the rhizomes in spring. Fully hardy.

Arctostaphyllos uva-ursi z 2
Bearberry
This attractive and low-growing plant barely reaches a height of 5in (13cm). It succeeds best on well-drained acid soils, in sun or light shade, and has a spread of 2ft (60cm) after two years. The leaves, which are small, shiny and evergreen form a weed-suppressant mat. In spring the plant is studded with pale pink, bell-shaped flowers followed in autumn by small bright red berries. 'Massachusetts' is lower-growing with long-lasting flowers. Plants root readily from stems touching the soil.

Asarum europeum z 4
The European ginger
A faint marbled effect is created by the bright glossy-green and pale veined leaves of this unusual perennial ground cover plant. The leaves are evergreen and grow on 6in (15cm)-long stalks which hide the bell-shaped, maroon flowers beneath. Individual plants spread to 12in (30cm) and are best grown in cool moist conditions. For interest, plant in a drift with the mouse plant *Arisarum proboscideum*.

Bergenia cordifolia (*below*) z 4
Elephant's ears
The large, leathery evergreen leaves of this plant, from which its common name derives, take on a range of reddish and mauve tints in winter. From late winter onwards pink or white flower heads are carried on 18in (45cm)-tall stalks. Individual plants spread to 24in (60cm) and tolerate sun or shade. They are excellent for planting as an edging to a large shrub border, on most soils. *B. purpurascens* and *B. p.* 'Ballawley', *B.* 'Abendglut', 'Silberlicht' and 'Morgenrote' are all worth growing.

Epimedium × rubrum (*below*) z 4
Barrenwort
An ideal choice for planting where dry soil and shade are the main factors, such as beneath trees. A relative of *Berberis*, this low-growing plant has red or bronze-tinted leaves during spring along with crimson flowers with white spurs which are carried on thin stems 9in (23cm) tall. In summer the foliage is pale green. In winter, cut away the old leaves, taking care not to damage the flower buds, to reveal the flowers. Propagate by dividing the rootstock and plant 9-12in (23-30cm) apart.

Euonymus fortunei 'Sparkle 'n' Gold'
(*above*) z 5
This popular, woody carpeting shrub grows to 9in (23cm) high in sun or shade. Its small, dark green leaves are edged with bright yellow and form a dense cover. Plants succeed on most soils and should be planted up to 18in (45cm) apart. In winter the leaves assume pinkish tints as the temperature falls. Useful for mass planting on banks and other large areas. 'Emerald Gaiety' has white-edged leaves, while 'Kewensis' grows to 4-6in (10-15cm) with tiny leaves in dense mats.

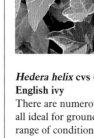

Hedera helix cvs (*above*) z 5
English ivy
There are numerous forms of this plant, all ideal for ground cover in a wide range of conditions, including shade. 'Glacier' (*above*) has greyish-green variegated, cream-edged leaves with reddish stalks. The narrow lobes of 'Digitata' contrast well with those of 'Pedata'; 'Goldheart' is popular for its bright yellow centred leaves; the dark green 'Atropurpurea' turns deep purple in winter. Plants grow 1in (2.5cm) high, spreading to 18in (45cm).

Helxine soleirolii (*below*)   z 8
Baby's tears or mother-of-thousands
Also listed as *Soleirolia soleirolii*, the
common names of this plant come from
its small rounded leaves and its capacity
to grow from the tiniest fragments. This
evergreen, prostrate-growing perennial
forms a dense ground-hugging carpet
which can choke other plants if not
controlled. It will grow well beneath
trees. At most it achieves a height of 2in
(5cm). Plant in moist soil; divide in
spring. The leaves may be burnt back
by winter frosts.

***Heuchera* 'Palace Purple'** (*below*)   z 4
Grown for its impressive foliage, which
is purple-red, brighter red on the
undersides, this clump-forming
perennial remains evergreen only in
mild winters. The leaves are heart-
shaped with deep veins, above which in
early summer are carried delicate sprays
of small, bell-shaped white flowers.
Plants grow to 18in (45cm) with equal
spread, thriving best in a semi-shaded
spot in moisture-retentive but well-
drained soil. Divide in autumn or
spring, using the young outer pieces of
the woody crown. *H. sanguinea* has
blood-red flowers and rounded leaves.

***Juniperus horizontalis* 'Grey Pearl'**   z 3
(*above*)
With its pale grey-green foliage, this
prostrate evergreen conifer grows to 8in
(20cm) and spreads widely, up to 10ft
(3m). It will thrive in sun or light shade.
Other cultivars include 'Emerald
Spreader', which barely reaches 4in
(10cm) high, and the bluey leaved
'Glauca', 6in (15cm) high. *Juniperus* ×
media 'Pfitzeriana' is a vigorous hybrid
which is capable of reaching 5ft (1.5m)
in height after ten years. Plant junipers
on well-drained soil.

Lonicera pileata (*above*)   z 5
Evergreen in all but the coldest areas,
this shrub is well-suited to planting in
bold drifts. The stiff, spreading, almost
horizontal branches fan out in layers,
forming a dense canopy as adjoining
plants knit together. The small glossy
leaves are a fresh green, paler on the
undersides. Small, fragrant white
flowers appear on the undersides of the
branches followed by beautiful
translucent purple berries. Grows to 2ft
(60cm) with a spread of 3ft (1m). The
flat growth is a good base for a summer-
flowering scrambling clematis.

Pachysandra terminalis (*below*)   z 4
Tolerant of deep shade and a tough
grower, this plant has a place in all
gardens. Growing to 10in (25cm) and
quickly spreading to 3ft (90cm) due to
its rhizomatous roots, it has leathery,
shiny green leaves at the top of 6-8in
(15-20cm)-tall stems. The small, scented
flowers appear in spring and are creamy-
white and rather insignificant. The plant
will grow quickest in moist, acid
conditions; it will grow equally well but
slower on dry acid soils. 'Variegata' and
'Silveredge' are less vigorous with
narrow white margins on their leaves.

Stachys byzantina (*below*)   z 4
Bunnies' or lambs' ears
Also known as *S. lanata*, this low-
growing evergreen perennial has silvery-
woolly leaves. It is ideal for a hot, dry
sunny position. The leaves are oval, up
to 4in (10cm) long, forming a spreading,
weed-smothering carpet, never reaching
more than 6in (15cm) high, spreading to
18in (45cm). Flowers appear in grey-
purple heads and are usually removed
because they grow on 20in (50cm)-tall
stems. 'Silver Carpet' is flowerless,
making it particularly suitable as an
effective ground cover.

BORDER PERENNIALS

The most successful borders are those that are designed with a balanced mixture of plants to produce a year-round display. The mainstay of the border is the perennials, while shrubs give a strong form to the composition and bulbs and annuals add seasonal interest. Many perennials are herbaceous (such as astrantia, peonies, dicentras, meconopsis and polygonatum), that is to say they die down in the autumn and overwinter under ground, and some are evergreen, including sub-shrubs (which are woody at the base and herbaceous at the tips) such as santolina, rue and sages.

Mixed borders are a rewarding form of gardening because a display can be produced in a short time and

then any errors can be corrected by moving plants about or by removing them, if they overstep their mark. Many perennials, given a good soil, spread quite rapidly. However, when selecting them care should be taken to match the plants to the climatic and soil conditions of a garden because in some cases, particularly with those perennials that spread by underground rhizomes, they can become rampant or self-seed with abandon.

Traditionally, in England, the border was set in a long, thin piece of ground – occasionally up to 300ft (90m) in length and at least 10ft (3m) wide – usually positioned in front of a wall or hedge and planted

Left: In early summer popular perennials for traditional borders include delphiniums, lady's mantle, lupins and poppies. A patch of the annual *Limnanthes douglasii* (with its unusual yellow and white flowers) fills a gap at the front of the border and will eventually be replaced by late-flowering annuals.

Right: In autumn the tall, creamy plumes of *Cortaderia selloana*, the pampas grass, are a perfect foil in a large border for the purples and mauves of asters and warm reds of *Dahlia* 'Bishop of Llandaff', and *Persicaria amplexicaulis*. Note the marked contrasts in forms and textures.

exclusively with herbaceous perennials. The plants were arranged according to height, with the tallest at the back and the shortest at the front, and usually in an almost random, polychromatic way. Borders were designed to be at their peak for two or three of the summer months, when the owners were most likely to visit their country residence, and as they were part of a sizeable garden they could easily be avoided during the rest of the year. As a consequence little attention was paid to spring and autumn colour or winter form.

In the early part of the twentieth century Gertrude Jekyll, the famous garden designer and author of many books, encouraged gardeners to think more carefully about selecting plants according to their colour, about extending the season by making use of foliage as well as flowers, and about planting late-flowering species beside earlier ones to hide these as they faded. For example, the frothiness of gypsophila will soon cover the fading crowns of poppies while the dark stems and star-like white daisy flowers of *Aster divaricatus* will arch nicely over the large glossy leaves of bergenias.

The variety of possible colour schemes for a border is enormous and in the end the choice is a personal one, but such books as Miss Jekyll's and, more recently, Penelope Hobhouse's on the subject of colour are classics and serve as good inspiration, as do other gardens – often as examples of what not to do. The important thing to remember is that once you choose a colour scheme it is essential to adhere to it if the border is to succeed. For example, the introduction of yellow tulips in a border of grey, whites, purples and mauves, pinks and maroons, spoils the whole effect even if they flower for only two or at most three weeks during the year.

If you wish to have several different schemes but the garden is too small to accommodate more than one border, it is possible to devise a graduated scheme.

The colours of the rainbow can serve as a good guide-line, starting with purples and deep blues at one end, progressing through lighter shades of blue to white and then introducing light yellows which increase in density through oranges to deep reds. If space allows, the colour can move back down the scale, creating an effective, definite rhythm.

An alternative is to introduce banks of neutral colours to separate successive schemes. In large gardens, dark green buttresses of yew against a wall or other hedge can be successful, while on a more modest scale patches of grey foliage (from such plants as santolina, artemisia or stachys) serve as a good foil to many colours and can link one scheme to another.

Not all borders need to be linear and backed by a wall or hedge. Much can be made of beds positioned in the centre of the garden that can be viewed from all sides. In recent years, island beds that fit into an in-formal garden plan – often irregularly shaped and surrounded by serpentine paths – have been made popular by the nursery, Blooms of Bressingham. Colours can be divided according to aspect, with warm reds, oranges and yellows on the sunniest sides and cooler pale blues, pinks and whites where it is shadier.

In a more formal setting, a central regularly-shaped bed, divided into four or more compartments depending on size with box edging and a pattern reminiscent of a parterre or knot garden, can equally well be planted with perennial plants. The rigidity of the design will hold together the essentially informal habit of the perennials.

It is possible to have a border in most situations, such is the diversity of perennial species. Whether the site is sun-baked and freely draining (in which case artemisia, sage, eryngium and phlomis are a good choice) or in the shade of trees and moisture retentive (where *Brunnera macrophylla*, astilbes and dicentras will thrive) it is possible to produce a successful border. If the conditions are particularly demanding then great drifts of a few suitable species can look just as spectacular as a large collection of different-coloured flowers in a kinder environment.

While there are a number of species that bloom for several months (for example penstemons, astrantias, erodium and *Sedum* 'Autumn Joy'), it is always important to include a good number of plants that are grown primarily for their foliage (such as artemisias, hostas, alchemilla, ferns and grasses) as the leaves will last for most of the season. With such foliage plants, flowers must be considered as extras that appear for a few weeks with continuity being achieved through the use of many species.

It is always a bonus to bring a little of the garden into the house to enjoy at close quarters. While most plants can be cut, it is useful to grow some that bear plenty of blossoms that last particularly well in water indoors – for example, coreopsis, astrantias and dianthus. In many cases cutting flower stems encourages more to grow and thereby lengthens the flowering time of the plant.

Perennial plants, like most others, should usually be planted out or moved when they are dormant, any time during autumn and winter when the conditions are suitable. Sometimes it is useful to do this while they are growing, between spring and autumn, when it is easier to evaluate their size and spread. In such circumstances, planting should be done with extreme care, speed and plenty of water to prevent the roots from dehydrating. If the plant is checked by being moved at this time it will usually have recovered by the following season.

Some staking is often required to prevent tall-stemmed plants from flopping over and swamping all around them. There are a number of different types of stakes available on the market, often in plastic-coated metal and in shades of green or in black; alternatively, tall hazel or beech twigs can be used and look a little more natural. However, on the whole it is best to avoid using stakes if at all possible and rely on the density of planting to ensure that most of the plants remain upright.

The permanent character of a border can make perennial weeds something of a problem, it is therefore important to ensure that the ground is clear before planting which usually means careful hand weeding. A generous layer of clean organic mulch (spent untreated mushroom compost, well-rotted manure or forest bark are among the best) applied in spring will help to prevent weed seeds from germinating; in addition it will improve the soil composition and nutrient levels and help to conserve moisture throughout the season.

Left: Crocosmia 'Lucifer' thrives in a hot sunny border, making a large clump of sword-like foliage, topped by brilliant, flame-red flowers. The sub-shrub cotton lavender (*Santolina chamaecyparissus*), with its grey, conifer-like foliage and small, yellow, pompon flowers, and the purple-blue spikes of *Salvia × superba* spill over the gravelly path, softening the edge of this striking border.

For cutting

Acanthus mollis z 5
Bear's breeches
It is the architectural qualities of this perennial that make it such a dramatic addition to the garden and to any arrangement of cut plants. The large, oval semi-evergreen leaves are deeply cut and bright shiny green. During summer strong spikes of funnel-shaped white and mauve flowers appear, reaching up to 4ft (1.2m) in height. Plants spread to around 18in (45cm) and prefer a warm sunny spot in well-drained soil. They die back to a crown in autumn. Propagate by division when dormant or through root cuttings.

Anaphalis triplinervis z 3
Pearly everlasting
Cut the heads of small papery flowers of this perennial during late summer and hang them upside down to dry out naturally. They are ideal for indoor winter decoration. Plants grow to 1ft (30cm) high with around a 6in (15cm) spread. The stems and lance-shaped leaves are silvery and woolly, and the flowers are whitish. Plants prefer full sun and well-drained soil, and can be divided in the spring.

Artemisia ludoviciana (*above*) z 5
White sage
A lovely foliage plant for cutting. The aromatic, silvery-white lance-shaped leaves of this bushy perennial are woolly all over. In summer the narrow plumes of whitish-grey flowers appear when the plants reach about 4ft (1.2m) in height. They thrive in a hot dry border where the soil tends to dry out in summer, and go well in blue- and grey-themed plantings. Increase by softwood or semi-ripe cuttings in summer and trim plants lightly in spring before growth starts. White sage can be invasive.

Aster × frikartii 'Mönch' z 6
Encourage the production of blooms on this autumn-flowering perennial by pinching back the shoots in spring and early summer. The large, daisy-like, scented, clear bluey-mauve flowers appear from late summer to mid- or late autumn. They are carried on 3ft (90cm)-tall strong stems. The plants are easily grown in well-drained soil, and should be divided every three to four years, replanting with the outer sections of the crowns. Plants spread to 15in (40cm). The many forms of *A. novi-belgii* and *A. novae-angliae* are worth growing.

Astrantia major (*above*) z 4
Masterwort
These beautiful flowers create interest in both the border and the vase. Each bloom resembles a small red pincushion stuck with green and white florets which are surrounded by a frill of papery bracts. The strong flowering stems emerge from a cluster of deeply divided, basal leaves which form good ground-covering mounds. For variegated foliage grow 'Sunningdale Variegated' and for plum-coloured flowers grow 'Rubra'. Plants need moist soil in sun or light shade, and reach about 2ft (60cm) in height. Divide them in spring.

Bupleurum angulosum z 4
The most striking feature of this umbelliferous plant is the collar of large pale jade green bracts, ¾in (1 ½cm) wide, that back the clusters of tiny yellow flowers. The flowers are arranged in small umbels which are part of larger umbels and form dense clumps in summer. The flower heads are held high above the lanceolate leaves. Plants grow to 18in (45cm). They are slow to spread and need cool, well drained conditions in an open site. Evergreen in mild areas.

Coreopsis grandiflora (*above*) z 3
Prized as a border perennial and for its strong upright stems which are ideal for cutting, the coreopsis has bright yellow flowers through the summer and into early autumn. They are carried on stems up to 3ft (90cm) tall on which the green narrow leaves grow. The petals or ray florets are split at their tips and have a small dark-maroon spot at their base. Several good forms exist: 'Goldfink', 'Mayfield Giant', 'Badengold' and 'Sunburst'. Grow plants in large clumps in moist rich soil in the sun. Divide in spring or take cuttings in summer.

Dianthus 'Doris' z 3
One of the most popular of all the pinks, this modern carnation has strongly fragrant flowers and strong stems suitable for cutting. The flowers are pale pink, semi-double with a reddish ring toward the centre. Plants grow compactly and produce a continuous flow of flowers through the summer months. They grow as evergreen clumps with numerous flowering shoots, 12-18in (30-45cm) tall. Plants need a sunny spot and fertile soil.

Gypsophila paniculata z 3
Chalk plant or baby's breath
The flowers of gypsophila form delicate clouds of white during summer. They cut well and add great beauty to flower arrangements of any size. Plants grow to 3ft (90cm) in height with a similar spread, flourishing on alkaline soils in full sun. The grey-green foliage grows at the base of the plant. 'Bristol Fairy' is a double form with bright white flowers; 'Flamingo' is also double but pink. Plants tend to be short-lived and die away after a few years. New specimens are best obtained from a nursery.

For shade and dry soil

Scabiosa caucasica (*above*)   z 3
The flowers are like pincushions, 2in (5cm) or more across, and are a beautiful lavender-blue throughout the summer. Good cultivars include the creamy-white 'Miss Willmott', the pure white 'Bressingham White' and 'Clive Greaves' which is bluish-violet. The leaves are narrow, more deeply divided further up the stems and quite hairy. This perennial prefers alkaline soils and is ideal for a cottage-style border. Plant young plants in spring, dividing older clumps to increase stocks.

Thalictrum speciosissimum (*above*) z 5
Meadow rue
This species of meadow rue is useful for cutting even when the flowers have faded, as its blue-grey divided foliage remains attractive for the entire summer. The small flowers are lemon-yellow in fluffy heads which fit well into a border where the colour theme is blue and yellow. An underplanting of lady's mantle, *Alchemilla mollis*, is recommended. Plants reach a height of up to 5ft (1.5m), forming good strong stems. Plant in fertile moist soil in full sun. Large plants can be divided.

Aruncus dioicus (*below*)   z 4
Goat's beard
Also listed as *A. sylvester* and *Spiraea aruncus*, the common name aptly describes the branching feathery plumes of small creamy-white flowers which grow on stems up to 6ft (2m) tall. The flowers appear in summer above an attractive mound of broad fern-shaped leaves. Plants grow well in dry or moist soil. 'Kneiffii' has finely divided foliage and creamy flowers growing to 3ft (90cm). Male plants tend to be the most floriferous, while the females have the seed heads which are used for drying. Divide plants in spring or autumn.

Aster macrophyllus   z 3
Grown for its ability to create good ground cover, this spreading aster reaches a height of 2ft (60cm), with equal spread, soon meshing together when planted in a group. The leaves are large and heart-shaped, and the main flush of pale lilac flowers is in autumn. It thrives in dry soil near to trees and shrubs, where its roots can be invasive, but should be avoided elsewhere. Lift and divide to propagate.

Dryopteris filix-mas   z 4
In even the most inhospitable places the male fern will produce its distinctive upright fronds which look like shuttlecocks. It adapts well to dry and shady conditions, staying evergreen in mild winters. Plants reach a height of 4ft (1.2m) with a spread of 3ft (90cm). The arching fronds are much-divided, lance-shaped and mid-green, unfurling from crowns coated in papery brown scales. The tough, rhizomatous brown roots form thick clumps. Divide mature plants by cutting younger crowns cleanly away from the older parent. 'Grandiceps' is a superior form.

Epimedium perralderianum (*above*) z 5
The barrenworts are noted for their tough growth and tolerance of dry shaded sites, making resilient ground cover plants. This species is semi-evergreen, forming carpets of growth 1ft (30cm) high, which are studded in spring with clusters of bright yellow, pendent flowers with short spurs. The glossy deep green foliage can be clipped back to allow the flowers to be seen more easily. The new leaves which grow out in spring and summer are tinted with shades of red or bronze. To propagate, divide the woody rootstock during spring or autumn.

Filipendula hexapetala 'Flore Plena' z 3
Dropwort
Also named *F. vulgaris* 'Flore Plena', this form has double white flowers which can be flushed pink, carried in large flat panicles above the finely divided carrot-like foliage during the summer. The plants are perennial with thick, fleshy swollen roots and reach a height of 2ft (60cm) with an 18in (45cm) spread. They succeed on dry chalky soils in shade. Division of the rootstock in winter and spring is essential because dropwort does not come true from seed.

Geranium endressii 'Wargrave Pink' z 3
A reliable plant which is excellent for suppressing weeds and for colonizing virtually any garden situation. Its cup-shaped, bright salmon-pink flowers are carried above light green, delicately lobed basal leaves, on plants 18in (45cm) high with a spread of 2ft (60cm). This cultivar has particularly bright flowers which work well in a dry shaded position planted with purple-flowered irises. Divide in spring or autumn or take semi-ripe cuttings in summer.

For shade and moist soil

Helleborus foetidus   z 3
Stinking hellebore
The common name should not deter the planting of this adaptable evergreen plant which can bring early colour to a shaded dry border. It associates well with early-flowering perennials: try its pale green, red-margined flowers next to those of honesty, *Lunaria rediviva*, or the spring pea, *Lathyrus vernus*. The flowers appear in large panicles from late winter onwards, held high above the leaves. Plants can be seen at their best when on a slope. Propagate by division, with minimal disturbance.

Iris foetidissima (*above*)   z 5
Gladwyn iris
In the autumn the greenish-brown seed pods of this iris split open to reveal fiery orange seed. To view the heavy pendulous pods, plants are best placed on high banks or in raised beds. In summer the purple flowers are carried among the evergreen, dark green grassy leaves. 'Variegata' has cream variegation, but has few if any seeds. Plants thrive in poor dry soil in shade, growing to 18in (45cm) high. Lift and divide them in spring, keeping them well-watered until established.

Phyllitis scolopendrium   z 5
Hart's tongue fern
Also known as *Asplenium scolopendrium*, the light green fronds of this fern brighten up shady dry corners during spring. When mature, the evergreen plants can be up to 2ft (60cm) in height. An added attraction is the rows of spore cases in a chevron-like pattern on the undersides of fertile fronds. Plants grow in any fertile, preferably alkaline soil. 'Undulatum' has fronds with ruffled margins, while 'Cristatum' has attractive crested leaf-tips.

Aconitum 'Bressingham Spire'   z 3
(*above*)
Monkshood
A valuable plant for late summer and autumn flowers, the erect panicles of 'Bressingham Spire' are carried on 3ft (90cm)-tall stems which often need staking. The hooded helmet-shaped flowers are deep purple-blue. The foliage is deeply lobed. Plants thrive in moist cool soil which should be mulched with organic matter. Every three or four years lift and divide the tuberous roots in early winter. Monkshood is poisonous, most especially the roots.

Astilbe × *arendsii*   z 4
In light shade and deep, rich, moist soil the astilbes provide a marvellous display of both foliage and flowers throughout the summer. They are beautiful delicate plants with deeply cut, dissected foliage in various shades of bronze and green. The foliage sets off perfectly the tiny flowers – dark crimson in 'Fanal', white in 'Bridal Veil' – which are carried in wispy plumes. Plants range in height from 18in-2ft (45-60cm) with similar spread. Lift and divide every three to four years, replanting young sections.

Brunnera macrophylla   z 3
Of Russian origin, this spring-flowering perennial makes excellent ground cover beneath evergreen shrubs at the front of a border. Small, vivid blue flowers appear in spring on 1ft (30cm)-tall stems above mid-green heart-shaped leaves, which are bristly-hairy. Each plant can spread to 2ft (60cm) when growing in rich, moist fertile soil. Lift and divide the plants every three to four years, discarding the central piece of the clump. Brunnera is easy to grow and goes well with *Berberis darwinii*.

Cimicifuga ramosa (*below*)   z 3
Bugbane
This fine perennial is happy in shade and will enliven the garden in late summer and early autumn with its sheer elegance. Its impressive, 1ft (30cm)-long pure white inflorescences are held on slender branching stems capable of reaching 7ft (2.1m) in height. After flowering, green seed pods remain on the plants well into winter. The foliage forms a mound of large divided leaves which takes on attractive yellow shades at the end of the season. Plants need cool, moist humus-rich soil. Divide them in autumn or spring.

Claytonia virginica   z 6
Spring beauty
An evergreen clump-forming perennial with flattish, black underground tubers which can be difficult to grow until it is established. It needs shade and moist but well-drained soil to succeed. The leaves are succulent, spoon-shaped, red-tinted when young turning green and glossy as they mature. In early spring the branched stems carry cup-shaped white to pink flowers which are striped with a deeper pink. Propagate by autumn division or from seed.

Corydalis ochroleuca   z 5
Ideal for a shaded spot, this dainty corydalis looks superb spilling out of a north-facing wall or in a border. Plants form clumps with fleshy fibrous roots and finely-divided grey-green leaves. The dense spikes of creamy-white flowers tipped with yellow are carried above the foliage from late spring onwards, at a height of up to 1ft (30cm). Individual plants spread to about 1ft (30cm), forming low but effective ground cover. Plants self-seed profusely; divide larger specimens.

Dicentra spectabilis (*above*) z 3
Bleeding heart, lady's locket, lady-in-the-bath or Dutchman's breeches
To add a coolness to the garden in early spring, the delicate fern-like foliage and deep blue-pink flowers of this perennial are unsurpassed. The leaflets are of a blue-green glaucous hue and are followed by the heart-shaped flowers which hang from arching 2ft (60cm)-tall stems. For white flowers grow *D. alba*. Plants need cool moist soil and do well near water. They become dormant in hot summers. Divide in late winter.

Doronicum 'Miss Mason' z 4
Leopard's bane
This makes an ideal early spring partner for the perennial honesty, *Lunaria rediviva*. Plants form spreading clumps of growth, 2ft (60cm) across. Each of the bright yellow, daisy-like flowers is 3in (7cm) across and distinct for its thin narrow petals are all carried at the same level on 18in (45cm)-tall stems. The flowers last for several weeks. The heart-shaped leaves are strongly toothed. Plants need moisture-retentive soil and should be divided in autumn.

Gentiana asclepiadea z 5
Willow gentian
One of the tallest-growing of all the garden gentians, this evergreen perennial has narrow leaves and graceful arching stems. The rich blue trumpet-shaped flowers appear in pairs in late summer to autumn. Plants grow best in shade and must have deep, moist rich soil with humus added in. They can achieve 3ft (90cm) in height, but tend to be more lax in habit. A long-lived perennial which improves with age, the roots of which should not be disturbed. Lift and divide in early spring.

Geranium macrorrhizum 'Bevan's Variety' z 3
Use it to effect under a light canopy of overhanging trees or in a shaded courtyard border, where it will form a valuable ground-covering mat, 1ft (30cm) high. The aromatic leaves are pale green as they emerge, changing to russet shades in autumn, and are often retained through the winter in warm zones. During summer the long-lasting cerise flowers are carried in rounded heads on long stems. Divide plants in autumn or early spring.

Lysimachia punctata (*above*) z 3
Garden loosestrife
Rather prone to getting out of control if not checked, the garden loosestrife produces erect spikes of bright yellow flowers and mid-green bracts during the summer. It is ideal for a moist shaded corner. The brownish dead flowering shoots can be left through the winter to add some colour, before being cut back in spring. *L. clethroides* has white flower heads late in the season. Both grow to around 3ft (90cm). Divide large clumps in spring; burn discarded roots.

Meconopsis betonicifolia z 7
Blue poppy
Few plants can equal the eye-catching sky blue flowers of this poppy, carried on tall stems above pale green foliage in late spring and early summer. Plants form a basal rosette of leaves from which the stems emerge, reaching up to 4ft (1.2m) high, spreading 18in (45cm). They grow well among established rhododendrons if the summers are cool, thriving in moist, neutral or acid soil, but will not tolerate humidity or great heat. Divide plants in spring or raise from seed sown in late summer in moist acid compost.

Mertensia virginica z 3
Virginian cowslip or Virginia bluebell
For a cool border in a woodland garden, there is no finer choice than this elegant perennial with its hanging clusters of violet-blue tubular flowers during spring. The flowers appear at the top of stems up to 2ft (60cm) high, which die back later in the summer. The oval leaves are bluish-green, quite soft and bristly. Each plant spreads up to 18in (45cm) across. When they are dormant, protect the crowns of the plants from slugs. 'Rubra' has pink flowers. Divide plants in early spring before they flower.

Peltiphyllum peltatum z 6
Umbrella plant
The common name derives from the big (up to 1ft (30cm) across) umbrella-like leaves which are held on 3ft (90cm) stalks. They are preceded by quite spectacular flowers carried on tall, white-haired purple stems, rising straight up from the dark roaming rhizome. The pale pink to white flowers are held in clusters. The leaves take on shades of yellow, orange and red in autumn. Divide the rhizome to increase. Useful for stabilizing banks.

Polygonatum × hybridum (*above*) z 3
Solomon's seal
No moist and shaded part of the garden is complete without the arching 3ft (90cm)-tall stems of Solomon's seal, carrying translucent, opposite, green oval leaves 2-6in (5-15cm) long. Below the leaves hide the small, bell-shaped cream flowers, edged with green, which appear from spring to early summer. The giant *P. canaliculatum* (also listed as *P. commutatum* or *P. biflorum*) has leaves which take on yellow tints in autumn. Divide in early spring. Check every day for sawfly caterpillars.

For hot, dry places

Primula florindae (*above*) z 6
Giant cowslip
Although this lovely Tibetan primula will thrive in moist shade, it is quite at home in wet soil next to water. Plants form a clump of large rounded leaves from which several flowering stems emerge, carrying drooping heads of scented, yellow bell-like flowers which last for several weeks during the summer. The stem and flowers are powdered with a silvery-white mealy bloom. Raise more plants from seed sown as soon as it is ripe or preserved and sown in spring.

Pulmonaria saccharata (*below*) z 3
Lungwort
This rough-leaved member of the borage family makes useful ground cover. In hot and dry conditions it tends to suffer from mildew. The flowers appear in early spring in arching heads, pink buds emerging from purplish calyces and then turning blue. The dark evergreen foliage is heavily spotted with grey blotches, making some of the leaves almost completely grey. Plants grow to 1ft (30cm) tall when flowering. Divide in spring.

Artemisia stelleriana (*below*) z 4
Dusty miller
A rhizomatous perennial which becomes woody at its base, forming a more or less shrubby evergreen. Plants form clumps or carpets of deeply lobed and toothed greyish-white foliage. In summer the small, yellow daisy-like flowers appear in slender sprays borne on grey stems. Dusty miller will grow well near the coast and succeeds in cold gardens. Plants grow to a height of 1-2ft (30-60cm) with similar spread. 'Boughton Silver' is a vigorous, arching cultivar. Divide in spring or autumn or take stem cuttings in summer.

Ceratostigma plumbaginoides z 5
Normally regarded as a shrub, this lovely late summer flowerer is often cut back to ground level by winter weather. It loves a hot sunny position and rich well-drained soil, growing to 1ft (30cm) high. This species is ideal for the front of a bed or border, but can be invasive. At the end of summer each reddish leafy shoot is tipped with a bristly head of dark blue flowers, with new ones opening every day. Cut back frost-damaged shoots in spring before the new growth emerges. Take cuttings in summer or divide in spring.

Chrysanthemum haradjanii z 8
Also listed as *Tanacetum haradjani*, this evergreen mat-forming perennial tends to become woody at its base and has a deep tap root. The leaves are lance-shaped, finely divided, silvery-grey and the perfect foil for the clusters of yellow flower heads which appear in summer. Plants achieve a height and spread of up to 15in (40cm) and should be divided in spring if necessary. This species is a useful border plant and at home in a rock garden or alpine house.

Crambe cordifolia z 5
The huge stately panicles of flowers produced by this member of the cabbage family demand ample space. Numerous white flowers appear on stems up to 7ft (2.1m) tall in early summer. The large dark green leaves can be 2ft (60cm) long and are hairy and deeply-veined. The base of the plant has a spread of 4ft (1.2m). Plants grow well in slightly alkaline soil, so long as it is well drained and in full sun. Suffers badly from attack by caterpillars. Divide in spring or sow seed. The crambe is magnificent when seen against a dark background such as a yew hedge.

Eriophyllum lanatum z 6
This perennial produces delightful sunny flowers. An abundance of eight-petalled, bright yellow heads covers the plant during summer. They are held on grey stems which give the plant a height of 12in (30cm). Clumps of divided silvery leaves give it a similar spread. It requires sun and well-drained soil but is frost hardy. A very attractive plant for the rock garden or the front of a border. Propagate by division in spring or by seed in autumn.

Eryngium × oliverianum (*above*) z 5
This spiny upright perennial is prized in the border for its large, thistle-like rounded flower heads of bluish-lavender which are at their peak in late summer. Each head is subtended by a collar of thorny bracts. The many flowers in each head eventually open covering the entire plant with blooms. The basal leaves are mid-green with jagged edges. Plants grow well even in the poorest soils, but must have sun. They reach 2-3ft (60-90cm) in height with a spread of up to 2ft (60cm). Propagate by division in spring or by root cuttings in winter.

Liatris spicata (*above*)　　　z 3
Gayfeather
Also known as *L. callilepis*, this is
something of an oddity among flowering
border perennials in that its flower
spikes, which look like thick pinkish
bottlebrushes, open from the top
downwards. The spikes grow from
clumps of dark green grassy foliage.
Good forms include 'Kobold', with
rosy-purple spikes up to 18in (45cm)
high, and 'Alba' for white flowers. All
are easy to grow, needing full sun and
regular deadheading in summer.

Nepeta × faassenii　　　z 3
Catmint
Cats will roll in this wonderfully
aromatic herbaceous perennial – hence
its common name. The leaves are grey-
green, soft and downy. In late spring
and early summer blue-purple flower
spikes appear, with a second flush of
blooms in autumn if the plants are
sheared back after the first flowering.
Catmint will grow even in the poorest of
dry soils. Ideal for edging beds and
borders. Propagate by tip cuttings in
summer or division in spring.

Phlomis russeliana　　　z 4
An evergreen perennial which makes
excellent ground cover, growing to 3ft
(90cm) high when in flower. The strong
flower stems appear in summer carrying
several whorls of soft butter-yellow
hooded flowers above the foliage. The
large hairy leaves are heart-shaped. In
winter the dead flower heads add
interest. Plants can achieve a spread of
2ft (60cm). The leaves are aromatic if
rubbed. They need full sun and are
ideal for baked, dry positions. Divide
plants in spring or take softwood
cuttings during summer.

Ruta graveolens (*below*)　　　z 3
Rue
If not grown in full sun in an open spot,
rue tends to become drawn and floppy.
It is an excellent border plant and very
useful as edging. Clusters of mustard-
yellow flowers appear above the foliage
during early summer, at which time
plants can reach up to 3ft (90cm) in
height, with similar spread. 'Jackman's
Blue' is illustrated, with blue-grey fern-
like foliage. The leaves release a
pungent odour. Contact with the foliage
or sap can cause a skin rash. Clip back
shoots in spring; take semi-ripe cuttings
in summer.

Santolina chamaecyparissus 'Nana' z 7
Cotton lavender
This dwarf and compact form has finely
toothed, narrow leaves which are
covered with a woolly white coating.
Plants form low mounds of silvery
fragrant foliage topped in summer by
small, yellow button-like flowers.
Blends well with the true English
lavender, *Lavandula officinalis*.
Deadhead in autumn and cut older
plants hard back in spring. Propagate
by semi-ripe cuttings in late summer.

Stachys byzantina　　　z 4
Bunnies' or lambs' ears
Also listed *S. lanata* and *S. byzantina*,
this popular evergreen perennial makes
good ground cover. It forms thick mats
of deeply felted, silver-grey leaves. In
summer the flower spikes, which are
also covered in silver hairs, grow
upright from the mats carrying clusters
of tiny pink-purple flowers. Lamb's ears
is at home in hot dry soils and loves to
be baked next to paving in full sun. It
goes well with old fashioned roses and
pinks and with *Sedum* 'Autumn Joy'.
Divide clumps in spring or autumn.

Achillea filipendulina 'Gold Plate'　z 3
(*above*)
Yarrow or milfoil
Thriving on dry, poor soils, this plant
flowers throughout the summer. The
bold flat heads of tiny, golden-yellow
daisy-like flowers face upwards on stiff
stems 4ft (1.2m) high. The foliage has
an elegant feathery nature and is
aromatic if rubbed or crushed. For paler
yellow flowers and grey foliage grow
A. 'Moonshine'. Plants can spread to 2ft
(60cm) across. Divide them in spring or
autumn, or take cuttings in summer.

Anemone × hybrida　　　z 5
'Honorine Jobert'
This Japanese anemone flowers for three
months from mid-summer to autumn,
producing saucer-shaped flowers with
clear white petals and yellow stamens.
Even though the branched flowering
stems are up to 3ft (90cm) tall, they do
not need staking. The deeply lobed
leaves form a neat mound, 2ft (60cm)
across, in heavy soil; in lighter soils
these anemones can be quite invasive.
Plants grow well in full sun or light
shade. Divide in spring or take root
cuttings in winter.

Bupthalmum salicifolium　　　z 6
Yellow ox-eye
While tending to be invasive in borders,
the yellow ox-eye is worth growing for
its deep yellow flower heads carried
singly on thin stems. Its vigorous nature
can be curbed somewhat by regular
division and by digging out unwanted
growth. Plants grow to a height of 2ft
(60cm) when flowering, and have dark
green, narrow leaves. They thrive on
slightly starved, infertile soil in full sun.
The flowers appear for many weeks.
Increase by division in spring.

Spring flowering

Chrysanthemum maximum (*below*) z 4
Shasta daisy
Even after bad weather, the flowers of the shasta daisy will show little sign of damage. This old border favourite grows 2-3ft (60cm-90cm) tall, the stems being topped with large, white daisy-like flowers with yellow button-like centres. The dark bottle-green leaves form a dense carpet in spring from which the flowering stems emerge throughout the summer if regularly deadheaded. Fine cultivars include the frilly-petalled 'Aglaya' and the pale yellow 'Cobham Gold'. Plant in sun. Divide clumps in spring or autumn.

Erodium manescavii (*below*) z 7
One of the most useful cranesbills for the border, this species will flower for several months during the summer. It forms mounds of blue-green, divided fern-like foliage topped by clusters of single lilac-pink flowers. Plants need a sunny position. They reach a height and spread of 20in (50cm) and self-seed quite readily, from which good forms can often be selected if the seedling plants are allowed to flower. As an alternative, semi-ripe cuttings can be taken in summer.

Patrinia gibbosa z 5
This unusual Japanese plant emits a rather unpleasant smell. It produces long-lasting flowers during late summer each with one long greenish-yellow petal. The flowers are small, appearing in massed heads above a clump of broad basal leaves, and are attractive even when they have faded. The roots need to be kept reasonably cool and moist. Plants grow to 18in (45cm) tall and spread to 1ft (30cm). Divide in spring or grow-on self-sown seedlings.

Penstemon 'Alice Hindley' z 9
The greatest asset of the penstemons is their long flowering season – from early to late summer – which can be extended through regular deadheading. They are also available in a wide range of colours, from white to deep red, with many intermediate shades of blue and mauve. Hardiness is also variable: it is often said that the wider the leaf the more tender the plant. This cultivar has the characteristic tubular flowers which are pale lilac, and is more or less evergreen with rich green leaves. Plants can grow to 4ft (1.2m) and may need staking. Take cuttings in summer.

Sedum 'Autumn Joy' (*above*) z 3
This large stonecrop is prized not only for its display of large, flat pink flower heads in autumn, but also for its dried seed heads in winter. The young leaves are also attractive and grow to 2ft (60cm) by late summer. In full flower the plants attract clouds of bees, butterflies and other insects. Plants will soon form bold clumps 2ft (60cm) across on fertile soil, and must be in a warm sunny spot. As the flowers age they turn to shades of coppery red. Cut back the old flowering stems in late winter. Divide the crowns in spring.

Aquilegia vulgaris 'Nora Barlow' z 4
(*above*)
This unmistakable cultivar of granny's bonnets is a spring favourite in the border, noted for its double spurred flowers with red petals which are pale green at their tips. The grey-green foliage is deeply divided and forms a loose clump below the 2½ft (75cm)-long flowering stems. Plants spread to 20in (50cm). They need well-drained soil and an open sunny position. Cultivars such as this only occasionally come true from seed. *A. vulgaris* has flowers of purple, white, pink and crimson.

Convallaria majalis (*below*) z 3
Lily-of-the-valley
An old favourite of cottage gardens, noted for its wonderfully scented flowers. The white bell-like flowers appear on arching stems during spring, emerging from a pair of broad, mid-green lance-shaped leaves. Plants grow to around 8in (20cm) tall and spread quickly. They prefer moist soil with plenty of organic matter added, and are ideal for carpeting a small bed or the ground below shrubs. Increase by replanting sections of the rhizome.

Euphorbia polychroma (*below*)   z 4
Dappled shade is perfect for this early-flowering spurge, which emerges in spring reaching a height of 18in (45cm). The sulphur-yellow flower heads are held above fresh green leaves, most of the colour being provided by the yellowish bracts. During summer the heads fade to green and finally to reddish-brown. This species associates well with *Brunnera macrophylla* or red tulips. Plant it in moist well-drained soil. Divide plants during autumn or take cuttings in summer. Avoid skin contact with the plant's white latex.

***Geum* 'Borisii'**   z 5
The bright orange flowers of this avens have striking yellow stamens and add a touch of warmth to a border in spring. A clump-forming perennial, its leaves are broad and unevenly lobed, forming a loose clump at the base of the 1ft (30cm)-tall flowering stems. The stems are hairy and each one carries several single flowers. This perennial is at its best in full sun and needs moist but free-draining soil. Increase by seed sown during autumn or by division.

***Heuchera sanguinea* cvs**   z 3
A number of fine cultivars have arisen from crossing this species with *H. americana*. 'Palace Purple' is an evergreen perennial hybrid with large clumps of deeply purple-bronze leaves, against which are set creamy flowers in spring and summer. 'Red Spangles' has silver-marbled leaves and spikes of bright crimson, bell-shaped flowers in summer. Both these make good ground cover and need moist soil, in sun or light shade. The flowering stems grow to 18in (45cm) tall and should be cut back as they fade. Divide the plants in spring or autumn.

Omphalodes verna   z 5
Verna means early, in this case the early-flowering of this semi-evergreen perennial which is decked in spring with sprays of white-eyed, bright blue flattish flowers. Plants form clumps of mid-green oval-shaped leaves and grow to 8in (20cm) high. They make good ground cover for a shaded or semi-shaded border and need well-drained but moist soil. Similar, but with heart-shaped deeply-veined leaves, is *O. cappadocica*, which carries clear blue flowers above its leaves during spring. Plants can be divided in spring or raised from seed.

***Paeonia officinalis* 'Rubra Plena'**   z 2
The deep velvety-red flowers of this old-fashioned, European herbaceous peony are fully double and are carried in great, sometimes unwieldy clusters. Plants form large 3ft (90cm)-wide clumps of glossy foliage which lasts for the entire season. This species does not like being moved, but will survive under adverse conditions for many years. Cultivars with single flowers include 'Phyllis Pritchard' and 'J.C.Weguelin'. Increase by root cuttings in winter or division in late autumn or early spring.

Papaver orientale (*above*)   z 3
Great oriental poppy
With its enormous papery-petalled flowers on gently curving 3ft (90cm)-tall stems, this poppy is a spectacular spring-flowering plant for the border. Plants form rather loose clumps of long basal leaves. They thrive in dryer borders and must have full sun. 'Marcus Perry' has red petals with a black blotch and those of 'Perry's Pink' are grey-white. Plants will self-seed, but cultivars must be increased by root cuttings during winter.

Symphytum × uplandicum   z 3
Russian comfrey
A tough herbaceous perennial which grows to 3ft (90cm) in height and carries spectacular cymes of pinkish-blue flowers in late spring and early summer. Plants grow best in deep moist soil and go well with yellow-flowered azaleas and rhododendrons. 'Variegatum' has similar flowers plus grey-green leaves broadly margined with pale cream. Plants will self-seed, although 'Variegata' must be increased by division in spring. Because of their deep roots, they can be difficult to eradicate.

Trollius europaeus (*above*)   z 3
Globeflower
In spring this relative of the common buttercup produces large, globe-like lemon-yellow flowers on 2ft (60cm)-tall shoots. For best results grow it in moist soil next to a stream or pool, in sun or shade. Plants form clumps 18in (45cm) across of mid-green deeply-divided leaves. Hybrids are usually listed as cultivars of *T. × cultorum*, including the lovely 'Alabaster' with its yellowish-white blooms. Propagate cultivars by division in early autumn, and species from seed sown in summer or autumn.

Veronica gentianoides   z 4
A pretty and dainty perennial which forms mats of broad dark green leaves from which rise spikes of washed-out blue flowers in spring. It is ideal for the front of borders and for mixing in with red or orange companions such as *Geum × borisii*. On strong plants the flowering stems grow to 18in (45cm), less if grown on poor dry soils. 'Variegata' has the added interest of cream splashed leaves. Propagate by division or softwood summer cuttings. Plants love a sunny spot in well-drained light soil.

Summer flowering

Acanthus spinosus (*below*) z 7
This species of bear's breeches is very variable but tends to be somewhat smaller than the commonly grown *A. mollis*. Both are prized for their architectural qualities. The shiny dark green leaves achieve 2-3ft (60-90cm) in length and form spiky clumps at the base of the 4ft (1.2m) flowering stems. The stems are clothed almost to the top in hooded purple and white flowers in late summer. Plants grow best in full sun. They can become invasive. Divide plants in autumn or spring, or take winter root cuttings.

Campanula lactiflora (*below*) z 4
An easily grown perennial bellflower needing moist soil to succeed, this species produces 4ft (1.2m)-tall stems which are clothed in pointed leaves. Bell-shaped mauve flowers appear in large branching heads at the top of the stems. 'Loddon Anna' is taller with pale pink flowers. To extend the flowering season cut back some of the stems in late spring. Plants need sun or light shade. Propagate by division in late autumn or spring, or through softwood or basal cuttings during the growing season. Stake on windy sites.

Delphinium hybrids (*above*) z 3
Delphiniums form large and, if not supported, unwieldy clumps of growth up to 2ft (60cm) across, and tall flowering stems up to 6ft (1.8m) high. The flowers appear in narrow racemes, in vibrant tones of blue, white and purple, or now in reds in the University Hybrids. Plants need deep humus-rich soil, sun and shelter from wind for the taller types. Common hybrids are the Pacific Giants and Blue Fountains Series. Increase plants by division or by taking cuttings from young basal shoots during spring.

Digitalis × mertonensis (*above*) z 4
A clump-forming perennial, this attractive foxglove has 2½ft (75cm)-long spikes of nodding, tubular, rose-pink to coppery flowers, held all around the flowering stems. The basal rosette of soft, hairy oval leaves grows to 1ft (30cm) across. Plants should be divided after flowering in autumn. For best results plant in moist fertile soil in light shade. If seed sets this can be sown when it ripens in the autumn. *D. ferruginea* is best treated as a biennial and has pale orange-brown flowers.

Echinops ritro (*below*) z 3
Globe thistle
Any cottage-garden-style border is incomplete without the beautiful globe thistle. In summer its rounded bright blue flowers attract hordes of bees and butterflies. The flowers are held well above the jaggedly lobed leaves, which are fresh green on their upper sides and white-felted below. The flowers stay open for many weeks, while the seed heads carry interest into autumn. Strong plants reach 3-4ft (90-120cm). To propagate, sow seed in spring, or divide or take root cuttings in autumn.

Euphorbia griffithii 'Fireglow' z 5
The massed flower heads of this beautiful spurge look like glowing embers in a fire when seen against a dark green background. The lance-shaped leaves appear all along the length of the 2-3ft (60-90cm) flowering stems and have a prominent pinkish-red midrib. Plants spread to 20in (50cm). After autumn frosts the foliage takes on attractive tints. 'Dixter' is similar but more compact. Divide in spring or autumn. The white sap can cause skin irritation and can damage the eyes.

Geranium 'Johnson's Blue' z 3
A lovely hybrid cranesbill resulting from a cross between *G. pratense* and *G. himalayense*, which grows to a height of 1ft (30cm). The large flowers appear throughout the height of summer and are of a deep lavender-blue with distinct darker veining on the petals. The deeply lobed rounded leaves appear in spring before the blooms and will sometimes take on attractive reddish tints in autumn. Cut back in late summer for late flowers. Plants work well beneath pale yellow or apricot roses. Divide in spring or autumn.

Hemerocallis cvs   z 3
Daylily
This robust border perennial can survive drought, large amounts of watering and being transplanted at any time of the year. Plants look good both in flower and foliage, and with careful choice of cultivars continuous flowering is possible throughout the summer. 'Pink Damask' has pinkish flowers; _H. flava_ has fragrant yellow blooms; while those of _H. fulva_ are tawny-orange. Both of these species can be invasive. Newer hybrids need only be split when flowering begins to diminish. Plants grow in sun or light shade, need feeding in spring and reach a height of 1-4ft (30-120cm) depending on cultivar.

Hibiscus moscheutos   z 4
Swamp rose mallow
A native of the eastern United States, this lovely plant has spectacularly large, rounded satiny flowers of crimson, white or pink. It needs fertile moist soil in full sun for best results, although it will grow in dryer conditions. Plants reach 3ft (90cm) in height with a similar spread. Raise plants from seed sown during spring.

Inula magnifica (_above_)   z 3
For a splash of late summer cheer in the border, this herbaceous perennial is an ideal choice. Huge 6ft (1.8m)-tall stems appear from a basal clump of oval leaves 1ft (30cm) long. They are crowned with large flower heads containing numerous bright yellow, narrow petals which give them a shaggy appearance. Where space is limited, the more modest _I. hookeri_ can be grown. Plant both in well-drained moist soil and propagate by division in spring or autumn. They look really good when seen against a dark green backdrop such as a yew hedge.

Kniphofia 'Little Maid' (_below_)   z 6
This is one of the more discreet and tasteful of the red hot pokers, providing colour in the late summertime. It has narrow bluey-green foliage and flowering stems 2ft (60cm) high, carrying spikes of pale lemon-yellow flowers which fade to cream from the base up as they age. Other cultivars have flowers ranging from deep red to bright yellow. Grow plants in free-draining soil in a warm sunny spot. During winter tie up the leaves to keep the crowns dry. Divide in spring.

Ligularia dentata 'Desdemona'   z 4
A lightly shaded position at the back of a border, where the soil is cool and moist, is perfect for this majestic clump-forming perennial. It looks wonderful in front of _Gunnera manicata_. The large rounded kidney-shaped leaves are dark green on their upper sides and deep red-purple below. In late summer the foliage is topped by bunches of up to 12 large, daisy-like, bright orange flowers, carried on reddish-purple stems 3-4ft (1-1.2m) tall. 'The Rocket' has palmate, strongly dentate leaves and pale yellow flowers. Divide plants in spring.

Lychnis × arkwrightii   z 6
The electric scarlet flowers of this hybrid maltese cross make it stand out in any border. A clump-forming perennial, it spreads to 18in (45cm) and has dark green oval leaves all the way up its quite weak, 18in (45cm)-tall stems. The stems carry clusters of brilliant orange-red, five-petalled flowers. _L. coronaria_ has grey-furry leaves in great clumps, studded with bright purple-cerise flowers. Plants are often treated as biennials. They need sun and well-drained soil. Self-seeds freely; alternatively, divide plants.

Lythrum salicaria 'Firecandle' (_above_) z 3
Purple loosestrife
An adaptable plant which needs fertile, moist or dry soil to succeed. The oval 3in (8cm)-long leaves are held in opposite pairs all the way up the 3ft (90cm)-tall stems. The stems carry terminal spikes of deep rose-red flowers opening in mid-summer. For pink blooms lasting from early summer to early autumn, try 'Morden's Pink'. These plants thrive near to water, in full sun or semi-shade. Divide the crowns in spring before growth starts.

Monarda 'Cambridge Scarlet' (_above_) z 4
Bee balm, bergamot or oswego tea
The flowers are peculiar, borne in circular heads at the top of stiff erect stems, each being strangely hooded and of great attraction to hummingbirds and bees: deadhead regularly through the summer. The sharply-pointed oval leaves release a scent when rubbed or crushed. Other good cultivars include the compact 'Adam' with cerise flowers, 'Snow White', and the brownish-red 'Mahogany'. Grow in moist soil in sun. Divide every three to four years for the best results.

Oenothera tetragona   z 4
Evening primrose
Carried on stems 1-2ft (30-60cm) tall, the reddish fragrant flowers begin opening in the late afternoon and by the evening are fully open, only to fade the next day. The bright yellow, cup-shaped flowers are held well above the broadly oval, dark green leaves which are bluish on their undersides. 'Fireworks' ('Fyrverkeri') has deep red buds and greenish-purple young foliage. Best in light, well-drained soils and sun. Divide the clumps during early spring or in autumn.

Phlox paniculata **cvs**   z 3
A popular border plant which flowers over a long period in summer, and again in early autumn if the first display is cut back as it fades. Plant in deep, free-draining humus-rich soil and water throughout the growing season as necessary. Pinch back weak shoots in spring. Plants reach 2-4ft (60-120cm) in height and are best grown in bold drifts, in sun or light shade. Always choose mildew-resistant cultivars. 'Eva Cullum' has bright pink flowers with red eyes. Divide in autumn.

Physostegia virginiana   z 3
Obedient plant
If you bend the flowers of this plant to one side they will stay there. This late-flowering perennial adds interest to a summer border with its slender, pink snapdragon-like flowers arranged neatly on 2½ft (75cm)-tall stems. The lance-shaped mid-green leaves grow on the stems up to the first flowers. 'Vivid' has rich pink flowers; 'Alba' is white; 'Variegata' has white-edged foliage. Plant in a moist well-drained spot in full sun, but avoid highly alkaline soils. Divide in spring.

Platycodon grandiflorus   z 3
Balloon plant
The buds appear in summer and look like clusters of small blue-purple balloons. They open to become cup-shaped flowers with dark veins. This perennial grows up to 2ft (60cm) tall and spreads to 18in (45cm). The leaves are greenish-blue, forming a tuft at the base of the plant, and also clothing the stems. Grow plants on light sandy soil in full sun. To propagate, detach non-flowering basal shoots with a piece of root attached during the summer, or sow seed in autumn.

Polygonum bistorta '**Superbum**'   z 3
(*above*)
One of the finest bistorts for the perennial border, this plant forms spreading clumps of leathery basal leaves. From these rise the 2½ft (75cm)-tall flowering stems which are topped with bottlebrush-like spikes of small pale pink flowers from early to late summer. Plant in sun or light shade, in moist conditions. *P. amplexicaule* 'Atrosanguineum' has rich crimson flowers. Divide in spring or autumn, watering them well until established.

Romneya coulteri (*above*)   z 8
Tree poppy
For the best results grow this plant in the shelter of a south- or west-facing wall. It detests being moved and must be planted in light, very free-draining soil to flourish, where it will produce a summer display of huge flowers, which have pure white, crinkled petals around a cluster of yellow stamens. The deeply-divided leaves are a beautiful bluish sea-green. Plants reach 6ft (1.8m) in height. Cut the stems to ground level in autumn and protect with mulch. To increase, cut away root pieces in spring.

Rudbeckia fulgida '**Goldsturm**'   z 3
(*below*)
Coneflower or black-eyed susan
This easily grown perennial has distinctive cone-shaped flowers with black velvety centres in late summer. This cultivar's flowers are 3-4in (8-10cm) across with thin golden-yellow petals. The flowers are carried on 2ft (60cm)-tall stems which have numerous oval leaves at the base. These long-lived plants need moist soil in sun or light shade. Divide the spreading rhizomes in autumn or spring.

Salvia × *superba*   z 4
This herbaceous perennial can reach a height of 3ft (90cm) or more and is a relative of the culinary sage *S. officinalis*. It has the characteristic stiff, square stems and oval dull-green leaves with toothed margins. The stems branch out in summer to form numerous narrow spikes of ½in (1cm)-long flowers of a deep violet-blue, surrounded by red-purple bracts from the base up. Cut right back as the flowers fade for a second flush in early autumn; this also prevents legginess. Some staking is advisable. Well-drained soil and full sun are essential. Divide in spring or take summer cuttings.

Sidalcea **hybrids**   z 5
These plants, which make neat rounded clumps of long-stalked weed-smothering leaves, are like miniature versions of hollyhocks. The flowering stems are 3-4ft (90-120cm) tall, have deeply-lobed leaves, and end in elegant branching spikes of pink cup-shaped flowers. Flower colour ranges from the deep red of 'Croftway Red' to the pale pink in 'Elsie Heugh'. Grow in moisture-retentive but well-drained soil, in full sun or light shade. Divide in spring.

Autumn flowering

Winter flowering

Aster novi-belgii (*above*) z 4
Michaelmas daisies are variable in both
habit and colour but they are always
invaluable additions to the autumn
garden. Anything from 1-4ft (30-120cm)
in height, flowers range from deep
crimson to white through every shade of
purple, mauve, pink, red and blue
('Sheena' is illustrated). Quickly spreads
to 18in (45cm); benefits from frequent
splitting – retain the outside and discard
the centre. Thrives in moist fertile soil.
Mildew can be a problem.

Catananche caerulea z 4
Cupid's dart or blue cupidone
Once used in love potions, this plant
produces crisp blue flowers in a papery
calyx on wiry 2ft (60cm)-high stems. Its
grass-like thin foliage is grey-green,
forming a tufted crown 1ft (30cm)
across. Plants withstand drought well.
Superior cultivars are 'Major', 'Perry's
White' and 'Bicolor'. Split the crown
every few years, discarding the old
centre and replanting the vigorous outer
sections. Root cuttings can be taken in
winter. The flowers can be dried.

Chelone obliqua z 4
Turtle's head or shell flower
An intriguing plant on account of its
deep-lilac flowers, which are curiously-
shaped, hooded and weather-resistant.
They stand out well against the dark
green, clearly-veined lance-shaped
leaves held in opposite pairs all along
the 3ft (90cm)-tall stems. This upright
perennial is occasionally found in its two
rarer forms: *C. alba* with its white
flowers and the dwarf clone 'Praecox
Nana'. Plants need moist soil in light
shade to do well. Propagation is through
spring or autumn division, seed or soft
tip cuttings taken during the summer.

Echinacea purpurea (*below*) z 3
Purple or hedgehog coneflower
A native of the central and eastern
United States, this sturdy plant has
single daisy flowers with raised
mahogany-coloured discs surrounded by
purplish-pink to palest pink drooping
rays. They can reach 6in (15cm) across
on stems 2-5ft (60cm-1.5m) high. The
best cultivars include 'Robert Bloom',
with deep crimson rays and orange
discs, and 'White Swan', with pure
white rays. They are useful for flower
arrangements and attractive to bees and
butterflies. Need a sunny position.

Eupatorium purpureum z 3
Joe Pye weed
Not the showiest of plants but useful for
the back of a border or in a damp
position where space is not restricted.
The dark, dull green lanceolate leaves
are up to 1ft (30cm) long and are held in
whorls of three or five. The stiff stems
stand 4-6ft (1.2-1.8m) and are topped by
large panicles of pink to purple flowers
that last from mid-summer well into
autumn. Fertile, moist soil is most
suitable although clumps can become
very large in ideal conditions and need
splitting regularly.

Tricyrtis hirta '**Variegata**' z 5
Hairy toad lily
The golden edged leaves of this plant
make it attractive for much of the year
but it is most striking in autumn when
strange upright flowers appear in
clusters in the axils of the top leaves.
They are spotted and speckled with
dark purple and last for up to three
weeks. It reaches 1-3ft (30-90cm) with a
spread of 18in (45cm). Grow in partial
shade. Prefers moist, humus-rich deep
soil on the acid side which never allows
the rhizomatous roots to dry out.

Bergenia '**Abendglut**' z 4
Elephant's ears
Also known as 'Evening Glow', this
hardy evergreen perennial will flower in
late winter if the weather is mild. It
makes good ground cover, forming
rosettes of crinkly, shiny purple-tinted
leaves, with the tinting becoming more
pronounced during winter. This cultivar
reaches a height of 9in (23cm) and
spreads to 1ft (30cm). The deep
crimson-magenta, semi-double flowers
appear in dense heads on stout stalks.
Plants will grow in sun or shade and can
be divided in spring.

Erica carnea (*below*) z 6
The winter-flowering heather is a woody
evergreen perennial which can flower
from early winter to spring. To achieve
this choose reliable cultivars such as
'Springwood Pink' and 'Springwood
White', both of which have large
sweetly-scented flowers; for deeper red-
mauve blooms grow 'Vivellii' and 'Ruby
Glow'. Plants form dense mats of dark
evergreen foliage which set off the
bright papery flowers. They grow to
6-12in (15-30cm) high, spreading to 2ft
(60cm); excellent for raised beds.

Erysimum '**Bowles' Mauve**' z 6
Also listed as *Cheiranthus* 'Bowles'
Mauve', in a warm spot this bushy,
evergreen perennial wallflower will
flower from early spring to summer. It
produces shoots up to 2½ft (75cm) high,
which are topped with spikes of small
deep-mauve flowers. The leaves are
dark green, narrow and lance-shaped,
some plants having a grey-green hue.
Plants will not survive severe winters, so
propagate by taking softwood cuttings
in summer and overwintering them in a
frame or cold greenhouse. They succeed
best in alkaline soil.

For foliage

Helleborus niger   z 3
Christmas rose
Protection from winter rains and wind is needed to get the best from this plant. It will flourish in a shaded position in moist soil which never dries out. Flowers appear in winter, if the weather is not too severe, but are easily spoilt by bad weather. Each one is creamy-white, made up of an intermediate whorl of petal-like tepals surrounding a central cluster of yellow stamens. They grow on 1ft (30cm)-tall stems above clumps of dark green, leathery evergreen leaves. Divide plants in spring or sow the seed.

Iris unguicularis (*above*)   z 8
Winter iris
Also listed as *I. stylosa*, the winter iris will produce flowers continuously from late autumn until spring. The delicate flowers are lilac with yellow centres and smell of primroses. Plants form a dense carpet of grassy evergreen leaves. They grow best at the base of a south- or west-facing wall, forming quite large clumps, 8in (20cm) tall. Two good cultivars are 'Walter Butt' and 'Mary Barnard'. To propagate, lift and divide the rhizomes. Slow to establish.

Petasites fragrans   z 5
Winter heliotrope
This is a truly mid-winter flower, with one of the sweetest scents imaginable. On a warm day the fragrance spreads across a large area. The flowers are small, pinkish-white and daisy-like. Dark green, heart-shaped leaves follow. It is a very easy plant to grow, tolerating even quite poor soils, and makes excellent ground cover. Indeed, it can become rampant so is best for a large garden. Reaching a height of 9-12in (23-30cm), plants can spread to about 4ft (1.2m). Propagate by division.

Acorus calamus 'Variegatus'   z 7
Myrtle or sweet flag
The sword-like leaves of this marginal water plant smell like oranges when crushed. A semi-evergreen perennial, it forms thick clumps of tough leaves which are green with creamy-white margins. Early in the season the young leaves are often tinged with pink. Clumps grow to 2½ft (75cm) tall and spread to around 2ft (60cm). Plants need to be in 10in (25cm) or more of water, in sun. To prevent them becoming invasive, lift and divide them every three to four years in autumn.

Alchemilla mollis (*below*)   z 3
Lady's mantle
Beaded with droplets of glistening water around their crinkled edges, the pale green leaves can be a beautiful sight early in the morning. This low-growing perennial makes good ground cover, reaching a height and spread of 20in (50cm), less on poor soils. In summer the plants are covered in a haze of tiny lime green flowers which have large conspicuous calyces. Plants grow well in all but the wettest soils. Trim after flowering; divide in spring or autumn.

Anthericum liliago   z 3
Spider plant or St Bernard's lily
An upright-growing perennial with long, narrow greyish-green leaves in tight clumps. Plants grow to a height of around 2ft (60cm), spreading to 1ft (30cm). In early summer they produce tall racemes of white trumpet-shaped flowers like tiny lilies. The seed heads are attractive in autumn, while the foliage adds colour to a border through the entire season. Plants need full sun and moist fertile soil which does not dry out. Increase by transplanting self-sown seedlings or by division in spring.

Artemisia absinthium 'Lambrook Silver' (*below*)   z 4
A lovely cultivar derived from *A. absinthium*, which has masses of finely dissected, aromatic silvery-grey leaves. Plants grow as bushy perennials, needing protection during winter in exposed gardens. Vigorous bushes can reach 2½ft (75cm) in height and spread to 2ft (60cm), making a bold silver statement in the summer border. The flowers are insignificant. Give these plants a warm sunny spot in fertile soil, trimming them to shape in early spring. To increase, take cuttings in summer.

Athyrium filix-femina   z 3
Lady fern
Although this fern prefers moist soil, it will grow in dryer conditions. It dies back to a scaly crown during winter; new fresh green fronds unfold in spring and have a fine lacy appearance. Plants reach 3 × 2ft (90 × 60cm) and continue to look good until late summer when the foliage withers. Remove fronds as they die back. Increase by division of larger crowns in autumn and winter. Add humus-rich material before planting in a shady spot in a border.

Euphorbia characias wulfenii   z 8
In their first season plants produce clusters of grey-green leaves, followed in their second season by enormous dense spikes of yellow-green flowers with collar-like, pale green bracts. These impressive heads are carried on 5ft (1.5m)-tall stems. Through winter the foliage takes on a bluish tinge. Best planted in full sun in moist but free-draining soil, plants will tolerate light shade. Take basal cuttings in summer, allowing the cut end to dry before insertion, or divide in spring or autumn. Avoid skin contact with the sap.

Foeniculum vulgare (*above*)   z 4
Fennel
Fennel makes a fine border plant with
its finely divided feathery leaves making
a soft background to many other border
plants. Plants can stand 6ft (1.8m) high
in mid-summer, the branching stems
being topped by flat umbels of
yellowish-green flowers followed by
yellow seed heads which self-seed
prolifically. Remove unwanted seedlings
soon after germination. 'Purpureum'
has deep bronze foliage. Plants grow
well in thin dry soil in sun.

Galax urceolata (*above*)   z 3
Also listed as *G. aphylla*. Only where
the soil is moist, rich in leaf mould and
of a low pH, will this valuable ground-
covering evergreen perennial thrive.
The leathery mid-green leaves are large
and rounded, taking on purplish-bronze
tints in autumn and winter. Densely-
packed 8in (20cm)-tall spikes of white
flowers appear in late spring and early
summer. Increase by separating sections
of rooted runner in the spring. Plants
can be underplanted with early spring
bulbs such as *Narcissus cyclamineus*
which push up through the leaves.

Hosta sieboldiana 'Elegans' (*below*) z 3
The popular plantain lilies are available
in a wide range of species and cultivars.
The broad or narrow, lanceolate leaves
vary in colour from deep blue to pale
green, and may have gold, white or
silver variegations. The purplish or
mauve flowers are fairly insignificant.
This cultivar forms large clumps of
rounded glaucous leaves up to 3ft
(90cm) high and spread to 5ft (1.5m).
Plants must have rich, moist, cool well-
drained soil in shade to do well. They
are prone to attack by slugs and snails.
Divide the crowns in early spring.

Houtuynia cordata 'Chamaeleon'   z 3
(*below*)
This herbaceous perennial spreads
rapidly making useful, though invasive,
ground cover. The leathery heart-
shaped leaves are splashed with bright
streaks of orange, yellow and red,
mostly at their margins. Crushing the
leaves releases a shocking strong aroma.
H. cordata 'Variegata' is also
recommended. In dryer borders plants
tend to lack vigour. Full sun brings out
the best colours. Sprays of white flowers
appear in summer. Propagate by
detaching rooted runners in spring.

Lamium galeobdolon 'Variegatum' z 4
(*above*)
Also called *Galeobdolon argenteum* and
Lamiastrum galeobdolon 'Variegatum'.
This semi-evergreen perennial makes
good ground cover for a border, some
1ft (30cm) tall with spreading runners
which root readily at their nodes. The
mid-green oval leaves are marked with
splashes of silver, above which in
summer appear racemes of yellow two-
lipped flowers. Plants will tolerate shade
and can become invasive. The soil
should be well-drained. Divide well-
rooted runners in late winter or spring.

Liriope muscari   z 6
An odd plant whose tufts of grassy
foliage seem quite dull until autumn
when spikes of dense violet-blue flowers
appear, giving a wonderful display
especially when in large drifts. *L.
spicata* is similar with flowers of pale
lavender appearing from late summer
onwards. Both species grow to 12in
(30cm) in height, slowly spreading to
18in (45cm). Plants need sun and well-
drained soil to do well. Divide the
rhizomes in spring. Plants take a few
seasons to produce a good display.

Macleaya cordata   z 4
Plume poppy
Sometimes listed as *Bocconia cordata*,
plume poppy flowers in late summer on
shoots which can be more than 7ft
(2.1m) tall, and is admired for both its
flowers and foliage. The lobed leaves are
grey-green above and downy-white on
their undersides; the small petalless
cream flowers are held in large terminal
panicles. *M. microcarpa* is more invasive
with rosy-buff flowers. Plants need full
sun and well-drained fertile soil. Divide
in spring or take root cuttings in winter.

Grasses and bamboos

Matteuccia struthiopteris (*below*) z 3
Ostrich plume fern or ostrich fern
The fresh-green, lance-shaped sterile fronds unfurl in spring and are deeply divided along their length. They are arranged in such a way as to resemble shuttlecocks and are easily damaged by drying winds and drought, so plant in a sheltered spot preferably in wet soil in semi-shade. In late summer the fronds become ragged. Throughout winter the stiff, spore-bearing fronds stand erect, up to 2ft (60cm) tall on older plants. Propagate by dividing dense clumps in spring or autumn.

Ophiopogon planiscapus nigrescens z 6
A highly distinctive evergreen with grassy black leaves growing in dense clumps. In summer racemes of lilac flowers appear above the leaves, themselves followed in some seasons by shiny, jet black rounded fruits in sparse clusters. Plants grow up to 9in (23cm) with a 12in (30cm) spread, forming a dense mat if planted together. Grow in sun in well-drained soil. Similar, but with green and white or yellow striped foliage, is *O. jaburan* 'Variegatus'. To increase, divide plants in spring.

Polystichum setiferum z 5
Unlike many ferns, this species retains its fresh green fronds from spring until late winter. The fronds are beautiful as they unfold in spring, being clothed with papery scales of a pale brownish-grey, which are retained along the orange-brown midribs. A useful fern for borders as it withstands fairly dry conditions and grows virtually anywhere, although it prefers semi-shade. 'Divisilobum' is perhaps the best cultivar. Plants grow to around 2ft (60cm) tall and need soil rich in organic matter. Divide in spring.

Salvia officinalis 'Purpurascens' z 8
(*above*)
Common sage
The young stems and leaves are flushed with purple, fading to darker green as they mature. This form needs full sun, fertile well-drained soil and plenty of nutrients to succeed. It is a perennial evergreen shrub and has purple flowers in summer. Plants form well-rounded 2ft (60cm)-high bushes. Take softwood cuttings in summer or semi-ripe cuttings in autumn which are then rooted in a cold frame over winter.

Veratrum nigrum (*above*) z 3
Black false hellebore
The chocolate-purple coloured flower spikes catch the eye in late summer and early autumn. They appear on stiff 6ft (2m)-tall upright stems, with several shorter spikes forming a branched head. Ribbed pale green leaves with distinctive parallel veins clothe the stems. The white false hellebore, *V. album*, has panicles of yellowish-white flowers. Both are well worth growing and are ideal for a shaded woodland border, needing moist humus-rich soil. Divide plants in autumn.

Arundinaria variegata z 7
White-stripe bamboo
Also listed as *A. fortunei* and *Pleioblastus variegatus*, this dwarf bamboo has white stripes in its narrow downy leaves. The stems branch near their bases and reach a height of 2½ft (75cm). Plants will spread slowly over a large area if unchecked, making good evergreen ground cover. They grow easily in any moist fertile soil. All tattered shoots should be clipped back in spring. Propagate by dividing the thick roots in early spring. Cut right back occasionally to promote new growth.

Arundo donax (*above*) z 8
Giant reed
Grown for its dramatic foliage, this herbaceous grass rarely if ever flowers in cultivation. It has thick rhizomes which form dense clumps, and can send its vigorous shoots to a height of 20ft (6m). The shoots are thick and sturdy, carrying floppy, bluish-green broad leaves. 'Versicolor' or 'Variegata' have creamy-white striped leaves. Plants thrive in dry or wet soil. Propagate by rooting sections of stem or young side shoots in wet sand in summer.

Carex pendula z 5
Pendulous sedge
A graceful plant which has tufted clumps of narrow, arching, glossy green leaves, 18in (45cm) long, with sharp margins. From these emerge tough 3ft (90cm)-tall flowering stems. The brown-green pendulous flower spikes are produced freely throughout the summer. Plants have a spread of 1ft (30cm) and should be planted in cool moist soil, preferably with some shade. *C. buchananii*, the leatherleaf sedge, has narrow coppery-bronze leaves. Divide plants in spring.

Chusquea culeou (*above*)   z 7
Chilean bamboo
A lovely bamboo which forms dense evergreen clumps 15ft (4.5m) high, which add an exotic feel to any garden. The sheaths are clear white when young and attached at swollen nodes. Clumps spread to over 10ft (3m) and are very difficult to dig out at this stage. The narrow dark green leaves are carried in whorls at each node. Thin out older shoots each year to open up the centre. To increase, hack away young pieces of the clump using a sharp spade.

Cortaderia selloana (*above*)   z 7
Giant pampas grass
Toward the end of summer this grass begins to send its enormous plume-like flower heads 8ft (2.4m) into the air, rising from large clumps of narrow saw-edged leaves. By late autumn the feathery plumes are fully developed and should be cut for drying or left to add interest to the garden in winter. 'Rendatleri' has pink plumes and 'Pumila' reaches only 5-6ft (1.5-1.8m). Plants need well-drained fertile soil and can be split in spring. Wear gloves if cutting out dead leaves or flower stems.

Erianthus ravennae (*below*)   z 6
Ravenna grass
Even though this sun-loving grass will only do well in a warm position during a hot summer, it is well worth trying. Its tall purplish stems can reach 6ft (1.8m) and carry long spikes of greyish-purple flower heads at their tips. Large leaves form a greyish clump at the base. Some discreet staking of the tall stems might be necessary, particularly in windy areas. Plants must have well-drained soil and should be planted facing west or south to take full advantage of the sun. Divide in spring.

Festuca glauca (*below*)   z 4
Blue fescue
One of the smallest and most beautiful of the cultivated grasses, this makes neat tussocks of thin, wiry blue-grey leaves no more than 1ft (30cm) tall. As the leaves age and die they turn to shades of fawn. Plants can be divided every two to three years in spring by careful teasing. Cut back by two thirds in late summer to promote fresh autumn growth. Complements purple-leaved plants like *Ajuga reptans* 'Atropurpurea'. Useful for its evergreen nature, blue fescue needs sun and well-drained soil.

Luzula maxima 'Variegata' (*above*)   z 5
Woodrush
Also given as *L. sylvatica* 'Marginata' and *L. s.* 'Aureomarginata', this dainty plant is ideal for shady borders. It makes excellent ground cover. Even where the soil is dry, plants will soon form solid mats of broad grassy foliage with hairy white edges, reaching 1ft (30cm) in height with sprays of insignificant flowers in loose heads during summer. Tolerant of a wide range of soil conditions; at its best in dry shade. Divide in spring or autumn.

Milium effusum aureum (*above*)   z 4
Bowles' golden grass or wood millet
The flat golden-yellow leaves of this form are spectacular in spring, especially when seen in bold drifts. In summer the flowers, which are yellowish-green, appear in tiered panicles above the leaves. Its colour is best in partial shade. In moist humus-rich soil plants can grow to 3ft (90cm) in height and spread to 1ft (30cm). The seeds are shiny and can be collected for sowing the following spring, although they will self-seed. Alternatively, divide plants in early spring.

Miscanthus sinensis 'Zebrinus'   z 4
(*below*)
Few grasses have as many uses in the garden as this large clump-forming perennial. 'Zebrinus' is noted for its green and yellow-banded leaves; in 'Variegatus' each leaf carries a whitish-silver stripe; for a display of large, pinkish silky flowers try 'Silver Feather'. Plants send up 5-7ft (1.5-2.1m)-tall shoots with narrow leaves which have hairy undersides. The foliage lasts well into winter and makes a lovely rustling sound in a breeze. In spring cut back dead shoots and divide.

Molinia caerulea (*below*)   z 4
Purple moor grass
Coming from quite inhospitable conditions in the wild, this grass can tolerate extreme cold and soil which is damp and acidic. The species has attractive purple flower heads in summer, but much more valuable in the garden are the cream-striped, arching leaves of 'Variegata'. Plants grow as dense tufts up to 2ft (60cm) tall and spread only slowly. In autumn the leaves fade to pale fawn and are very beautiful in winter sunshine. In spring divide and clip back old leaves.

Pennisetum alopecuroides (*above*)   z 5
Chinese fountain grass
A clump-forming herbaceous perennial that grows to 3ft (90cm) high with a spread of 2ft (60cm). The leaves are mid-green and narrow. In late summer or early autumn the bottlebrush-like flower spikes appear which can be 5in (13cm) long. They are a deep purple colour with terminal white tufts. Plants prefer a warm spot, in full sun, with light free-draining soil. The flowers retain their colour into winter. Lift and divide clumps in late spring.

Phalaris arundinacea picta (*above*)   z 3
Gardener's garters
In moist soil this grass can become invasive, but this can be avoided by placing it in a drier spot, such as near the roots of trees and shrubs. An evergreen perennial, its broad leaves are striped with white and in summer it produces narrow spikes of pale flowers on upright stems. Plants grow to 3ft (90cm), rapidly producing a bamboo-like thicket. They are set off by a dark green background, such as a hedge of *Taxus baccata*. Propagation, if found to be necessary, is by planting rooted tufts.

Phyllostachys nigra (*below*)   z 7
In their second season the olive-brown stems of this bamboo turn black, so that in established clumps there is a range of colours, from the light green of the young shoots to olive-brown and black. Plants are evergreen and form clumps 20ft (6m) high. The leaves are narrow, mid-green and arching. Clumps need thinning to prevent the centre becoming too cluttered. Considerable strength is needed to propagate the plants using a sharp spade to split the rootstock. If plants become too invasive, contain the roots to a depth of 3ft (90cm).

Stipa gigantea (*below*)   z 7
The flowers of this most beautiful grass are held on strong 8ft (2.4m)-tall stems. The narrow leaves make a ground-covering clump and are around 18in (45cm) long. When they open the flower heads are a shiny purple, changing to golden-yellow as they mature, with a silvery sheen. In full flower there are numerous pendulous yellow anthers. Stems can be cut and used in dried arrangements or left through the winter to add interest to the garden. In spring cut back dead stems and divide. Plant in sun in fertile soil.

ANNUALS AND BIENNIALS

Annuals and biennials are useful in the garden, whatever its style and stage of development. In the early years, their fast rate of growth is a great asset when furnishing large empty spaces, while their temporary nature allows experimentation in the use of colour and form before committing oneself to a more permanent and expensive scheme. As the garden matures they can be used to produce seasonal highlights either in beds of their own or mixed in with border perennials, shrubs or bulbs, in informal or formal designs.

Traditionally annuals and biennials were favourites with cottage gardeners. Self-sown hardy species such as cornflowers, pot marigolds, night-scented stock, sweet sultan (*Centaurea moschata*) foxgloves, eryngium and Queen Anne's thimble (*Gilia capitata*) give the garden a soft and natural appearance which is a trademark of the style. Once established, they find the spot best suited to their requirements, but where they are not wanted it is easy to weed them out.

The use of annuals and biennials in bedding schemes reached its peak in the late nineteenth century when plants were grown and planted out in their thousands, providing changing displays in gardens and parks throughout the year, each one more vivid than the

Far left: A stylish and colourful parterre of box, cotton lavender and lavender is brought to life in spring with plants grown as biennials. Daisies, forget-me-nots, pansies, polyanthus and wallflowers create a colourful display for several weeks.

Left: The nemesia is a half-hardy annual, usually raised from seed under cover in spring. This mixed strain will make an attractive and useful pattern of soft colours from early summer through to the first frosts.

Below: Ageratums, lobelias, petunias and small zinnias are among the summer-flowering annuals well suited to growing in containers alongside tender perennials, which should be raised from cuttings annually for the best effect.

last. Those most frequently used included wallflowers, forget-me-not and polyanthus in the spring, and salvias, cinerarias, pelargoniums and begonias in the summer. Often, so called "accent plants" were introduced to add height to the scheme; these included burning bush, love-lies-a-bleeding, castor oil plant, *Coleus blumei* and *Cordilyne* cultivars. Such carpet bedding schemes are very labour intensive, but in a small space, using a few trays of bought plantlets, a very pleasing effect can be quickly achieved and reward the effort involved.

Annuals are often grown exclusively for picking, either in rows or within a border. Continual cutting will encourage more flowers to form and lengthen the season. Particularly well suited to this use are the long-stemmed species such as bells of Ireland, cosmos, zinnias, sweet peas, love-in-a-mist, stocks and gypsophila; everlasting species should be cut on a dry day towards the end of the season and hung upside down to dry. Take these flowers in their prime.

Most annuals and biennials are adaptable to most soils, but the richer and more moisture-retentive the soil the lusher the growth and longer the flowering

period. In poor dry soil they will be thinner, flower more quickly and die off sooner. While the plants will survive dry periods, they do need adequate water, especially when they are getting established. Most, particularly summer-flowering species, need sun to flower well, but there are a number that will tolerate shade so most spaces can be filled. As ever with plants, it is a matter of careful selection.

Many people do not have the space to raise their own seedlings and need to buy strips of plants in the spring ready to plant out, but it is very rewarding to grow one's own. Annuals are usually divided into hardy and half-hardy categories; the category a plant belongs to will determine when it should be planted. Spring-flowering hardy annuals and biennials are sown in summer in a nursery bed in the garden and transplanted to where they are to flower in the autumn. Once established they will self-seed, but highly bred annuals tend to degenerate and it is best, on the whole, to start with fresh plants each year. Summer-flowering hardy annuals can be sown in spring directly in their flowering position. Half-hardy summer-flowering annuals should be raised under heat in the spring and transplanted into the garden as soon as the last frost has passed.

Above: Delightful warm hues predominate in a planting that includes the bright yellow *Calceolaria* Sunshine, *Rudbeckia* Rustic Mixed Dwarf and *Salpiglossis* Splash.

Left: A cottage-garden effect is achieved by the apparently haphazard mingling of African marigolds, impatiens, nasturtiums and petunias.

Mixed border

IN SUN

Amaranthus caudatus
Love-lies-a-bleeding or tassel flower
This striking half-hardy annual has tight hanging tassels of crimson flowers which can be 18in (45cm) long, on plants 4ft (1.2m) tall with a spread of 18in (45cm). Ideal as the centrepiece in a formal bedding scheme or as a specimen plant in a container. Plants need rich, fertile well-drained soil and should be raised under glass or sown outdoors after the last of the spring frosts. For bright green flowers grow *A. viridis*.

Atriplex hortensis 'Rubra'
Red orache or red mountain spinach
The unmistakeable, triangular, deep red leaves of this fast-growing half-hardy annual can be up to 6in (15cm) long and are edible. Ideal for a coastal garden, plants need full sun and fertile well-drained soil. They grow to a height of 4ft (1.2m) or more. The flowers are insignificant and followed by small reddish fruits. Sow plants *in situ* in late spring and early summer. They require pinching regularly to keep them bushy. Propagation is not necessary as plants self-seed readily.

Calendula officinalis (*above*)
Pot marigold or English marigold
Used in the past as a culinary herb, this quick-growing bushy annual suits a cottage garden or annual border, where it can grow up to 2ft (60cm) tall. The narrow, pale green leaves are aromatic. The flowers are daisy-like, single or double, appearing from spring to autumn, in colours ranging from yellow to orange, cream and mahogany. Plants can be sown in autumn and over-wintered or in spring. Deadhead flowers and pinch regularly. Prone to mildew.

Campanula medium
Canterbury bell
A hardy biennial which is planted in autumn for flowering the following summer. It is a favourite in cottage gardens and widely used in beds and borders. Plants need well-drained soil and a sunny position. Tall cultivars can grow to 3ft (90cm) in height and need supporting. From the basal clump of bristly-hairy leaves appear spikes of single, semi-double or double flowers in pink, white, mauve or blue. Space plants 1ft (30cm) apart. 'Bells of Holland' has single bell-shaped flowers.

Centaurea cyanus (*above*)
Cornflower
Blue cultivars such as 'Blue Ball' and 'Blue Boy' grown among yellow- and bronze-flowered pot marigolds, *Calendula officinalis*, can produce a beautiful display in a bed or border. In other cultivars the flower colour ranges from white to pink: 'Frosty' has white-specked flowers. Plants will seed themselves freely. For an early spring display sow *in situ* in autumn and protect the plants with cloches during severe weather; alternatively sow outdoors in spring or earlier under glass and transplant. Deadhead to prolong flowering into late summer.

Clarkia elegans
Popular in cottage gardens and excellent as cut flowers, this plant is grown for its frilled flowers in upright spikes of pink, red and mauve. It is best grouped in a bed or border. Tall cultivars can grow to 2ft (60cm) in height and may need supporting. Sow plants *in situ* in slightly acid, fertile soil in spring and thin to around 9in (22cm) apart. They thrive in sun. The dwarf clarkia, *C. pulchella*, grows to 1ft (30cm).

Cleome spinosa (*above*)
Spider flower
Also listed as *C. hassleriana*, this half-hardy plant adds an exotic touch when grown as a dot plant in a bedding scheme or as a gap-filler in a mixed border. The pinkish-white rounded heads of flowers are ideal for cutting. Plant in fertile well-drained soil in sun and water well in dry weather. When mature, plants reach 4ft (1.2m) in height and spread to 18in (45cm). Both the flowers and leaves are aromatic. Raise under glass and plant out after frosts. Colour Fountain is a reliable mixture.

Eschscholzia californica (*above*)
California poppy
Ideal for infilling in a sunny border, preferably where there is poor well-drained soil, this species is easy to grow. With regular deadheading flowering will continue all through the summer and into autumn. Scatter the seed thinly over the ground and lightly rake in. Plants grow to a height of 6in (15cm) and carry their silky-petalled poppy-like flowers above finely divided blue-grey leaves. They are hardy and self-seed. Monarch Art Shades has frilled petals.

Godetia grandiflora

The godetia never fails to bring a bright splash of colour to a border in late summer. A hardy annual, it can be sown *in situ* in autumn or spring, and should be thinned in spring to 9in (22cm) apart. Each flower is up to 4in (10cm) across with four fluted petals of pink, orange, white or red, the colours being in stripes and picotees in some forms. The flower spikes are leafy and up to 2ft (60cm) in height. Water the plants well in dry weather, but avoid overfeeding. Best results are seen in light, slightly acid soil.

Lavatera trimestris (above)

This elegant and showy mallow is a hardy annual and goes well with striking perennials. The flowers, which are up to 4in (10cm) across and come in pink, rosy-red or white, are trumpet-shaped with a delicate sheen. Plants may be sown *in situ* in autumn or spring (preferably in a sheltered spot), or raised under glass in pots for planting out. Deadhead to maintain flowering. Plants often self-seed. They reach a height and spread of 2-4ft (60-120cm). 'Silver Cup' has pink blooms.

Matthiola bicornis
Night-scented stock

Plant the night-scented stock near the house: the flowers of this hardy annual are closed during the day, opening only at night to fill the air with a delicious fragrance which may waft into the house through an open window. Although not the most attractive of annuals, it can be worked in between other plants simply by sowing seed in small patches during spring. Plants reach 1ft (30cm) in height with equal spread. They become straggly after flowering. Sow in succession until early summer.

Nicotiana (above)
Tobacco plant

The modern hybrids are derived from *N. alata* and are less scented than older forms, but they do have flowers which stay open all day and face upwards rather than drooping. Raise this half-hardy annual under glass and plant it out after frosts have passed, in sun or part shade where the soil is fertile. Domino (*above*) grows to 1ft (30cm), Sensation to 2-3ft (60-100cm); 'Lime Green' has yellowish-green flowers. Space plants 1ft (30cm) apart, and deadhead regularly. Prone to aphids.

Onopordum acanthium (above)
Cotton thistle or scotch thistle

This dramatic hardy biennial spends its first season producing a rosette of leaves at ground level. In its second season tall flowering shoots appear which can reach 6ft (1.8m) or more if the soil is rich. The stems are clothed with silvery-grey thistle-like leaves and the tips of the shoots carry deep purple flower heads topping a very spiny receptacle. Plants spread to 3ft (90cm) when mature. Raise from seed sown in autumn or spring. Slugs may damage lower leaves.

Portulaca grandiflora (below)
Sun plant

A sunny position and well-drained, preferably sandy soil is essential if this half-hardy annual is to do well. This succulent grows close to the ground and dislikes overwatering; feeding is usually unnecessary. The flowers are 1in (2.5cm) across, semi-double with golden-yellow stamens and silky ruffled petals. They open fully only in sun. Raise plants under glass from seed, planting out after frosts. Mixed-coloured strains include Calypso and Sundance. Plants grow to 8in (20cm).

Salvia horminum (below)

Sow this unusual ornamental sage *in situ* in autumn or spring. A hardy annual, this beautiful plant is grown for both its colourful leaves and its bright pink or blue flower bracts. The bracts appear in dense spikes during summer, and can be cut and dried when mature for indoor decoration. 'Pink Lady' and 'Blue Beard' are reliable cultivars. Pinch young plants to keep them bushy. Plants grow up to 18in (45cm) tall and spread to 8in (20cm). This species is a good choice for grey, silver and blue borders as a gap-filler in summer.

Bedding plants

IN SHADE

Digitalis purpurea (above)
Wild foxglove

This relishes shade and moist, humus-rich lime-free soil. A hardy biennial, it flowers in the second season of growth. The tall spikes of tubular flowers can reach 3-5ft (90cm-1.5m) in height. The flowers are purple with darker spotting. *D. p.* f. *alba* is white. Sow outdoors in summer and move plants to their flowering positions in autumn. The Excelsior hybrids have flowers of red, purple, pink, yellow or white.

Impatiens (above)
Busy lizzie

Modern strains, which are lower, more compact and hardier than older forms, come in a range of colours from pink, white and orange to salmon and purple. These half-hardy annuals are ideal for shaded corners or for under trees. Flowers open continuously. Good strains of *I. walleriana* include Super Elfin and Blitz. For foliage, grow the New Guinea hybrids. Plant after frosts into fertile soil. 'Novette Mixed' is shown above.

Lunaria annua (below)
Honesty

This popular hardy perennial is prized for its large, flat silvery seed pods and early-scented four-petalled flowers of deep purple, white or pink. Plants self-seed in large numbers and need rigorous thinning. They grow in sun or shade and are at home growing around the base of evergreen shrubs. 'Variegata' has bright green leaves with white margins. Plants grow rapidly to 2½ft (75cm) tall with a 1ft (30cm) spread. Remove the seed heads as the seed pods begin to open.

Myosotis
Forget-me-not

Although it tends to become leggy in deep shade, the forget-me-not is ideal for creating a splash of blue among permanent plantings in borders. Seed of this hardy biennial is sown outdoors in summer and the young plants transplanted to their flowering positions in autumn. Plants are 1ft (30cm) tall when flowering, with similar spread. Most garden forms are hybrids of *M. alpestris* and *M. sylvestris*; cultivar names speak for themselves – 'Blue Ball', 'White Ball' and 'Pink Gem'.

Nemesia strumosa

A fast-growing, bushy half-hardy annual which tends to bloom very quickly if the summer is hot and dry. To avoid this, stagger sowing. Plants should be grown in fertile, well-drained lime-free soil in a cool position. Taller cultivars grow up to 18in (45cm). The lovely trumpet-shaped wide-lipped flowers come in shades of purple, white and yellow. Space plants 6-12in (15-30cm) apart and cut back after the first flowers have faded. Carnival and Funfair are good mixtures. Water well in dry weather.

Ageratum houstonianum cvs
Floss flower

Often used as an edging plant in bedding schemes, this half-hardy annual has powderpuff-like clusters of flowers throughout the summer. The blue cultivars are still the most widely grown; white forms turn brown as they fade and the pink strains have yet to gain popularity. Plants form hummocks between 6-12in (15-30cm) tall with similar spread. Raise seed under glass and plant out after frosts. Deadheading keeps flowers coming. Plants grow in sun or part shade and should be well-watered in dry summers.

Antirrhinum majus cvs
Snapdragon

A huge range of cultivars and hybrids of this popular perennial exist. It is grown as a half-hardy annual and needs rich well-drained soil in full sun. The flowers are basically tubular or trumpet-shaped, and can be single, semi-double or double. Seed is sown under glass, the plants going out after frosts. Pinch the tips of young plants to make them bushy. Plants grow from 4in-3ft (10-90cm) tall depending on the strain. Use Monarch if rust disease is present.

Begonia semperflorens (above)

The introduction of this fibrous-rooted begonia has revolutionized bedding schemes. It flowers throughout the summer until the first frosts of autumn, is compact and available in a wide range of colours, and has attractive bright green or bronze foliage. Plants are best raised from plugs and moved to their flowering positions after frosts. They are happy in shade and need compost-enriched soil. Plants grow to 4-12in (10-30cm) depending on cultivar and can be potted up for winter flowers indoors.

Bellis perennis

For carpet bedding, edging, or for filling in gaps along borders the English daisy is ideal. Flowers appear from mid-spring onwards and can be rosy red, bright pink, white or crimson. Blooms last for many weeks. Plants are grown as hardy biennials, although they are actually perennial and can be replanted when taken from bedding displays. Sow seed in early summer outdoors and transplant to beds in autumn. Deadhead to maintain vigour. For large flowers grow 'Monstrosa' and 'Super Enorma', and for daintier plants 'Pomponette'.

Cheiranthus cheiri (above)
Wallflower

A wonderfully scented hardy biennial for a spring bedding scheme. The narrow, dark green leaves are topped by clusters of four-petalled flowers in shades of yellow, orange and red which open during spring into early summer. Raise plants from seed sown outdoors in summer and move to their flowering positions in autumn. They are susceptible to club root disease and should be grown in fertile well-limed soil. 'Orange Bedder' and 'Scarlet Bedder' are trusted cultivars.

Kochia scoparia tricophylla
Burning bush or summer cypress

Used widely as a dot plant for its striking summer foliage, the leaves of this half-hardy annual are feathery and mature plants resemble a conifer in shape. In autumn the foliage turns bronze-red. Plants can grow to 3ft (90cm) and need sun; well-drained sandy soil is best. They are rapid growers which can be clipped over if they become too large. Raise plants under glass planting out after spring frosts, 2ft (60cm) apart.

Mesembryanthemum criniflorum
(above)
Livingstone daisy

More correctly named Dorotheanthus bellidiformis, there are few summer-flowering bedding plants to rival the large, glistening daisy-like flowers of this half-hardy succulent annual. In addition, the narrow fleshy leaves and stems have an attractive sparkling coating. Seeds are usually bought as mixtures – red, white, yellow, orange and many intermediates. Plant after frosts, 8in (20cm) apart. Plants love dry, sunny positions.

Mimulus cvs (above)
Monkey flower

Its strength as a bedding plant is being able to provide red and yellow colour in shaded or dark spots such as on patios which face north; it also suits hanging baskets. Plants are raised under glass in spring and planted out after frosts. They will flower in as little as seven weeks from sowing, producing blotched and spotted trumpet-like flowers. Plants can be up to 1ft (30cm) tall and should be spaced around 9in (22cm) apart in damp soil. 'Yellow velvet' is illustrated.

Tagetes patula; T. erecta
French marigold; African marigold

T. patula carries a mass of single flowers on plants growing up to 9in (22cm) high, while T. erecta is a larger plant, up to 2ft (60cm) high, with fewer but much larger, usually double flowers. The flowers appear throughout the summer and are bright orange or yellow in colour. The mid-green pinnate leaves have a strong pungent aroma when rubbed. Plant in spring after frosts and remove all flower buds for a few weeks after that. T. patula 'Naughty Marietta' is an old trusted favourite.

Salvia splendens (above)
Scarlet sage

One of the most reliable summer bedding plants for red flowers. This tender perennial is grown as a half-hardy annual and is planted after frosts. The dense racemes of tubular scarlet flowers appear from mid-summer providing colour right into autumn. Plants grow to 1ft (30cm) in height and should be spaced 1-1½ft (30-45cm) apart. 'Blaze of Fire' is a popular scarlet cultivar, while 'Laser Purple' has mauve flowers. White strains are also available. Plants grow well in most soils in sun.

Viola × wittrockiana

With careful planning pansies can be in flower in every season. All the modern strains and hybrids come from this species. Universal, Multiflora and Floral Dance are the hardiest and most reliable strains. Plants are treated either as hardy annuals or biennials. Sow plants for winter and spring bedding displays in early summer and plant out in autumn. Colours include blue, purple, yellow, white, orange and red, with bicoloured and blotched forms. The petals are edible. Protect from slugs.

For cutting

Asperula azurea setosa

Most asperulas are perennial plants, this dainty hardy annual being a welcome exception. Seed is best sown where the plants are to flower, and the young seedlings not disturbed by transplanting. Autumn sowing is usual, for an early spring flowering. Plants grow to a height of 2in (5cm), and being quite small fit easily into any bare patches in borders or on rock gardens. The small green narrow leaves are studded with clusters of tiny four-petalled pale blue flowers which have the scent of new-mown hay.

Callistephus chinensis
Annual aster or China aster

This plant can provide a welcome crop of flowers for cutting in late summer. The flowers come in many forms; some are the typical daisy-type, others are double or have plumed petals, while still others resemble small chrysanthemums. Treat plants as half-hardy annuals, planting after the most severe frosts. They grow to ½-3ft (15-90cm) depending on cultivar. Never grow asters in the same spot year after year to avoid aster wilt, a soil disease.

Cosmos bipinnatus
Cosmos

With its large blooms and delicate feathery foliage, cosmos is an easy annual to grow, providing a useful supply of flowers for cutting through the summer. Plants will bloom until the first frosts if deadheaded regularly. Tall cultivars (up to 3ft (90cm) in height) may need staking, but all will grow well on poor but well-drained, preferably sandy soil. Seed is usually sold as mixtures; Sensation is a tall mixture with white, red and pink flowers.

Helichrysum bracteatum
Straw flower

This is one of the most popular "everlasting" flowers grown for its papery heads. What appear to be petals are in fact bracts which come in a range of colours including pinks, mauve, red, yellow and white. Cut the stems just before the flowers are fully open and hang to dry. Easy to grow, this hardy annual can be sown outdoors in spring or raised earlier under glass and planted out. Hot Bikini and Bright Bikini are good mixtures. Plants grow to 1-3ft (30-90cm) at a spacing of 1ft (30cm) apart.

Gilia capitata
Queen Anne's thimble

With its feathery leaves and rounded heads of pale lavender flowers, this branching hardy annual is ideal for cutting. Twiggy supports may help the more lax-growing plants on windy sites. Seed can be sown *in situ* in autumn or in spring, or under glass for planting out later into rich, fertile soil in full sun. Flowers will continue to be produced into early autumn on well-grown plants if cut regularly. Space or thin plants to 8in (20cm) apart. They will grow up to 18in (45cm) tall.

Moluccella laevis (*above*)
Bells of Ireland or shell flower

The most conspicuous part of this plant is the large, pale green, bell-like calyx surrounding the small white, tubular flowers. These cluster all the way up the attractive, erect stems along with the rounded leaves. As the flowers fade, interest is maintained by the green calyces, making this a much sought after cut flower for summer. Plants are half-hardy and fast-growing, needing rich soil and full sun. Sow seed under glass in early spring or *in situ* after frosts, planting 1ft (30cm) apart.

Nigella damascena
Love-in-a-mist

The flowers of this hardy annual emerge through its finely divided foliage. Most seed gives rise to plants with a mixture of pink, white, blue and lavender flowers, and sowing should be staggered because the flowering season is short. The stems are useful as a fresh cut flower in summer, and the seed heads can be used as dried flowers. Enrich the soil with compost before sowing, which can take place in autumn or spring. Plants grow up to 2ft (60cm) tall.

Ornamental Grasses

What they lack in colour, ornamental grasses make up for in fine textures and sounds. Quaking grass, *Briza maxima*, is perhaps the most popular with its papery lanterns rustling in the breeze; while the half-hardy Job's tears, *Coix lacryma-jobi*, has pearly seeds which appear among the reed-like foliage. Other species include hare's tail, *Lagurus ovatus*, and cloud grass, *Agrostis nebulosa*. Sow or plant in full sun in well-drained soil, with 1ft (30cm) between plants, or sow small patches to fill gaps. Plants self-seed freely.

Scabiosa
Sweet scabious or pincushion flower

Similar to the cornflower and useful as a summer cut flower, most modern strains of sweet scabious are derived from *S. atropurpurea* which is a hardy annual. Most flowers are double and available in pinks, reds, mauves and white. Plants suffer in prolonged wet weather. Sow the seed outdoors in autumn or spring, or raise under glass and plant out 1ft (30cm) apart. Plants reach up to 3ft (1m) in height if grown in slightly alkaline well-drained soil. Single colour varieties are avilable.

Zinnia (*above*)

The modern types of *Zinnia* have complex parentage giving rise to flowers which can be as large as dahlias or small and button-like (Lilliput miniatures are shown). The flowers are daisy-like, single, semi-double or double, and come in a huge range of colours. A compost-enriched soil and full sun are vital. Plants grow to ½-2ft (15-60cm). Space plants 1ft (30cm) apart when planting out the young plants raised in spring under glass. They will not stand frosts or prolonged, cool wet weather.

BULBS AND CORMS

Bulbs are often associated with the dramatic and vibrantly colourful displays seen in public open spaces, but they can also be enjoyed in the garden where they can be put to many different uses. Bulbs reliably come into flower within one season and associate well with bedding plants and in a mixed border, either in the bright sunshine or light shade, throughout much of the year.

All bulbs require an annual resting period. This may be during the summer, as is the case for the spring-flowering species which most commonly originate from areas with a Mediterranean climate. In the winter many tender summer-flowering species, which require hot- house conditions to grow out of their natural habitat (or must be lifted in the autumn before the frosts and kept in a cool, dark frost-free place throughout the winter), are dormant. Other bulbs, such as the sweetly scented *Acidanthera murielae*, are usually cheap enough to be able to be replanted annually, after the risk of frost has passed, as one would bedding plants from the garden centre.

Throughout the resting period the bulbs disappear under ground, leaving gaps which need to be furnished with other plants. This is most noticeable with

Left: The pink *Cyclamen hederifolium* and the white variety *album* do well in dry shade, as here at the base of a blue atlantic cedar. The cyclamen, which flowers in autumn and self-seeds readily, has the peculiarity of sending out roots from the top of the corm. It benefits from a mulch of leaf mould after flowering.

hardy late winter- and spring-flowering species. There are several different techniques of covering the spaces while allowing the bulbs to proceed through their cycle without damage and to increase steadily.

Many winter- and spring-flowering bulbs look at home in a border that is shaded by tall deciduous trees or shrubs, where they come into flower before the leaf canopy becomes too dense. Here, daffodils, winter aconites, snowdrops, cyclamen, bluebells and trilliums will thrive along with shade-loving herbaceous foliage plants such as hostas, geraniums and alchemilla which gradually cover the dying foliage, or ever-

green ground cover plants such as ivy, periwinkle and pachysandra. As a rule, in permanent bulb plantings it is useful to plant them very deep so that they are not damaged by any weeding or lifting of herbaceous plants that need dividing.

On a grander scale, all these plants can be naturalized in a woodland setting in great drifts. Alternatively it is possible to grow many species of daffodils, crocuses, the summer snowflake and snake's head fritillary in rough grass. The important thing to remember is that the flowers must rise above the grass to have any effect (so the later they bloom, the taller they

Left: Early-flowering narcissi and chionodoxas brighten an acid border that is suitably planted with heathers and rhododendrons.

Right: Bulbs are ideal for creating large drifts of colour in spring. These squills flourish in the shade of a winter-flowering cherry (*Prunus* × *subhirtella* 'Autumnalis'). Recommended precursors for them are winter aconites, snowdrops and *Arum italicum marmoratum.*

must be). They should be left in leaf and the grass un-cut for up to eight weeks to allow the next year's flowers to form in the bulbs.

In formal plantings, or where they have been grown with spring bedding plants, tulips, daffodils and hya-cinths can be lifted after flowering and replaced by a totally different scheme for the summer. Bulbs that are lifted in mid- to late spring should be heeled into another part of the garden or kept in boxes with moist peat, compost or soil around their roots until the foliage dies down. They then need to be dried, cleaned and stored in a well-ventilated place until autumn.

Where spring bulbs are used either on their own or in association with bedding plants it is important to think about the effect that is wanted when choosing colour combinations. Daffodils cover a broad range of yellows through creams and whites and some orange or pink cups, while hyacinths offer solid shades of blue, pink, white, peach and yellow and tulips range from black to white and red-striped. It may be that vibrant contrast is wanted in which case hyacinths are appropriate, but often the toning colours and refined forms of daffodils would have a more relaxing effect.

Above: The narcissus 'Thalia' and delicate grape hyacinths (muscari) crowd around the base of a large terracotta pot in which species tulips are coming into flower.

Left: Lilies are indispensable bulbs for summer borders. The species and hybrids include short-growing kinds as well as some of the tallest and most stately of bulbs. There is a wide colour range and many lilies are richly scented.

For shade

Anemone nemorosa
Wood anemone   z 4

This charming woodland plant, which is
a rhizomatous perennial, thrives in
shaded, moist, humus-rich but well-
drained soil. Plants grow vigorously,
forming a carpet 6in (15cm) high, which
in spring is studded with star-shaped
single flowers each with a central cluster
of yellow stamens. 'Allenii' has blue-
pink flowers and those of 'Vestal' are
double. The foliage is a mid-green.
Increase through self-seeding or by
dividing the rhizomes, but undisturbed
specimens flower best.

Arisaema triphyllum (above)   z 5
Jack-in-the-pulpit

The arisaemas are prized for their
curious hooded flowers. In autumn,
they have the added attraction of
clusters of fleshy red fruits. Plants die
away each winter to an underground
tuber. They thrive in shade where the
soil is moist and humus-enriched. The
leaves are soft, three-lobed and remain
through summer after the flowers have
faded. Plants grow to 18in (45cm),
spreading slowly to 1ft (30cm). Plant
tubers 6in (15cm) deep.

Arisarum proboscideum   z 6
Mouse plant

Every garden should have a clump of
this plant which succeeds in well-
drained but moist humus-rich soil. The
arrow-shaped, bright green, shiny leaves
hide the shy flowers which emerge near
soil level. Each flower is made up of a
dark brown spathe wrapped around a
central spadix. The tip of the spathe is
drawn out into a 6in (15cm)-long "tail".
This plant is easy to grow and reaches a
height of only 4in (10cm). Propagate by
splitting the tuberous root systems.
Useful for ground cover.

Arum italicum marmoratum (*above*) z 7
This superior form of the cuckoo pint is
prized for its bright green, shiny leaves
which are beautifully veined with white
or cream. They appear in autumn and
so add some winter interest. The flowers
appear in late spring and are green or
creamy-white, followed in autumn by a
spike of bright red berries. Plants reach
a height of 6-10in (15-25cm) and a
spread of 1ft (30cm). They need moist
but well-drained soil and can be
propagated by sowing ripe seed or by
dividing the tubers in early autumn.

Cardiocrinum giganteum (*above*)   z 7
The flowering stems of this spectacular
bulb grow up to 12ft (4m) high. Each of
the tubular lily-like flowers are up to 6in
(15cm) long, cream-coloured with
purplish streaks inside the throat. After
flowering, large green-brown seed pods
form. The bulbs should be planted in
autumn (in shade) just below the surface
of humus-rich soil. The young shoots
need protecting from frost and slugs.
After flowering, the main bulb dies,
leaving offsets which will flower when
five years old, while seed-raised bulbs
take seven years.

Cyclamen hederifolium (below)   z 6

Also known a *C. neapolitanum*, this low-
growing tuberous perennial reaches only
4in (10cm) high and will add colour to a
garden – anything from white through
pale pink to mauve – in autumn when
the flowers appear ahead of the leaves.
It is impressive when seen as a mature
clump at the base of a tree. The leaves
are small and ivy-shaped, dark green
patterned with shades of silver. They
make good ground cover. The petals are
sharply reflexed and slightly twisted.
Plants need well-drained soil and are
best raised from seed.

Erythronium dens-canis   z 6
Dogs'-tooth violet

An unmistakeable plant with its pair of
purple-spotted basal leaves. From the
centre of these emerge the nodding
white, pink or purple flowers with
brownish-yellow centres, to a height of
up to 10in (25cm). This violet grows
well when naturalized in thin grass
where there is some shade. The tubers
become dormant in summer and should
not be planted where they will dry out.
E. tuolumnense has deep yellow flowers.
Plant both 6in (15cm) deep.

Hyacinthoides non-scripta   z 6
Bluebell

In spring, the tufts of strap-shaped
leaves appear first followed by the
flower buds which push up from within
the leaves. The flower stems grow up to
16in (40cm) tall and arch at their tips.
The bell-shaped flowers are fragrant, in
shades of blue, pink or white, blue
usually being predominant. This plant
needs cool and shaded conditions to do
well. Divide the clumps in late summer
and replant only those bulbs that are 6in
(15cm) or more across. Plants need
moist soil.

Formal planting

Leucojum vernum   z 6
Spring snowflake

Unlike its relative the snowdrop, this graceful plant has green tips to its six white petals. Each leafless stem grows up to 6in (15cm) tall and carries one to two pendent bell-shaped flowers. Plants grow best in moist soil. The leaves are quite erect and strap-like, rising from the base. *L. aestivum* (the summer snowflake) has smaller flowers in heads of three to seven and seed pods which float on water to spread the seeds. Divide in spring or early autumn.

Narcissus   z 5

Several of the hardy species narcissi make excellent bulbs for planting in moist and shady spots. They are at their best when growing on the edge of a damp woodland. The delicate blooms of *N. cyclamineus* are characterized by their sharply reflexed petals and very narrow trumpets, which nod gracefully in spring. *N. pseudonarcissus*, often referred to as the wild daffodil, has flowers which range from white to deep golden yellow, and it naturalizes freely. It often hybridizes very successfully with *N. cyclamineus*.

Trillium grandiflorum (*above*)   z 4
Wake robin, trinity flower or wood lily

On alkaline soils this species will form large clumps of whorled dark green leaves, above which are held the large white flowers from spring to early summer. The flowers take on tinges of pink as they age. Only one flower emerges from the centre of each leaf. Plants are 15in (38cm) tall when in flower, and spread to 1ft (30cm). The soil must be leafy and humus-rich for success. 'Flore Pleno' has double flowers. Propagate by division after the foliage has died away in summer.

Daffodils (*above*)   z 5

This large and diverse group of bulbous plants work especially well in formal planting schemes, particularly when interplanted with lower-growing annuals or biennials in spring bedding displays. Choose the large-flowered cultivars of *Narcissus* for formal use. The golden-trumpeted types are the most popular and reach 1-2ft (30-60cm) in height. Plant the bulbs during late autumn. Deadheading the flowers retains energy in the plant. After flowering, the leaves should be left for at least six weeks.

Hyacinths   z 6

The thick fragrant spikes of this plant are its major asset. The flowers are bell-shaped, fleshy and waxy, and come in varying shades of blue, pink, red or white. Hyacinths are ideal subjects for a formal spring display, especially if planted in quite narrow beds. For large groups, single-colour planting is most effective, perhaps interplanted with tulips or pansies. Popular cultivars are the yellow 'City of Haarlem', the pure white 'L'Innocence' and 'Delft Blue'. In autumn, plant fresh quality bulbs 6in (15cm) deep in moist well-drained soil.

Iris danfordiae   z 6

In the first season after planting this charming miniature iris will produce a bright splash of golden colour with its sweet-scented flowers. After this, the bulbs divide naturally and take several years to flower again. Ideal for formal planters on a patio in spring or in bold drifts in a paved garden, this iris reaches only 4in (10cm) in height. The leaves die away in late spring and can be oversown with summer-flowering annuals. Choose a sunny position and well-drained fertile soil.

Iris reticulata (*below*)   z 6

Many fine cultivars exist of this lovely blue miniature iris which is prized for its early flowers. In mild conditions the flowers can open from late winter onwards. This plant is well suited to containers and makes an excellent choice for edging along paths or for a bold dash of colour in a paved garden. Where possible work it in next to early yellow flowers, such as those of *Hamamelis mollis*. Hybrids include the pale blue 'Cantab', and the cream and azure 'Clairette'. Plant in free-draining soil 4in (10cm) deep in autumn.

Lilium (*below*)   z 6

With their unmistakeable and elegant flower spikes, the lilies are naturals for use in formal planting. Most produce a flowering stem 2-6ft (60-180cm) tall and may require some staking. There are hundreds of species and cultivars to choose from and types to suit both acid and alkaline soil conditions. *L. regale* (*below*) has fragrant funnel-shaped flowers. The spring growth is attractive in its own right. Plant in autumn or spring into humus-rich soil which is in a shaded, cool position, but where the flowers can grow up into the sun.

Drifts of colour

Muscari armeniacum (*above*) z 5
Grape hyacinth
A tough plant which will grow well under shrubs and other plants. The flowers appear from mid-spring onwards and are a vivid blue, massed at the end of green stems like a tiny bunch of grapes. Two cultivars are commonly grown, the pale blue 'Cantab' and the darker 'Heavenly Blue'. Plants rarely grow to more than 9in (23cm) tall and make excellent ground cover, spreading rapidly when in well-drained soil in a sunny position.

Tulips (*above*) z 5
A huge range of cultivars of *Tulipa* exist. They are much used in spring bedding schemes, where their tall strong flower stems hold the blooms above lower-growing bedding plants. Flowers appear from mid-spring onwards, in colours ranging from pure white to the deepest purple, and can be single or double. Bulbs should be planted in autumn, 4-6in (10-15cm) deep. Lift cultivars after the leaves have died away and store in a dry place or replant each autumn. *T. kaufmanniana* has pink flowers with orange centres.

Camassia quamash z 4
Quamash
Group this plant in clumps in a border or near the edge of a pond. It loves heavy soil and partial shade. In summer, the star-shaped blue, violet or white flowers, 3in (8cm) across, are held in narrow spikes up to 32in (80cm) tall. At the base there are narrow, upright green leaves. Remove the faded flower stems. Divide clumps of bulbs in late summer and plant them during autumn 4in (10cm) deep. For dense spikes of white or bluish-violet flowers grow *C. leichtlinii* which can reach 5ft (1.5m).

Chionodoxa luciliae z 5
Glory of the snow
Often known as *C. gigantea*, these delightful, small spring-flowering bulbs are easy to grow. They are suited to a whole range of different situations, including the front of borders, rock gardens and in containers. The violet-blue star-like flowers have a white central zone, surrounding creamy filaments, and are carried on stems that grow to little more than 4in (10cm) high. There is a white form, 'Alba', and the pink 'Rosea'. Plants need well-drained humus-rich soil in full sun.

Colchicum autumnale (*below*) z 6
Meadow saffron or autumn crocus
Each corm of this plant can produce up to eight crocus-like flowers, in shades of purple, pink or in pure white. For a spectacular display in the autumn, plant corms in large groups, allowing for the foliage: the flowers are followed by large, glossy, deep green strap-shaped leaves which can grow to 6in (15cm) in length. 'Albo-Plenum' has double white flowers each with up to 30 petals. Plants naturalize well in grass in a sunny open position with well-drained soil.

Crocus tommasinianus z 5
One of the finest and earliest of the spring-flowering crocuses. It has narrow leaves and six-petalled purple flowers which have a white tubular throat. The stamens give the centre of the flower a deep orange splash. The colour of the flowers varies: shades of lilac and violet are also seen, while the petals are often dark-tipped and sometimes silvered on their outsides. Plants are 4in (10cm) tall when in flower, the flowers opening fully in bright sun. They are ideal for naturalizing in grass, eventually forming broad drifts. Plants succeed in alkaline soils, which must be well drained. Plant the corms 2in (6cm) deep in autumn.

Daffodils z 5
The most impressive massed displays are achieved when daffodil bulbs are planted informally whether in a natural or semi-natural setting. Both the large trumpet-flowered hybrids and the smaller and daintier species can be used to great effect in this way. Once naturalized, the plants should flower for several seasons. Use different cultivars to extend the display for up to two to three months during the spring.

Eranthis hyemalis (*above*) z 5
Winter aconite
This beautiful member of the buttercup family has bright yellow flowers which can peep through a blanket of snow during late winter. Plants are 4in (10cm) high when flowering, the base of each flower being subtended by a frilly green rosette of leaves. The flowers last for several weeks and are ideal as a winter underplanting, below *Rubus cockburnianus* or *Cornus alba* 'Sibirica'. The leaves are a useful ground cover. Plants self-seed regularly. Plant the tubers in autumn in moist soil.

Galanthus nivalis (*above*)   z 5
Common snowdrop
Along with *Eranthis hyemalis*, this early-flowering bulb signals the start of spring. The flowers hang like small white drops on green stalks. It is best seen in bold drifts and benefits from being in the shade cast by trees or shrubs, especially if they are deciduous. It can push up through low-growing ground cover plants. For unusual yellow and white colouring grow 'Lutescens'. Ideally, plant snowdrops in heavy soil straight after flowering.

Ipheion uniflorum 'Wisley Blue'   z 5
(*above*)
A South American bulb needing a sunny position and freely-draining soil: it does best at the base of a south- or west-facing wall, or at the front of a border. The soft blue flowers are star-shaped and face straight up to the sky, having a sweet soapy fragrance. The pale green grassy leaves flop loosely below the flowers and smell of garlic if rubbed. Plant bulbs 2in (5cm) deep in autumn or lift and divide large clumps. Plants reach a height of 5-8in (13-20cm) and make useful ground cover.

Ornithogalum nutans   z 6
Star of Bethlehem
This plant is grown for its white and green flowers, which are star-shaped and appear some time after the narrow basal leaves are formed. Each flower is translucent and up to 1¼in (3cm) long, held on spikes 6-14in (15-35cm) tall. Plants will form drifts when established in grassed areas so long as the soil is well drained. They prefer partial shade and the bulbs should be planted in autumn. For best effect grow on grassy slopes or banks where the flowers can be seen against a dark background.

Scilla peruviana (*above*)   z 7
This native of the Mediterranean needs a warm sunny spot and moist soil. The conical flowers heads appear in early summer, each with up to 50 flattish blue-violet flowers. Each head is ¾-1¼in (2-3cm) across on a stem 4-10in (10-25cm) tall. At the base are a cluster of narrow leaves. Propagate by division in late summer; plant bulbs shallowly in autumn or spring. *S. tubergeniana* flowers in early spring with pale blue, dark-veined flowers and *S. siberica* has bell-shaped, deep blue flowers.

Tulips   z 7
Apart from spring bedding displays, tulips can be put to good use in mixed borders, where they provide a bold splash of colour early in the season interplanted with other early perennials or spring-flowering shrubs. Many of the older types look good at the base of a stone wall and will blend in well in borders containing wall-trained fruit. For double flowers choose the yellow 'Monte Carlo' or for white, 'Snow Queen'; while for flowers with crested and ruffled petals 'Red Parrot' and 'Flaming Parrot' are ideal.

Acidanthera murielae   z 8
Also listed as *Gladiolus callianthus*, this beautiful plant adds a touch of elegance to any border. The exotic-looking flowers have six white petals with deep purple throats and are carried in groups of about ten on stems up to 3ft (90cm) tall. They appear in early autumn. Plant the corms in soil-based potting compost in autumn and keep in a cold frame, planting them out in a warm, sunny position the following spring. They must be lifted again before the first frosts in the autumn, or new bulbs must be bought in each year.

Allium giganteum   z 5
A member of the ornamental onion family, this plant will reach 4ft (1.2m) in height and has large rounded heads of densely packed lilac-pink flowers. The attractive grey-blue leaves are susceptible to damage by late spring frosts, so a warm sheltered spot is desirable. The large size of the flower heads makes a bold statement in a purple, blue or grey border. Plants need well-drained soil and the large bulbs need a handful of coarse grit scattered around them at planting time.

Crinum × powellii (*above*)   z 7
Although winter frosts will cut back the leaves of this South African native, the bulbs can be left planted outdoors year round in warm climates. Plant the bulbs with their necks just above soil level in a warm and sunny position, ideally at the base of a west- or south-facing wall. The strong, 3ft (90cm)-tall stems emerge in late summer with up to ten trumpet-shaped fragrant flowers. 'Roseum' has pink flowers, 'Album' white. Cover the leaves if late frosts are likely. Plants spread to 2ft (60cm). Plant fresh bulbs in spring in well-drained soil.

Crocosmia 'Lucifer' (*below*) z 7
Montbretia
This hybrid will create an eye-catching display of large fire-red flowers during late summer and autumn. Other hybrids include 'Spitfire', with its large fiery orange flowers, and the darker orange 'Emberglow'. Plants grow to 1-3ft (60-90cm) high and have stiff sword-like leaves. Plant corms in spring in well-drained soil in an open sunny position. Divide large clumps every few years, just after flowering or in early spring. Plants go well with late-flowering perennials, such as *Helenium autumnale*.

Curtonus paniculatus z 8
Also listed as *Antholyza paniculata* and *Cyrtonus paniculata*, this close relative of the crocosmias has been hybridized with *Crocosmia masonorum* to produce many fine cultivars which are usually listed under *Crocosmia*. However, it is a fine plant in its own right, reaching a height of 4ft (1.2m) with attractive zig-zagging sprays of tubular scarlet flowers. The leaves are erect, sword-shaped and pleated along their length. Plants need a well-drained soil and a sunny position.

Eremurus stenophyllus bungei z 6
Foxtail lily or king's spear
Prized as a border plant for its elegant spikes of cup-shaped flowers held on a 5-6ft (1.5-1.8m)-tall flowering stem, this perennial needs a sunny growing position and well-drained soil to succeed. The flowers are yellow, turning darker at the base of the spike as they fade. The leaves are linear and form a loose basal rosette. The roots are fleshy and finger-like. It is necessary to protect early growth from frost with straw or sacking. In winter, the crown of the bulb should be mounded over with sharp sand or ash to keep it dry.

Fritillaria imperialis (*above*) z 5
Crown imperial
A truly majestic spring-flowering bulb. The flowers appear on stems up to 3ft (90cm) tall and hang like bells below an apical tuft of green leafy bracts. 'Aurora' has orange flowers and 'Rubra' bronze-red. The stems are partly clothed with mid-green leaves. Plant the tubers on their sides in spring, 8in (20cm) deep, in humus-rich but well-drained soil. Propagate by division of clumps after the foliage has died away or by removal of offsets.

Gladiolus byzantinus (*above*) z 7
Sword lily
This gladiolus is a native of the Mediterranean and has striking reddish-purple flowers carried on slightly arching stems which grow up to 3ft (90cm) tall. The flowers are set against bright green, narrow leaves. Plants rarely require staking and may even be naturalized in grass providing it is not too vigorous. Plant corms in autumn in fertile but well-drained soil. The sword lily never fails to look good when grown in the company of *Cistus* × *purpurea* or *Rosmarinus officinalis*.

Lilium candidum z 6
Madonna lily
Succeeding on alkaline soil, this beautiful plant grows to 3ft (90cm) and has strongly fragrant, pure white flowers. It benefits from soil that has been enriched with compost or well rotted manure, the bulbs being planted shallowly and away from other lilies if possible. Growth begins in the autumn, the crown of basal leaves staying green through winter but then dying away as the flowering shoots emerge. The flowers are funnel-shaped, 2-3in (5-8cm) long, with five to twenty flowers on each stem in summer. The lance-shaped leaves are scattered along the stems.

Narcissus z 5
These bulbous plants can be guaranteed to add early colour to a mixed border. While the smaller species narcissi tend to be lost in larger borders, many of the newer cultivars are perfectly suited to them. It is best to plant the bulbs in clumps, preferably in the spaces that will be covered by herbaceous plants later in the season. Underplanting of deciduous shrubs can also work well. 'February Gold' has large, slightly reflexed petals; those of 'Thalia' are creamy-white.

Triteleia laxa z 8
Also known as *Brodiaea laxa*, this tender plant produces its funnel-shaped flowers in early summer. The flowers are carried in a large loose umbel, ranging from pale to deep purplish-blue, with each one being held erect and growing up to 2in (5cm) in length. The stem will reach a height of 20in (50cm) on a vigorous plant. Plant the corms during autumn in a sunny spot. The soil should be very well drained and dry out during summer. Propagate plants by seed or division. *T. hyacinthina* has white flowers which are sometimes tinged purple on thin stems.

Tulips z 5
Like daffodils, tulips are very useful early-flowering bulbs. For bright bold patches of colour consider the larger flowered cultivars. However, there are several species of tulips which should not be overlooked because of their smaller size. For a clump of graceful flowers (red and white flushed with pink) grow the lady tulip, *Tulipa clusiana*. *T. tarda* has yellow and white flowers.

ROCK GARDEN PLANTS

The rock garden reached its apogee, in England, in the period spanning the latter part of the nineteenth century through to the First World War. At this time labour, in comparison to materials and transport, was inexpensive and large amounts of money were expended on creating monumental rock gardens. Rocks were imported from mountainous regions and as many gardeners as necessary were employed to carry out the weeding needed to prevent the establishment of perennial weeds which can be very difficult to remove from between the rocks. The subsequent demise of the monumental rock garden was due in large part to the increase in the cost of labour:

unkempt growth went against the spirit of precision and order inherent in rockery design.

The advent of the environment-friendly translocated herbicide, glyphosate, that is deactivated as soon as it hits the ground, has made the control of weeds in a rock garden less of a problem. While taking extreme care not to touch the cultivated plants, weeds can be painted with a glyphosate-based mix which kills them off *in situ* without running the risk of leaving bits of root behind or disturbing the root system of the rock plants. This should be done in conjuction with ensuring that the soil used is free from perennial

Right: A naturally sloping and open site is ideal for a rock garden. Dwarf shrubs, such as hebes and some willows, add weight to a planting of geraniums, hypericums, pinks, rock roses, saxifrages, sedums and other perennials that thrive in sunny and free-draining conditions.

Left: The cool, moist cracks at the base of a rockery have been colonized by a mauve campanula, creeping jenny, a lungwort and a pink sedum.

Below: On an impressive limestone rockery the pale yellow of a large broom blends with the vibrant, spring colours of alyssum, aubrieta and saxifrage.

weeds before planting and that it is covered with plants or mulch as quickly as possible to prevent new seeds from germinating.

Rock gardens are best suited to informally designed gardens and look most convincing on a large scale. Unfortunately the cost of construction and the lack of space in many modern gardens often leads to very awkward-looking mounds of inferior stones appearing in the middle of a carefully kept lawn. However, there are many ways of creating the right environment for growing rock garden plants, which are for the most part alpines, in a restricted space whether in a formal or informal setting.

In the smallest spaces sinks and troughs can be easily accommodated and are particularly well suited in areas devoid of soil such as patios. Small rocks can be incorporated to create a miniature landscape and dwarf conifers can be used to give structure to the composition while the rock garden plants spill over the edge of the container.

Raised beds are another possibility and can be constructed to any shape. Large numbers of plants can be grown, both in the soil within the bed and in the cracks of the walls around it. By including miniature bulbs in the planting schemes it is possible to have colour throughout most of the season. In addition,

cultivation and appreciation of the plants is possible
with a minimum of bending and backache.

Dry stone walls or the top of brick walls, whether
boundary or retaining walls, can also be the home for
many trailing rock garden plants, as can the inter-
stices between paving slabs of patios and courtyards,
provided these have been laid on sand. In all these
situations the planting will be most effective if the
plants are allowed to find their own niche and self-
seed, colonizing the structure or surface.

All these growing environments have one characteristic in common. They all drain freely which is
essential to all plants that have their natural habitat in
mountainous regions. Whatever the situation it is
advisable to incorporate coarse drainage material in
the base of the container or rock garden, followed by a
layer of inverted turves and finally a mix of two parts
soil to one each of sharp sand and coarse peat. An
open site with plenty of light is also necessary for successful cultivation as is keeping the plants dry when
they are dormant, a period in nature when they are
either protected, in winter, by a layer of dry snow or,
in summer, baked by the sun. In the latter case it is
best to grow the most difficult and sensitive plants in a
scree or even under glass.

Above: A dicentra and a dwarf
geranium are among the plants
that have seeded themselves at
the base of these rocks. Great
patience is needed to get
plants to seed where they are
wanted as tiny plants are easily
washed away before they are
fully established. Often the
best strategy is to position the
first plants on flat ground
nearby and let them self-seed
naturally among the adjacent
cracks and crevices.

Left: Diascias, rock roses and
violas are among the plants
clothing the large blocks of
stone in this garden. Large
pieces of rock can be costly
and need to be positioned
carefully if they are to look
natural. A free-draining
compost needs to be
incorporated during building.

For flowers

Adonis amurensis z 3
The flowers of this charming perennial open from late winter onwards: often the bronze-green shoots can be seen pushing through the snow. Each bloom resembles a buttercup and is borne singly at the end of a shoot. After flowering, the finely cut leaves expand, giving the plant an eventual height of 1ft (30cm), before it dies away at the end of summer. Plant in well-drained humus-rich soil in late summer away from baking sun. To avoid mud splash on the flowers, surround the plant with stone chippings. Very hardy.

Alyssum saxatile (*above*) z 6
Gold dust
Sometimes known as *Aurinia saxatile*, this hardy evergreen perennial forms low mounds of growth with small, hairy grey-green leaves. In spring it is covered by bright golden-yellow flowers, and is the natural partner to *Aubrieta*. Plants reach a height of 8-12in (20-30cm) and should be clipped over after flowering to stop them becoming too large. They need full sun and well-drained soil. Increase by sowing seed in autumn or from softwood cuttings.

Androsace sempervivoides z 5
A fully hardy, compact and cushion-forming evergreen perennial with leathery, oblong leaves. In spring smallish heads of four to ten flowers appear, which are flat, pinkish with yellow eyes turning red. The plants need sun and well-drained soil, and grow up to 3in (8cm) high with a spread of about 1ft (30cm). Propagate in summer by taking tip cuttings or by removing young stolons, or in autumn by sowing seed. *A. sarmentosa* (z 3) has bright pink flowers with yellow eyes and is good for all but the wettest areas.

Anthemis cupaniana (*above*) z 8
With its finely cut, dense silvery foliage and small, daisy-like white flower heads with yellow centres, this evergreen perennial is an excellent choice in a warm climate. The flowers appear from early summer to autumn. The plants form spreading carpets, grow to a height of 1ft (30cm) with similar spread, and need clipping over after flowering. In winter the foliage turns green. Increase by taking basal cuttings from late summer through to spring. Plant in well-drained soil in full sun.

Arabis caucasica (*above*) z 3
An ideal choice for sturdy ground cover in a large rock garden, this evergreen mat-forming perennial is very hardy. It has small, oval mid-green leaves and four-petalled white or pink fragrant flowers in late spring and summer. Plants reach a height of 6in (15cm) and are at home on dry banks in thin soil. They should be trimmed over after the flowers have faded. 'Variegata' has cream-splashed leaf margins; 'Plena' has double white flowers; 'Rosabella' is deep pink. Propagate by seed in autumn or by softwood cuttings in summer.

Armeria maritima (*below*) z 3
Thrift, sea thrift or sea pink
In the wild, the evergreen hummocks (1ft (30cm) high) of this popular perennial cling to rocky outcrops along coastlines. In the rock garden, it should be sited in full sun, where the soil is very well drained. During spring and summer the hummocks are studded with globular flowers, ranging from lilac through pink to white: deadhead to prolong flowering. 'Vindictive' has rose-pink flowers. To propagate, divide plants in spring or take semi-hardwood cuttings in late summer.

Aubrieta deltoidea (*below*) z 7
Purple rock cress
In spring the dense mats of this evergreen plant are smothered in flowers – of varying shades of blue, red, purple or pink – which look supurb next to those of *Alyssum saxatile*. Its spreading foliage makes excellent ground cover. Plants will flourish on dry chalky soils and in walls and other crevices, so long as the drainage is good. After flowering, cut hard back to maintain shape and vigour. Propagate by taking tip cuttings in spring, or by layering the plants during the summer.

Campanula carpatica z 3
Bellflower

Ideal for the rock garden, this low-growing hardy perennial reaches a height of 3-4in (8-10cm) and spreads to 1ft (30cm). Its branching stems carry toothed, round-oval leaves, above which, during summer, the wide, bell-shaped, blue or white flowers appear. Named forms include the deep violet 'Jewel', 'Turbinata' which is lavender, and the pure white 'Bressingham White'. Plants need moist, well-drained soil, in sun or light shade. Divide in autumn or spring, or take softwood or basal cuttings in summer, or plant seed.

Chiastophyllum oppositifolium z 6

Also called *Cotyledon simplicifolia*, this succulent trailing perennial has an evergreen spreading habit and large, oblong, serrated fleshy leaves. During spring and early summer small yellow flowers open on very distinctive, arching sprays 6-8in (15-20cm) tall. It is at home in the cracks and crevices between rocks, but needs some shade and moist soil to do well. Take cuttings during summer using side shoots.

Dryas octopetala z 1
Mountain avens

The dark green, leathery leaves of this prostrate-growing evergreen perennial are held close to the ground. During late spring and early summer creamy-white, cup-shaped flowers appear just above the leaves, followed by attractive fluffy seed heads. Plants have a woody base, grow to only 2in (6cm) tall and make excellent ground cover, forming large patches in time. Choose a sunny spot and well-drained, gritty soil with some leaf mould added. Sow the seeds when fresh or take semi-ripe cuttings during the summer months. The fine *D. × suendermannii* is similar with pale cream flowers that open flat.

Erinus alpinus z 4
Fairy foxglove

Sow this dainty semi-evergreen perennial in spring, after which it will self-seed readily without becoming a problem. The plants need light, well-drained soil and a sunny position. They grow to only 6in (15cm) tall when in flower; clusters of pink, starry flowers rising above the small mid-green leaves. 'Albus' has white flowers, while those of 'Mrs Charles Boyle' are large and pink.

Gentiana sino-ornata z 6

A native of Tibet, the rich blue flowers of this hardy autumn-flowering gentian are a very impressive sight. They are borne singly above a cushion of fine grassy evergreen leaves, each 2in (5cm)-long trumpet having a green-striped throat. When in flower, the plants stand 2in (5cm) high and can spread to 1ft (30cm). Plant into moist, acid soil that is well charged with leaf mould, preferably in a spot that is shaded around midday. Propagate by dividing in spring every two to three years.

Helianthemum nummularium z 4
(*above*)
Sun rose or rock rose

One of the most colourful and reliable of all rock garden plants, this evergreen sub-shrub forms a spreading prostrate mat of growth covered in small, single rose-like flowers throughout the summer. Plants grow to 6in (15cm) high and spread to 2ft (60cm). They need full sun and free-draining, gritty soil that is not too rich. In autumn cut back to a few inches from the ground. For grey foliage and large pink flowers grow 'Wisley Pink'; 'Beech Park Red' has crimson blooms; 'Wisley Primrose' has yellow flowers. Propagate from non-flowering shoots in late summer.

Hedyotis michauxii z 3

Also listed as *Houstonia serpyllifolia*, this vigorous creeping perennial forms dense mats of spreading stems which root readily at the nodes. The mid-green foliage is dotted with violet-blue star-shaped flowers from spring to early summer. Plants reach a height of 3in (8cm), spreading to 1ft (30cm). Ideally, the soil should be sandy with added leaf mould, to hold moisture, and shaded. Divide in spring or sow seed in autumn.

Lewisia cotyledon (*above*) z 6

A gem among rock garden plants, *Lewisia* needs the morning sun to show off its bright flowers that close soon after lunch, but must be shaded from the midday sun. The rosettes of evergreen spatulate leaves set off the 1ft (30cm)-tall panicles of pink to salmon flowers that age rose-red. It requires excellent drainage to thrive, particularly around the neck which is apt to wilt during the winter when growth stops, and even during wet periods in the summer; cracks in walls are ideal.

Saxifraga longifolia (*above*) z 6

This hardy saxifrage is a rosette-forming perennial with long, narrow leaves encrusted with lime, which makes them especially attractive. When the rosettes reach three to four years old they produce long, arching flowering shoots smothered in panicles of white flowers. The flowers appear in spring and summer, and then the rosettes die without leaving any offspring. For this reason plants must be raised from seed, sown in spring or autumn. They are ideal for cracks and crevices, and need well-drained, alkaline soil and full sun.

For foliage

Asplenium trichomanes (*below*)   z 6
A dainty little fern suited to a limestone rock garden, where it will thrive in crannies, or planted in soil. It will tolerate full sun. It has slender tapering fronds (which should be removed once faded) with brown midribs carrying the bright green, rounded pinnae. The plant is semi-evergreen, often retaining most of its leaves through the winter. Plants grow to a height of 6in (15cm) spreading up to 1ft (30cm). Increase is by spores or more reliably by carefully dividing those clumps which have several crowns.

Bolax gummifera (*below*)   z 4
Prized for its hard cushions of foliage made up of evergreen blue-green leaves held in tight rosettes, this plant rarely produces its insignificant yellow flowers. Plants reach a height of only 1in (2.5cm), spread slowly to 6in (15cm) and need humus-rich but well-drained soil in full sun. They are very hardy and most at home in a gritty scree garden. Propagate by rooting rosettes during summer. Work plenty of sharp stone chippings in around the crown to prevent rotting. *Sagina boydii* is similar, growing to only ½in (1cm).

Dryopteris cristata (*above*)   z 5
Crested buckler fern
Moist conditions, such as are found next to a pond, suit this plant. It has light to mid-green fronds of two distinct types: sterile fronds which grow to 18in (45cm) in length and spread, and fertile spore-bearing fronds which can be 3ft (90cm) tall and stand fully erect. The latter, which have been likened to large shuttlecocks, give the fern a very distinctive appearance when planted in a group. Plants need some shade. Fading fronds should be removed regularly.

Sedum sieboldii **'Variegatum'**   z 5
(*above*)
Also called *S. sieboldii* 'Foliis Medio-variegatis', this tuberous perennial has rounded fleshy leaves in whorls of three. They are blue-green splashed with cream, sometimes with reddish edges. The flowers are pink and star-shaped, opening during late summer. Plants reach a height of 4in (10cm) and spread to 8in (20cm). It is also a useful plant for the front of a mixed border. Needs fertile well-drained soil and full sun. Propagate by division or through softwood cuttings in summer.

Sedum spathulifolium **'Purpureum'**   z 6
(*below*)
A purple-leaved form of the stonecrop, the leaves of this succulent perennial are spoon-shaped forming tight rosettes packed together on the plant. It produces mats or hummocks of growth to a height of 3in (8cm) and spreads up to 2ft (60cm). In summer, tiny yellow flowers appear in clusters: remove the flower heads in the following spring. Plants will tolerate some shade but prefer sun. Plant in well-drained soil and propagate by carefully detaching rooted rosettes.

Sempervivum tectorum (*below*)   z 4
Houseleek
Traditionally grown on the tiled roofs of houses to give protection from lightning and witchcraft, this plant grows as tight rosettes of succulent leaves, each rosette being anything from ½-8in (1-20cm) across. The leaves are normally green, but can be flushed with shades of red, pink and purple. Pinkish flowers appear in summer. Plants need good drainage and full sun to thrive. 'Triste' has green leaves tipped with reddish-brown. Increase plants by detaching rooted rosettes and replanting.

PAVED GARDEN PLANTS

In both large and small gardens it is often appropriate to have a paved area, such as a patio, terrace or flight of steps. Here, container-grown plants can contribute significantly to the success of the garden, introducing splashes of colour, architectural features, focal points and seasonal emphasis. They have the advantage that they can be moved around according to the mood and prevailing display of the moment.

There are also a number of plants that thrive in conditions where the soil is limited, poor and well drained, such as in the cracks between paving stones or in walls. For example, creeping thyme and chamomile can be used to soften the geometry of a paved area, as they will tolerate some walking on, while saxifrage and acaena are useful creeping around the edges. Erigeron and corydalis are suitable for colonizing cracks in walls and between steps, and tall plants such as verbascum make bold vertical statements.

Pots can be used to allow the inclusion of plants not suited to the soil in the garden (for example, camellias and rhododendrons in a garden where the soil is alkaline) or ones that have to be kept in frost-free conditions during the winter such as the sweetly-scented spidery-flowered bulbous hymenocallis.

Right: This decked courtyard contains numerous pot-grown, shade-tolerant plants, including impatiens, lamium and gardener's garters. Taller plants include a ginkgo, a willow (*Salix matsudana* 'Tortuosa') and a fig tree.

Left: Tender and hardy plants in carefully placed clusters of pots and individual containers do not obscure the decorative surface of bricks laid in a variety of patterns.

Below: Thymes and other tough, creeping plants occupy niches in the irregular paving of a sun-baked terrace on which a stone sink makes an attractive feature.

The importance of choosing the right container cannot be overstressed as it can make or break any aesthetic contribution the plant may bring to the garden. First, there is the style of the pot to consider, which should fit in with the chosen style of the garden. In a cottage garden, a mass of clay pots brimming over with flowering annuals and colourful bulbs will mingle happily with the exuberance of honeysuckles, roses, hollyhocks, phloxes and feverfew. In contrast, the recreation of a formal seventeenth-century garden will call for substantial containers of evergreen standards and topiary specimens displayed symmetrically about the main axes of the garden.

The containers may be of lead, stone or terracotta. There are many other materials available and much depends on the available resources, but it is better to have a few, well chosen containers than a host of second rate ones. Plastic pots may be light and cheap but should be hidden in wooden containers: marine ply stained dark green, black (which makes the vegetation stand out against it) or greeny-blue all work well. Alternatively, glazed containers created individually by potters that are in themselves pieces of art are an excellent choice as they would adorn the garden on their own or planted up.

The size of the container depends, within reason, on the size of the plant that is to be grown in it. It is

Left: Pansies and petunias form an underplanting beneath a mixture of shrubs – including trained cypresses, maples, pittosporums, roses and a yucca – grown in containers and raised beds that surround a small courtyard paved with York stone.

Below: Pot-grown plants, including elaborately trained ivy, have been used as accents and focal points within the formal geometry of this garden, in which the beds are divided by gravel paths.

important to remember that any container-grown plant requires sufficient nutrients to keep it growing healthily throughout the season without becoming so vigorous that it outgrows the container. Most good quality proprietary composts should contain enough nutrients, but at the height of the season it may be necessary to supplement this once a week with some liquid fertilizer. Watering is the single most important task when looking after pot-grown plants. During the main growing period, when evaporation is at its height, this usually needs doing twice a day.

Bearing these growing requirements in mind, it can be said that almost anything can be grown in a pot as long as it is accepted that it may not be as long-lived as normal, or, in time, will outgrow the container. So small trees (or larger ones grown as bonsai), shrubs, fruit trees and climbers can be included in a scheme of container-grown plants. Those that in their natural habitat tolerate drought are often best adapted to pot conditions; for example, many Mediterranean plants including bays, box, *Rhamnus alaternus* and pyracantha. Many species that need moist, shady conditions, such as rhododendrons and camellias, often fail through lack of watering. Usually, the most successful container displays are mixes of annuals and/or bulbs, newly planted as the seasons change.

Between the paving

Acaena microphylla   z 7

This charming native of New Zealand is prized more for its soft, burr-like scarlet seed heads, which glisten in the sun, than for its flowers. The plants form spreading evergreen mats of bronzed leaves, 1-2in (2.5-5cm) high. They prefer light soils in sun, needing only a few rooted shoots to establish quick-growing colonies. 'Blue Haze' grows slightly taller, with wonderful blue-grey foliage and reddish seed heads. Underplant with dwarf spring bulbs.

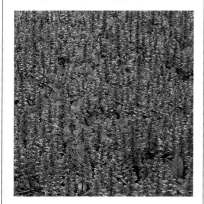

Ajuga reptans (*above*)   z 4
Bugle

For paved areas in light shade where the soil is moist the bugle is perfect. Plants form an evergreen mat of dark green, glossy foliage with blue-purple flowers on elegant flower spikes in spring. In flower, the plants are up to 1ft (30cm) high and spread indefinitely unless checked. 'Burgundy Glow' has leaves variegated pink, purple, cream and green; 'Purpurea' has deep purple-bronze foliage. Bugles associate well with the small-flowered erigerons and blue-leaved grasses such as *Festuca glauca*. Remove rooted pieces of shoot to increase stocks.

Campanula portenschlagiana   z 5

A vigorous bellflower which thrives in shade, needing moist soil. Plants produce a carpet of heart-shaped leaves covered from early summer to autumn with clusters of upright, open blue-violet flowers. At flowering the plants are 6in (15cm) tall, spreading up to 2ft (60cm). They are evergreen and hardy, but prone to slug damage in a wet spring. Plants self-seed and can become a pest in a sunny situation. Propagate by softwood cuttings of non-flowering shoots during summer.

Chamaemelum nobile 'Treneague'   z 6

A patch of this wonderfully fragrant, evergreen perennial releases the well-known "chamomile" scent when walked on or rubbed: a delight on warm summer evenings. It grows best on well-drained soils in full sun. Because the plant sets no seed it must be propagated by cuttings or division. The straight species is more vigorous and has white flowers with yellow centres; it grows to a height of 4in (10cm).

Corydalis lutea (*below*)   z 5

The yellow corydalis produces its small, snapdragon-like yellow flowers nearly year-round above rounded mounds of finely divided, delicate grey-green leaves. The mounds grow to 1ft (30cm) high, with a similar spread, and are ideal between paving stones or spilling from crevices in walls. It self-seeds with ease, or the ripe seeds can be scattered by hand as required. A superb partner for early bulbs such as *Chionodoxa*. Plants do well on poor soils, especially in the sun. At the end of summer cut straggly plants to the ground.

Erigeron karvinskianus   z 9/annual

A lovely fleabane with spreading loose stems carrying masses of daisy-like flower heads which open white, then turn pink, finally fading to purple. Flowers appear from summer through into autumn. The three-tone colour on established plants is quite eye-catching, especially when seen along the edge of garden steps. The stems also bear small, lance-shaped bristly leaves which are mid-green. Plants only grow 6in (15cm) tall, but spread widely, and should be clipped back in spring before new growth begins. Propagate by softwood cuttings in summer. Needs well-drained soil and full sun.

Helxine soleirolii   z 8

Also listed as *Soleirolia soleirolii*, this plant can become a nuisance in the wrong place. It is very tolerant and will fill the gaps between paving slabs or stones, especially if laid on cool moist soil in a shaded spot; but it is too delicate to withstand constant treading. Normally an evergreen perennial, it forms a dense carpet of tiny rounded green leaves which can be burned off by severe winter frosts. Plants never exceed 2in (5cm) in height. To propagate tease away small clumps and replant. Makes a good pot or greenhouse plant.

Lobularia maritima (*above*)   annual
Sweet alyssum

Formerly known as *Alyssum maritimum*. During spring, scatter the seeds of this quick-growing plant in the gaps between paving for a show of tiny white, scented flowers in small heads in the summer and autumn. Deadhead the flowers regularly to maintain the display. Plants have small, narrow greyish-green leaves, grow to a height of 6in (15cm) and spread to 1ft (30cm). They are hardy and need fertile soil and full sun to give of their best. 'Wonderland' has pink-purple blooms.

Mazus reptans   z 5

With some shelter (from frosts), moist soil and full sun, this creeping perennial will produce an abundance of purple flowers in spring. The flowers have a large, three-lobed whitish lower lip, spotted with red and yellow, and a small, slightly hooded top lip. Plants grow to no more than 2in (5cm) high, spread to 12in (30cm), and have narrow toothed leaves held in pairs along the stems. Divide plants in spring and replant vigorous tufts; alternatively, collect seed and sow in autumn.

Container plants

Saxifraga moschata (*below*)　　　z 6
Plant this evergreen perennial where there is some shade from the midday sun and where the soil is constantly moist. It will form a tight hummock 4in (10cm) high, made up of rosettes of small, lance-shaped green leaves. From these grow thin stems during summer, each carrying up to five creamy-white or yellowish star-shaped flowers. 'Cloth of Gold' has bright golden-yellow leaves and is ideal for shade. 'Elf' is shown. Propagate by detaching and rooting vigorous rosettes.

Thymus herba-barona　　　z 4
Caraway thyme
The common name of this evergreen sub-shrub comes from its small, dark green, caraway-scented leaves. The fragrance is released when the leaves are brushed against, but the plant will not tolerate trampling. Plants reach a height of 2-4in (5-10cm) and in summer are covered in small, lilac-pink flowers borne in clusters at the ends of the shoots. An ideal setting is among sand-coloured paving, especially if in tones of blue, grey and purple. Plants do best in full sun, where the soil is moist but free-draining. Take softwood or semi-ripe cuttings in summer.

Verbascum bombyciferum z 5/biennial
There are few more dramatic sights than this silver-leaved biennial mullein shooting up its tall racemes of densely-packed yellow flowers to a height of 4-6ft (1.2-1.8m). This it does in its second season, remaining evergreen through the previous winter. Both the large, oval basal leaves and the flower stems are covered in soft silvery hairs. Either allow to self-seed or scatter fresh seed, thinning in the following spring to produce strong plants.

Agapanthus **Headbourne hybrids**　z 7
(*above*)
Although the agapanthus is a native of South Africa, these hybrids originated in England and so tolerate cooler conditions. They are clump-forming perennials, evergreen in the mildest winters, with large, dark green strap-shaped leaves. In late summer the large, striking rounded heads of flowers rise to a height of up to 3ft (90cm). They range from deep blue to almost white. Plants need full sun, moist well-drained compost and protection during winter. Large plants can be divided.

Argyranthemum frutescens　z 9/annual
Marguerite
Also known as *Chrysanthemum frutescens*, this tender bushy perennial is perfect for growing as a standard in containers. It has delicate, blue-grey leaves and numerous daisy-like flower heads – yellow, pink or white depending on the form grown – during summer. It may take several seasons to form a 3ft (90cm)-high standard but it is well worth the effort. Plants thrive in a sunny spot with fertile moist soil and can be moved indoors during winter for protection.

Ballota pseudodictamnus　　　z 8
For a hot and sunny spot, this mound-forming sub-shrub provides considerable interest. It has grey-green rounded leaves covered in woolly hairs. During summer, small pink flowers emerge which have large, pale green calyces. The calyces remain long after the flowers have faded. Plants reach 2ft (60cm) in height and can spread rapidly to 3ft (90cm). To check growth cut back in early spring. Semi-ripe cuttings can be taken during summer. Needs well drained compost.

Bidens ferulifolia　　　annual
A Mexican native, this attractive member of the daisy family is grown as a half hardy annual, being raised from seed under glass in spring. It makes an ideal plant for a container, such as a hanging basket, with its lax habit allowing it to spill over the edge. Choose a terracotta pot or tub to complement its yellow star-like flowers and finely dissected greeny-bronze foliage. It associates well with *Helichrysum petiolare*. Plant after the frosts in rich, moist compost in the sun.

Fuchsia (*above*)　　　z 10/annual
The range of cultivars available of this popular garden plant is staggering. Most are tender and need overwintering where the temperature does not drop below 6°C (43°F) for some or 1°C (34°F) for others. They are often grown in containers and put out after the last frosts. The flower is prized for its great beauty. All fuchsias grow with a shrubby habit, being easily trained into standards. They need good rich soil and a sunny position. For containers, bushy plants up to 2ft (60cm) tall are ideal. 'Morning Light' is shown.

Helichrysum petiolare　z 8/annual
Grown primarily for its soft, silver-felted foliage, this rather tender sub-shrub is perfect for a mixed container planting. As the plant develops the shoots will trail and drape over the sides. It is best treated as an annual, young plants being overwintered from cuttings taken the previous season. Other cultivars well worth seeking are 'Limelight', with greenish-yellow leaves, and 'Variegata' which has cream variegation. Plants should be in sun and need well drained compost to produce their best displays.

Hydrangea macrophylla (*above*) z 6
With care, hydrangeas will grow well in
a good-sized container. Position them in
a lightly shaded spot, as excessive
sunlight will scorch the foliage, out of
the path of strong cold winds. Use a
free-draining humus-rich mixture when
planting up. The flowers are produced
either in large mop-like heads or in
flattish clusters, known as lacecaps.
'Blue Wave' is a lacecap with blue-pink
heads; the mophead 'Madame Emile
Mouillière' has white flowers with pink
or blue centres. The dead flower heads
add interest in winter.

Lilium regale (*above*) z 5
The regal lily
In summer, nothing can equal a
grouping of weathered terracotta pots of
this beautiful lily. The flowers appear
on stems up to 6ft (2m) tall on really
vigorous plants. Each stem can produce
up to 25 funnel-shaped fragrant flowers,
with petals that are whitish on the inside
with a yellow base and tinted pink on
the outside. The scaly bulbs can be
repotted in fresh rich compost each
spring. A few strong twigs are usually
needed to support the flowers.

Lobelia erinus (*below*) annual
Few containers would be complete
without the annual lobelia. The plants
are raised under glass and planted out
after the last frosts. They grow as
spreading or pendulous mats, reaching a
height of 8in (20cm), forming large
clumps which cascade over the edge of
the container. The flowers are two-
lipped, small, and appear throughout
summer into early autumn. 'Red
Cascade' and 'Cambridge Blue' are
notable; a mixed display is shown.

Osteospermum ecklonis z 9/annual
This evergreen semi-woody perennial
must be planted in full sun in well-
drained soil. It is ideal for pots or tubs
as a central dot planting, reaching a
height and spread of 18in (45cm). The
main flush of the white daisy-like
flowers with blue centres is in summer;
they open to their maximum on sunny
days. Take cuttings of non-flowering
shoots in summer. Plants tend to
become straggly and need some cutting
back in late spring. In the ideal climate
of subtropical areas they will flower
almost all year round.

Pelargonium z 10/annual
Ideal for summer containers, the best
types of these perennials are the ivy-
leaved, Swiss Balcony and zonals. All
these have bright red to white flowers
with numerous pink, mauve and salmon
intermediates. Repot plants in late
autumn and cut down by half before
overwintering in a frost-free place. In
spring cut back to healthy buds as
growth starts. Alternatively, take
cuttings in late summer and overwinter
ready for spring planting. The zonals
are usually raised as half-hardy annuals
from seed, preferably in fairly poor and
dry conditions.

Petunia annual
The modern strains of this popular half-
hardy summer bedding plant are
available as grandifloras (with large,
trumpet-shaped flowers) or multifloras
(where the flowers are smaller and more
numerous). Flower colour ranges from
white, through red, pink, purple and
yellow, and they can be double, striped
or frilly. For best results plant in
sheltered containers in full sun, where
the plants will adopt a trailing habit.
Allow 9in (23cm) between the plants,
which can grow up to 16in (40cm) high.
Wet summers tend to spoil the flowers.
Raise from seed in early spring.

Tropaeolum majus (*below*) annual
A very easy to grow hardy trailing
annual. Sow the large seeds after the last
frosts, choosing trailing varieties which
soon produce vigorous, spreading
shoots. During summer these are
decked with large bright flowers in
shades of red, orange and yellow. This
plant will thrive in the poorest of soils
and clamber through other container
plants with ease, and off into nearby
hedges and shrubs if allowed. Both the
flowers and leaves can be used in salads.

Verbena annual
Most forms of vervain are descended
from *V.* × *hybrida*, which is grown as a
half-hardy bushy annual reaching a
height of 6-18in (15-45cm) with similar
spread. The plants have oval, rough-
haired leaves and bright flowers held in
tight clusters of pink, red, mauve,
salmon or white from early summer
onwards. They need full sun and well-
drained soil. Selected forms are raised
from cuttings taken in late summer and
overwintered, the mixed types (such as
'Showtime') from seed raised under
glass in spring.

WATER PLANTS

Water in a garden is an undisputed asset to its design and attractiveness. The introduction of water plants not only helps to keep the water clean by natural means, but also helps to support a whole range of wildlife, including tadpoles and frogs, dragonflies, snails and fish. The position of a pond in the garden is important as most water plants require plenty of light to prosper. The shade cast by their leaves is welcomed by fish and other wildlife and reduces the growth rate of vigorous plants, such as duckweed and pondweed.

Regularly-shaped formal pools are well suited to the area adjacent to the house, where they will make an immediate impact and provide a focal point. In the smallest gardens they can be reduced to the size of a barrel (at least 1-2ft/30-60 cm deep), stone trough or tank, and planted with a single plant or two or three small-leaved species such as *Juncus effusus* 'Spiralis', frogbit (*Hydrocharis morsus-ranae*) and *Nymphaea tetragona* 'Alba'. The depth of the water and the vigour of plants can be regulated by planting each one in a basket that is supported by bricks so that it is immersed to the right depth. Larger pools call for simple treatments using only water lilies in a single striking colour or a subtle association of two colours.

Right: Astilbes, azaleas and ferns enjoy a cool, moist atmosphere, generated by a cascade and pool in a shady position. This well planned, established planting scheme looks completely natural.

Left: Yellow flags and arum lilies make a harmonious combination of white, cream and yellow that blends with the rockwork surrounding this sunny pool.

Below right: Although many waterside plants die down in winter, the foliage of some persists and can be very decorative. Here, the strap-shaped leaves of phormiums stand up stiffly behind irises and reeds.

An irregularly shaped informal pool looks most realistic if placed at the lowest point in a wild or informal garden, where water would naturally gather, and a path should lead the visitor down to discover it. A variety of plants will be appropriate here. The centre of the pool is suitable for deep-water plants, some of which root in the mud at the bottom of the pool or in specially designed baskets, while others, called floaters, are not rooted and have a tendency to spread very fast. Particularly fast-growing floaters are the oxygenators, which are essential to the ecology of the pool, but often need constant curbing. A common recommendation is that they should at the most take up a third of the pool's volume. Most frequently sold are the common duckweed, *Lemna minor*, and Canadian pondweed, *Elodea canadensis*, both of which can grow very quickly as the summer heat increases, choking all around them. They can only be recommended where it is easy to remove them regularly. *Myriophyllum spicatum*, the water milfoil, and *Cabomba caroliniana* are more desirable, being equally good purifiers and much less invasive.

For the edges of an informal pool, where the water is the shallowest, there is a wealth of "marginals" to choose from. With these, as with all other groups of plants, the art in designing is to select species of varying sizes and leaf shapes that harmonize and contrast with one another. In addition, they should complement the reflective quality of the water and the season, colour and habit of the flowers needs to be taken into account. These considerations should also be ex-

tended to the area immediately surrounding the pool, which can be made into a bog garden. For example, the upright heart-shaped leaves of *Peltandra virginica* and the diamond-shaped, serrated leaves of *Trapa natans* contrast well with the strap-like leaves of *Iris laevigata* and tall, leafless stems of the variegated sedge *Scirpus tabernaemontani* 'Zebrinus'. The shapes and habits of these marginals can then be echoed in the boggy surroundings of the pool with the tall leaves of the American skunk cabbage, *Lysichiton americanus*, the great clumps of *Hosta fortunei*, the straps of *Iris ensata* and ferny foliage of *Osmunda regalis*.

From a plantsman's point of view, bog gardens provide a gradual transition in habitats from the aquatic to the moisture-rich, and with this comes the opportunity to grow a wider range of plants.

The chief attraction of many bog plants lies in their foliage appeal, despite the presence of any flowers. This is because good foliage generally has a longer period of interest than flowers and so is better at masking the edge of the bog feature more effectively. Favourites include a wide variety of hostas, irises, the various forms of purplish-bronze or creamy variegated bugle (*Ajuga reptans*) and gunneras (for larger gardens only).

There are also some fine flowering bog plants that make a colourful impact when planted *en masse*. During early and mid summer, the feathery, creamy-white flowers of *Aruncus dioicus* can light up a semi-shaded area; it can be very vigorous and is probably best reserved for large areas. Astilbes are rather more restrained in size and are available in a variety of bright forms, from white through pale pink to flame red and crimson. Although they look stiffer and more formal than the aruncus, they create a truly colourful

summer display. More familiar in the herbaceous border but equally at home in the bog garden, hemerocallis hybrids produce their trumpet-shaped flowers all summer long and their strap-like leaves look good near water. The cheerful, low-growing flowers of *Mimulus guttatus* produce a splash of yellow from summer until early autumn, and there are primulas of all types and colours to suit any area provided the soil conditions are right. Generally speaking, most moisture-loving subjects prefer acid soil.

Well-planted bog gardens are particularly attractive to wildlife and, with careful plant selection, it is possible to create a wildlife environment. All water features attract wildlife, but the still, informal types with a shallow beach area and large areas of bog garden are the most appealing to the widest range of

Below: Although any water feature attracts wildlife, a pool specifically designed with this purpose in mind is delightful in an informal setting. Native plants, allowed to grow and spread in a natural way, create an ecologically balanced environment.

Above: The marginal planting of this natural-looking pool is based on bold leaf shapes reflected in the water, while the irises and primulas add an unexpected dash of colour in a mostly green setting.

Right: Informal pools merge into the rest of the garden with the addition of a bog garden. Here, ferns, hostas and astilbes help to blend this pond with the more formal borders that.

creatures, which include insects, amphibians, birds and even small mammals.

Native plants provide the best resources as they are part of our naturally occurring ecosystem. Certain plants encourage specific wildlife the marsh marigold (*Caltha palustris*) and water mint (*Mentha aquatica*) attract pollinating insects, while water dock (*Rumex hydrolapathum*) provides good cover for fauna. This is perhaps the one instance where plants are chosen for their ability to attract wildlife rather than for their decorative appeal, although the natural-looking tranquility of a wildlife pool undoubtably has its place in an appropriate setting.

Water garden

Aponogeton distachyos (*below*)   z 9
Cape pondweed, water hawthorn
This deciduous perennial has floating, oblong, dark green leaves which are sometimes splashed purple. The attractive waxy-white flowers have a characteristic "forked" appearance, sweet scent and noticeable black stamens. They appear from early spring until autumn. At home in deep or shallow water, plants spread to 4ft (1.2m). The fading leaves need tidying up in autumn. Propagate in spring by division of the tubers or by sowing fresh seed: plants often self-seed.

Cabomba caroliniana   z 6
Fish grass, fanwort, Washington grass
A useful oxygenator for ponds, this deciduous or semi-evergreen submerged perennial is used by fish as a source of food and a suitable place to spawn. Plants form spreading hummocks of fan-shaped, coarsely divided leaves which are bright green. Tiny white flowers appear in summer. Propagate by taking stem cuttings in summer or by division when dormant. Tends to be cut back in severe winters.

Callitriche palustris   z 5
Water starwort
The bright green, oval-linear leaves of this plant are not only attractive but also help to aerate the water. At home submerged or part-submerged in deep water, plants will grow equally well rooted in wet mud. In mud they tend to grow as rosettes, while in deep water the stems can be 20in (50cm) long. The minute green flowers appear during spring and summer but are rather insignificant. Plants grow as annuals or perennials and can become a weed if not kept in check. Dredge the pond regularly leaving a few stems to re-grow.

Caltha palustris (*above*)   z 3
Marsh marigold or kingcup
In shallow water around the edge of a pond there is little to equal the spectacular spring display of this deciduous perennial. It is equally well suited to a bog garden, moist rock garden or herbaceous border. The rounded, dark green leaves set off the large, cup-shaped golden-yellow flowers. Plants can grow to 2ft (60cm) in height with a spread of 18in (45cm). The double-flowered cultivar 'Flore Plena' reaches only 10in (25cm). Sow seeds in an open sunny position.

Ceratophyllum demersum   z 4
Hornwort
An excellent choice for attractive, feathery submerged foliage, this deciduous perennial is easily controlled; its brittle nature makes thinning out a simple task. It will sometimes float and will spread over a large area given space. The hornwort is a good oxygenator and grows best in cool deep water. Plants are rootless. Divide the scaly winter buds or take stem cuttings during the growing season.

Cyperus longus   z 7
Galingale
This evergreen perennial sedge is fully hardy and can reach 5ft (1.5m) in height, and spreads slowly but strongly. For large ponds it is excellent for stabilizing banks, and will grow well in otherwise uninteresting ditches, where in summer the milk-chocolate coloured flowers appear in flattish umbels. Flowers appear above the dark green, glossy, rough-edged narrow leaves. They are long-lasting and useful for cutting. Plants will tolerate their roots being in water. Divide in spring.

Hottonia palustris (*below*)   z 5
Water violet
The dense whorls of finely pinnate leaves of this violet form a spreading pale green mass. In summer, flower spikes appear above the foliage carrying lilac or white yellow-eyed flowers in whorled clusters. This hardy, submerged deciduous water plant is a member of the primrose family. Plants should be thinned regularly as they mature to stop crowding. They need a sunny position and cool, clean, still, deep water. Propagate through stem cuttings during the growing season.

Hydrocharis morsus-ranae (*below*)   z 5
Frogbit
The kidney-shaped, olive green shining leaves and small white flowers of the frogbit are a delight in summer. This deciduous perennial can spread up to 4in (10cm), but groups of plants tend to grow together spreading to 3ft (90cm). The petals are distinctive, three-petalled with a central yellow eye and grow up to 1in (2.5cm) across. The leaves are often bronze-tinted. Plants grow in still, fresh deep water needing an open sunny spot. They are easily propagated by detaching young plantlets.

Iris laevigata (*above*)　　　z 4
One of the best of the hardy water irises for growing in shallow water. Plants form large spreading clumps to a height of 2-3ft (60-90cm). The flowering stems arise from the rhizomes, each carrying between two and four flowers of a brilliant blue. The beardless flowers appear in sun or part shade. Divide in late summer. 'Regal' has red flowers, those of 'Snowdrift' are double white, while 'Variegata', which flowers again in early autumn, has variegated foliage.

Juncus effusus 'Spiralis'　　　z 5
Corkscrew rush
A tufted evergreen perennial with mid-green leafless stems which are twisted and curled like a corkscrew. The stems often lie on the ground. The greenish-brown flowers appear in summer. Plants are best used at the edge of a pond, so that the stems can be seen against the reflective water surface. Strong plants can send up 3ft (90cm)-tall twisted shoots which are used in modern flower arranging. Divide clumps in spring.

Myriophyllum spp　　　z 4
The myriophyllums are a group of deciduous perennials with finely divided, spreading foliage which makes an ideal habitat for fish spawn. They need full sun and can spread widely if not checked. *M.proserpinacoides* has blue-green leaves which take on red tints in autumn near the water surface, while *M.verticillatum* has paler, olive-green foliage. Both can be fully or partially submerged, and look most attractive when spreading over the water surface. Insignificant greenish or creamy flowers appear in summer. Propagate by stem cuttings in summer.

Nuphar lutea　　　z 4
Yellow water lily or brandy bottle
The yellow flowers, which are quite small (2in (6cm) across), bottle-shaped and sickly-smelling, are held some way above a mat of broad, oval, mid-green leaves which are about 16in (40cm) wide, giving the plant a spread of up to 5ft (1.5m). The seed heads are rounded, warty and quite decorative. This hardy deciduous perennial thrives in deep water, in sun or shade, and is useful for a water-lily effect where *Nymphaea* will not grow. To propagate, divide the thick crowns in spring.

Nymphaea 'Escarboucle' (*above*)　　　z 3
This water lily can achieve a spread of 10ft (3m) when given space. The floating leaves are dark green and in summer set off the semi-double, cup-shaped, deep crimson flowers. Each flower can be up to 6in (15cm) across and has a golden centre. Plants must have an open sunny position and still deep water. Dead leaves should be carefully removed as they fade. Propagate by lifting and dividing the thick tuber-like rhizomes in spring every few years or by using seed.

Nymphaea 'Marliacea' cvs　　　z 3
'Marliacea Chromatella' has olive green foliage, strikingly marked with deep bronze-maroon blotches, and canary yellow, semi-double, cup-shaped flowers. In summer, the flowers can reach 8in (20cm) across when fully open and have deep golden-yellow centres. 'Marliacea Albida' has pure white fragrant flowers and dark green leaves with red or purple undersides; 'Marliacea Carnea' has pink, semi-double, star-like flowers with gold centres. Propagate as for *N.* 'Escarboucle'. The attractive leaves are an excellent foil for the flowers.

Orontium aquaticum　　　z 6
Golden club
A favourite among water plants, the flowers of this aroid lack the typical spathe, leaving the central yellow and white spadix to provide colour. A deciduous perennial, the golden club grows equally well in shallow or deep water. In spring, the pencil-like flower spikes (spadices) emerge from among the floating mass of waxy leaves which are a bluish or greyish green. Plants grow to 10in (25cm) high spreading up to 2ft (60cm). Large seeds develop later in the summer and are used to propagate plants while they are still fresh, which is easier than trying to divide the tough rootstock.

Peltandra virginica (*below*)　　　z 5
Green arrow arum
This herbaceous perennial is grown for its bright green, distinctively veined, arrow shaped leaves, and its yellow to white spathes that enclose a short spadix and green berries in summer. It thrives in water up to 10in (25cm) deep, or in a bog garden. Plant in baskets of lime-free humus-rich soil in still or slow-moving water, in full sun.

Ranunculus aquatilis　　　z 3
Water crowfoot
A member of the buttercup family, this perennial has two leaf types: the submerged leaves are much-divided, while the floating leaves are solid and dark green. The flowers either float on the surface or protrude a little above the water. They are white, five-petalled with a yellow centre and appear during early summer. Plants grow in still or slow-moving water up to 3ft (90cm) deep. Thin plants occasionally, returning a few vigorous pieces to re-grow. This plant is poisonous if eaten.

Bog garden

Sagittaria sagittifolia z 5
Common arrowhead
Ideally suited to shallow water conditions, this deciduous perennial grows to a height of 18in (45cm) with a spread of 1ft (30cm). It has upright mid-green leaves shaped like arrows and in summer flowers are borne in spikes, each with three white petals and a purple centre. In *S. latifolia* the flower centre is yellow. Plants need full sun. Propagate by dividing in spring or summer, or by detaching young scaly shoots known as turions.

Scirpus tabernaemontani 'Zebrinus'
(*above*) z 5
Zebra rush
Also listed as *S. lacustris* subsp. *tabernaemontani* 'Zebrinus', this tall and handsome rush is useful in areas where the water is brackish. The leafless stems of this evergreen perennial sedge are striped markedly with white in horizontal bands. In summer, brown spikelets appear part way up the stems; these are the flowers. Remove any shoots that are all green to stop the plant reverting to the plain green form. Shoots reach a height of 5ft (1.5m) and spread indefinitely. Divide in spring.

Stratiotes aloides z 5
Water soldier
Characterized by its rosettes of spiny, olive green leaves, this free-floating semi-evergreen perennial is commonly found in alkaline water. It spends most of its time submerged, rising up to 10in (25cm) above the surface during summer when the whitish-pink cup-shaped flowers appear. The leaves are sharp and edged with spines. Plants spread to 12in (30cm) in diameter and need deep water. Propagate by small buds which develop on the plants' base.

Trapa natans z 6
Jesuit's nut or water chestnut
Grown primarily for its attractive foliage, the mid-green leaves are diamond-shaped with deeply toothed edges and grow in beautiful neat rosettes. The centre of each leaf is often marked with deep purple blotches. White flowers are produced in summer. Each floating plant can spread to 9in (23cm) and looks best if part of a group in shallow water. To propagate this annual, collect seed in autumn, overwinter in water or wet moss and plant in spring.

Typha latifolia variegata z 3
Reed mace
The vigorous and invasive reed mace should be considered for planting only in larger ponds, in sun or shade. This deciduous perennial forms huge clumps of growth from which emerge green leathery leaves and spikes of brownish flowers in late summer. The flowers are followed by dark brown torpedo-shaped seed heads, which split open to release masses of fluffy airborne seeds and are very decorative through autumn and winter. Plants can reach 8ft (2.5m) in height. *T. minima* is more dainty. Propagate by seed or division in spring.

Utricularia vulgaris z 4
Greater bladderwort
With tiny, bladder-like, bronze-green modified leaves on its submerged roots, this carnivorous perennial traps water-dwelling organisms. Only the flower stems rise above the surface to a height of 16in (40cm), carrying bright yellow flowers in summer. Plants spread to 12in (30cm), grow in deep water and are deciduous. They form large clumps which should be thinned when overcrowded. Propagate by division.

Zantedeschia aethiopica z 8
Arum lily
This South African native grows well in shallow water. It flowers throughout the summer, with the erect funnel-shaped spathes being held well above the arrow-shaped glossy, deep green leaves. Each spathe surrounds a central yellow spadix. The leaves and flowering stems arise from a tuber. Plants can reach up to 3ft (90cm) in height, spreading to 18in (45cm). Ensure they are bedded deeply in the soil below water level. Propagate from seed or by division in spring.

Carex stricta 'Aurea' z 5
Bowles' golden sedge
Also listed as *C. elata* 'Aurea', this evergreen hardy perennial has golden, lime-green striped leaves which create a splash of colour in summer, fading to greener shades later in the season. It grows equally well at the waters' edge as in a bog garden. Plants have a tufted habit, need moist soil and a sunny spot to colour well. They grow to 16in (40cm) in height and spread up to 6in (15cm). Dark brown flower spikes appear in summer. Propagate by division in spring.

Hosta fortunei (*above*) z 3
Unlike many hostas, this species is prized more for its flowers than its foliage: tall mauve flower spikes appear around mid-summer, towering above the soft grey-green leaves. This hardy herbaceous perennial forms large clumps and grows to a height of 3ft (90cm) with an equal or greater spread. It needs a moist fertile soil and light shade. 'Albopicta' has yellow leaves edged with light green which become two-tone green in summer; 'Marginato-alba' has leaves margined with white and violet flowers. Protect against slugs and snails. Propagate by dividing the crowns in early spring.

Iris ensata z 5
Japanese flag iris
Also listed as *I. kaempferi*. Plant this iris in partial shade, ensuring that the soil is rich in humus. Its flowering stems reach 2-3ft (60-90cm) in height and are branched, carrying up to 15 reddish-purple flowers, each up to 6in (15cm) across. There are many forms in a variety of colours. The rhizomes will spread indefinitely. To propagate divide them in late summer.

Kirengeshoma palmata   z 5

Even in the height of summer, this lovely herbaceous perennial exudes a coolness that is rarely matched by any other plants. An upright grower, it reaches a height of 3ft (90cm) with similar spread, and the stems carry lobed bright green leaves, topped by clusters of soft cream-yellow flowers from late summer to autumn. Prefers a lightly shaded position and moist, acid soil. Plants can be raised from seed or divided in autumn or spring.

Lysichiton americanus (below)   z 3
Yellow skunk cabbage

The large, bright yellow spathes emerge before the leaves, from early spring onwards, surrounding a central yellowish-green spadix which are the true flowers. Space must be made for the huge, fresh green leaves which can be up to 4ft (1.2m) long, 30in (75cm) in *L. camtschatcensis*, which has flowers with pure white spathes. These vigorous herbaceous perennials form large impressive clumps in full sun and will grow near still or running water, or in wet mud. Propagate through freshly collected seed or division in spring.

Mentha aquatica   z 3

A wonderfully aromatic bog plant which releases a cool peppermint-like fragrance when crushed. It grows as a hairy purplish perennial, the flowers appearing in rounded heads on 30in (75cm)-tall stems above oval toothed leaves. The pinkish-lilac flowers have hairy sepals. Divide plants using pieces of the creeping rootstock which can be invasive but is easily contained in a deep open-bottomed container sunk in the ground. One of the parents of the cultivated peppermint, *M.* × *piperata*, which is used as a culinary herb.

Mimulus guttatus   z 5
Monkey flower

With a height and spread of 2ft (60cm), this mat-forming perennial carries bright yellow snapdragon-like flowers which are spotted with brownish red. They appear throughout the summer until autumn. The mid-green leaves are oval. *M. luteus* (z 7) is similar but smaller and has large reddish blotches on the petals; rather more spectacular is *M. cardinalis* with its scarlet-orange flowers held on stems 2ft (60cm) tall. Propagate by division, through soft tip cuttings in summer, or by seed.

Osmunda regalis (above)   z 3
Royal fern

The thick mat of roots produced by this majestic fern is excellent at stabilizing the soil in very wet areas or near the edge of water. This deciduous perennial is tolerant of sun and can grow to 6ft (2m) in a season, with a spread of 3ft (1m). The young fronds are pinkish as they emerge in spring, turning a bright green as they mature. On established plants the ends of taller fronds terminate in a rusty-red, spore-bearing female spike, like a tassel. Propagate by division in autumn or winter.

Pontederia cordata   z 3
Pickerel weed

In late summer, blue flower spikes emerge from glossy, dark green leaves, which are narrow and lance-shaped. Plants form large clumps in time and grow best at the wet edges of a bog garden or in shallow water. They reach a height of 30in (75cm) and can spread to 18in (45cm). This deciduous perennial needs full sun to succeed and the flowers should be removed once they have faded. Increase in spring by seed or division.

Primula pulverulenta (above)   z 5
Candelabra primula

The common name derives from the appearance of the flower stems, which carry striking crimson-red flowers with deep purple eyes. The main flowering stem and the flower stalks are covered in beautiful white farina. Plants seed themselves readily, forming clumps of upright growth, 2-3ft (60-100cm) in height and 18in (45cm) across. 'Bartley' has pale-pink flowers with carmine eyes and mid-green, toothed lance-shaped leaves. Plants need moist fertile soil in sun or shade. Divide plants or lift self-sown seedlings to increase numbers.

Rheum palmatum 'Atrosanguineum'   z 6

Consider this large ornamental form of the rhubarb only where its height and spread of 6ft (2m) can be accommodated with ease. This herbaceous perennial has deeply cut, five-lobed leaves of reddish-purple, with darker veins. Each leaf can grow to 2ft (60cm) across. In early summer, upright panicles of crimson flowers rise above the leaves. Propagate by division of the thick rootstock with a spade in spring.

Rodgersia aesculifolia   z 5

Choose a spot away from strong winds to prevent damage to the large, crinkled bronze foliage (similar to that of the horse chestnut *Aesculus*), in sun or part-shade. Plants also grow well beside water. The rhizomes of this perennial form large clumps. Plants grow to 3ft (90cm) in height with similar spread. During mid-summer, plume-like, fragrant pink flowers appear from the foliage, held in rather flattish clusters. *R. pinnata* 'Superba' has bronze foliage, while 'Alba' has white flowers. Divide plants in spring.

Acid A term applied to soil or water with a pH value of below 7.

Aerial root A root growing above the soil from the stem of a plant.

Alkaline A term applied to soil or water with a pH value of above 7.

Annual A plant that completes its life cycle within one growing season.

Anther The terminal part of a stamen that contains pollen.

Arboretum A tree collection.

Aril A covering on some seeds that is often brightly coloured and fleshy.

Bent Any perennial grass which has spreading panicles of tiny flowers; ideal for garden lawns.

Biennial A plant which completes its life cycle in two growing seasons, forming a leafy plant in the first year before flowering, seeding and then dying in the second year.

Bract A modified, usually reduced, leaf that grows just below the flower head.

Breastwood Shoots that grow outwards from a plant that is trained against a support such as a fence.

Calcareous Containing, or resembling, carbonate of lime or limestone; chalky or limy in nature.

Calyx The outer whorl of a flower, consisting of sepals that may be free to the base or partially joined.

Catkin An inflorescence consisting of a hanging spike of much-reduced flowers occurring in trees like hazel and birch.

Chlorosis A condition in which leaves become unnaturally pallid, whitish or yellow. The disease is usually due to lack of essential minerals.

Compost (seed or potting) A mixture of materials consisting chiefly of loam, peat, sand and fertilizers. It is used as a medium for sowing seeds, planting on seedlings and potting plants.

Compound leaf A leaf composed of two or more similar parts.

Cone Flowering or fruiting spike of a conifer. The males are small and the females have hard scales that release protected seeds.

Coniferous Relating to the group of plants that typically bear cones. Most are evergreen with linear leaves.

Container-grown A plant in a container as opposed to a bare-rooted one that is lifted from the open ground.

Corona The growth between the petals and stamens of a flower; for example, the trumpet of a daffodil.

Corymb An inflorescence with a flat-topped flower cluster.

Crown The basal part of a plant from which roots and shoots grow.

Cultivar A cultivated, as distinct from a botanical, variety of plant.

Cutting A separated piece of stem, root or leaf taken from a plant in order to propagate a new plant.

Damask rose A type of rose grown for its red and pink fragrant flowers.

Deadhead To cut off a wilting or faded flower head from a plant.

Deciduous A plant that loses all its leaves at one time of the year, usually during late autumn.

Digitate Describes a compound leaf that resembles a spread hand.

Division Propagation by means of dividing a single plant into smaller portions; also a way of thinning plants.

Dormancy The resting period of a plant, usually in winter.

Double (flower head) A flower with a double row or multiple rows of petals.

Dressing A top covering, like pea gravel, applied to the surface of the soil.

Ericaceous Species of plant belonging to the heather family, Ericaceae, which includes azaleas and rhododendrons. Most will not grow in limy soil.

Evergreen A plant that retains its leaves throughout the year.

Fescue Any grass of the genus *Festuca*; ideal for garden lawns.

Floret A small flower making up the head of a composite flower.

Floribunda A plant with multi-headed flowers, for example, certain roses.

Genus A group of related species that share characteristics and form a family.

Germination The development of a seed into a seedling.

Glaucous A bluish-white, bluish-green and bluish-grey waxy bloom.

Grafting The process by which parts of two different plants are bound together to unite and become a single plant.

Ground cover A low-growing plant that covers the surface of the soil.

Habit The natural mode of growth and consequent shape of a plant.

Half-hardy A plant that is unable to survive the prevailing winter temperatures without some sort of protection, but does not need to be kept in a greenhouse all year round.

Harden off To acclimatize plants raised in warm conditions to cooler conditions.

Hardy A plant capable of surviving very cold weather in the open without any protection.

Herbaceous A non-woody, fleshy plant grown in borders; usually a perennial.

Humus Fertile, partially decomposed organic matter in soil.

Hybrid A plant that is produced by the cross-fertilization of two species or variants of species.

Indumentum A hairy covering on leaves and other plant parts.

Inflorescence Flowering part of plant.

Knot garden A formal garden of ornamental flower beds with low plants and hedges in an intricate design.

Lanceolate Describes the shape of a narrow, tapering leaf.

Lenticel One of many pores in the bark of woody plants through which gaseous exchange takes place.

Loam Any reasonably fertile soil that contains a free-draining mixture of clay, sand and organic material.

Marginal plants Plants that grow in the shallow water around the edges of a pool.

Microclimate A climate particular to a specific situation which differs from the overall climate of the garden or region.

Moss rose A type of rose that has a mossy stem and pink, fragrant flowers.

Mulch A soil-covering that protects plants, reduces evaporation, suppresses weeds, prevents erosion and, in the case of organic mulch, enriches the soil.

Node The point on a plant stem from which leaves or lateral branches grow.

Palmate Describes the shape of a leaf with five lobes or segments spreading out from a common point.

Panicle A branched flower head, each branch having several stalked flowers.

Papery (petal) The term given to a petal with a thin, paper-like texture.

Parterre A formal garden made up of elaborately shaped flower beds designed to be viewed from above.

Perennial A plant that lives for at least three seasons.

Pergola A horizontal framework or trellis supported by posts and covered in climbers, often part of a walkway.

Petoile The stalk of a leaf.

pH The scale by which acidity or alkalinity is measured.

Pinnate Describes the shape of a leaf with leaflets growing opposite each other in pairs on either side of the stem.

Plantlet A young plant produced naturally by the parent plant as a method of propagation.

Pleaching The training of hedge branches to form a dense hedge, often leaving the trunks bare as stilts.

Pricking out The transplanting of a seedling from a seed tray to a pot or another tray.

Propagation The production of a new plant from an existing one, either by seed or cuttings.

Raceme An inflorescence in which the stalked flowers are borne along a stem.

Rhizome An underground stem, often thick as in irises or thin as in grasses, and usually horizontal.

Rootstock The underground part of a plant from which the roots and shoots grow.

Rosette A circular cluster of leaves growing from the base of a shoot.

Runner A trailing stem that grows along the surface, takes root and forms new growth at nodes or the tip.

Scarify To rub or scratch the surface of a seed to increase water absorption in order to speed up germination.

Seed The structure resulting from fertilization of the female part of the flower, consisting of a single embryo protected by an outer covering.

Seedling A very young plant with few leaves raised from seed.

Semi-evergreen Describes a plant intermediate between evergreen and deciduous. It bears some foliage

throughout the year, but also loses some leaves during winter.

Sepal The outermost, leaf-like structures of a flower.

Sessile A flower or leaf with no stalk, growing directly from the stem.

Single (flower head) A flower with a single layer of petals.

Species A group of closely related organisms within a genus.

Spike (flower) An inflorescence consisting of stalkless flowers arranged along a stem.

Stamen The male reproductive organ of a flower.

Standard Any tree which has a 4-6 ft (1.2-1.8 m) high main stem or trunk with a large head; commonly applied to fruit trees, roses and fuchsias.

Stigma The terminal part of the ovary, (the female reproductive organ of a flower) where pollen is deposited.

Stipule (leaf) Out-growths, usually paired, at the base of the leaf stalks that protect the young leaves.

Stooling To cut to the ground and allow to regrow to encourage the growth of new whip-like stems.

Sub-shrub A plant with a woody base and herbaceous tips.

Subsoil The layer of soil below the topsoil which is lighter in colour.

Sucker A strong shoot that grows from the roots, rhizomes or main stem of a mature plant.

Tender A plant unable to withstand the coldest prevailing weather.

Tendril The twisting, thread-like growth of a climbing plant that coils or loops around any nearby support.

Tepal The outer part of a flower resembling a petal.

Thin To reduce the number of seedlings by uprooting at random.

Tilth The fine, crumbly surface layer of soil. The ideal tilth for a seedbed is the consistency of coarse breadcrumbs.

Tomentum A felt-like covering of hairs on leaves and other parts of a plant.

Topiary The practice of cutting trees and hedges into ornamental shapes.

Topsoil The upper layer of soil, the darkest and most fertile part, in which plants grow.

Triloliate Leaves that are divided into three, as in clover.

Umbel A flat-topped or dome-shaped flower head in which the flowers are borne on stalks arising from the top of the main stem.

Variegated Leaves with white, yellow or pinkish markings.

Variety A distinct variant of a species, either a cultivated form (a cultivar) or one that occurs naturally.

Watering in To water around the stem of a newly transplanted plant to settle soil around the roots.

Whorl Three or more flowers, buds, leaves or shoots arising from the same place on a plant stem.

PUBLICATIONS AND ORGANIZATIONS

Royal Horticultural Society
80 Vincent Square
London, SW1P 2PE

Botanic Gardens Conservation Int.
Descanso House
199 Kew Road
Richmond, Surrey, TW9 3BW
Wild species in danger of extinction.

British Association of Landscape Industries
Landscape House
Henry Street
Keighley, West Yorkshire, BD21 3DR
Domestic and industrial landscaping.

British Fuchsia Society
11 Hungerford Drive
Reading
Berkshire, RG1 6JA
Propagation and training of fuchsias.

British Pelargonium and Geranium Society
134 Montrose Avenue
Welling
Kent, DA16 2QY
Promotion of the popular pelargonium.

Gardening Which?
2 Marlebone Road
London, NW1 4DX
Choosing shrubs for your garden.

Institute of Groundmanship
19/23 Church Street
The Agora
Wolverton, Milton Keynes
Buckinghamshire, MK12 5LG
Lawn problems and pesticide safety.

Ministry of Agcriculture, Fisheries and Food
Whitehall Place
London, SW1A 2HH
Plant health in the single market.

National Chrysanthemum Society
2 Lucas House
Craven Road
Rugby
Warwickshire, CV21 3HV
Promotion of chrysanthemums.

National Council for the Conservation of Plants and Gardens
Wisley Garden
Woking
Surrey, GU23 6QB
Plants for alkaline and acid soils.

National Pelargonium Collection
Honeybourne Road
Pebworth, Nr. Stratford-on-Avon
Warwickshire, CV37 8XT
Pelargoniums.

Alpine Garden Society
AGS Centre
Avon Bank, Pershore
Worcestershire, WR10 3JP
Publications and publicity for the Alpine Garden Society.

Amateur Gardening
IPC Magazines
Westover House
West Quay Road
Poole, Dorset, BH15 1JG

BBC *Gardeners' World* **Magazine**
101 Bayham Street
London, NW1 0AG

Garden News
EMAP
13 Holham Road
Orton, Southgate
Peterborough, PE2 0UF

Gardener Magazine
Greater London House
Hamstead Road
London, NW1 7QQ

Organic Gardening
PO Box 4
Wivelscombe, Taunton
Somerset, TA14 2QY

NURSERIES AND MAIL ORDER

African Violet Centre
Station Road
Terrington Street
Clement, King's Lynn
Norfolk, PE34 4PL
Saintpaulias.

Allwood Bros
Mill Nursery
Hassocks
West Sussex, BN6 9NB
Carnations, pinks and dianthus.

Jacques Amand Limited
The Nurseries
115 Clamp Hill
Stanmore
Middlesex, HA7 3JS
Flowering bulbs including many rare and unusual spring flowering bulbs. Catalogue available on request for mail order.

Apple Court
Hordle Lane
Lymington
Hampshire, SO41 0HU
Nursery specialising in hostas, grasses, ferns, day lilies, monocots and perennials.

Architectural Plants
Cooks Farm
Nuthurst
Horsham
West Sussex, RH13 6LH
Hardy evergreen trees and shrubs.

David Austin Roses
Albrighton
Wolverhampton, WV7 3HB
Fragrant old roses and repeat flowering hybrids; clibing roses. 800 varieties.

Avon Bulbs (RHS)
Burnt House Farm
Mid Lambrook
South Petherton, TA13 5HE
Bulbs by mail order.

Barthelemy & Co
The Nursery, TG
262 Wimborne Road
West Wimborne
Dorset, BH21 2DZ
Japanese maples and Acer palmatum. Suitable for garden patio or bonsai. Catalogue and mail order service.

Peter Beales Roses
London Road
Attleborough
Norfolk, NR17 1AY
Over 1000 varieties, consisting mainly of old-fashioned shrub and climbing roses, many of which are rare and of historical interest. Catalogue available.

Blackmore and Langdon
Stanton Nursery
Pensford, Bristol
Avon, BS18 4JL
Begonias, delphinimums and phlox.

Walter Blom & Son Coombelands Nurseries
Thurleigh Road
Milton Ernest
Bedford, MK44 1RQ
Tulips.

Blooms of Bressingham
Bressingham
Diss
Norfolk, IP22 2AB
Hardy plants.

Bodwen Nursery
Little Ventowyn Lodge
Hewas Water
Sticker, St Austell
Cornwall, PL26 7DW
Japanese maples.

Bonsai Kai
39 West Square
London, SE11 4SP
Bonsai.

J.W. Boyce
Bush Pasture
Lower Carter Street
Fordham, Ely
Cambridgeshire, CB7 5JU
Roots and beans.

Broadleigh Dwarf Bulbs
Broadleigh Gardens
G4, Bishops Hull
Taunton
Somerset, TA4 1AE
Over 300 varieties, rare/unusual species, especially dwarf daffodils and tulips.

Buckingham Nurseries
28 Tingewick Road
Buckingham, MK18 4AE
Hedging and young trees, ornamental trees, fruit trees and ground cover.

Burncoose and Southdown Nurseries
Givennap
Redruth, Cornwall, TR16 6BJ
Trees, shrubs and oramental plants.

Burnham Nurseries
Forches Cross
Newton Abbot
Devon, TW12 6P2
Orchids.

Caddick's Clematis Nursery
Lymm Road
Thelwall
Warrington
Retail, mail order and wholesale. Over 350 varieties grown. Catalogue available.

John Chambers' Wild Flower Seeds
15 Westleigh Road
Barton Seagrave, Kettering
Northants, NN15 5AT
Wild flower seeds, and other seeds.

Chessington Nurseries
Leatherhead Road
Chessington
Surrey
House, patio, garden and conservatory plants and all other garden requirements.

Chris Bowers & Sons Dept RH
Whispering Trees Nursery
Wimbotsham
Norfolk, PE34 8QB
Fruit plants. Mail order service available.

Paul Christian
PO Box 468
Wrexham, Clwyd
North Wales, LL13 9XR
Rare fritillaries.

Colegrave Seeds
West Adderbury
Banbury
Oxfordshire, OX17 3EY
Multiflora petunias.

Cottage Herbery
Mill House
Boraston, Tenbury Wells
Worcestershire, WR15 8LZ
Herbs and cottage garden plants.

Cranborne Manor Garden Centre
Cranborne
Wimborne, Dorset
Old fashioned roses, Italian statuary and pots, rare and unusual plants. Box and yew hedging.

Deacons Nursery
Godshill
Isle of Wight, PO38 3HW
Family fruit trees.

Derek Lloyd Dean
8 Lynwood Close
South Harow
Middlesex, HA2 9PR
Pelargoniums.

Donnington Plants
Main Road
Wrangle, Boston
Lincolnshire, PE22 9AT
Argyranthemums, Primula sieboldii and auriculas.

Drysdale Nursery
Bowerwood Road
Fordingbridge
Hampshire, SP6 1BN
Collection of bamboos and a wide range of unusual shrubs. Catalogue available.

Efenechtyd Nurseries
Llanelidan
Ruthin
North Wales, LL15 2LG
Streptocarpus, foliage and begonias.

Fibrex Nurseries
Honeybourne Road
Pebworth, Nr. Stratford-on-Avon
Warwickshire, CV37 8XT
Pelargoniums, hederas and hardy ferns.

Forest Lodge Garden Centre
Hold Pound
Farnham
Surrey, GU10 4LD
Quality plants: specimen conifers, trees, shrubs, climbers and conservatory plants.

Glantlees Trees and Hedging
Newton on the Moor
Felton
Northumberland
Trees and hedging plants including oak, lime, maple, beech and many more.

M. Gould
Stockerton Nursery
Kircudbright
Galloway, DG6 4XS
A large mail order selection of British wild plant species including shrubs, primulas and bulbs etc.

Growing Carpets
The Old Farmhouse
Steeple Morden
Royston
Hertfordshire
Ground cover plants. Catalogue available.

Hannays of Bath
Sydney Wharf Nursery
Bathwick, Bath
Avon, BA2 4ES
Provide large-sized specimens of a wide range of uncommon species.

W. & L. Harley
Parham Nursery
The Sands
Market Lavington, Devizes
Wiltshire, SN10 4QA
Hardy perennials for the woodland and bog garden, herbaceous and rock garden. Many rare varieties.

Heather and Brian Hiley
25 Little Woodcote Estate
Wallington
Surrey, SM5 4AU
Tender and unusual perennials.

Hiller Nurseries (Winchester) Ltd
Ampfield House
Ampfield, Romsey
Hants, SO51 9PA
Mail order of over 4,000 trees, shrubs, climbers, conifers, roses and fruits.

Hostas
Sticklepath
Okehampton
Devon, DX20 1RD
Specialists in hostas.

Hydon Nurseries Limited
Clock Barn Lane
Hydon Heath, Godalming
Surrey, GU8 4AZ
Specialist growers of rhododendrons, azaleas, camellias and magnolias. A selection of new and unusual hybrids such as the smaller Yakushimanum varieties.

Jarvis Brook Geranium Nursery
Tubwell Lane
Crowborough
East Sussex, TN6 3RH
Pelargoniums.

John Sanday (Roses) Limited
Over Lane
Almondsbury
Bristol
Avon, BS12 4DA
Rose specilists. Thousands of roses including beds of hybrid teas and floribundas and borders of climbers and ramblers.

P. de Jager & Sons
The Nurseries
Marden
Kent, TN12 9BP
Fritillaries.

Langthorns Plantery
Little Canfield
Dunmour
Essex
Range of hardy trees, shrubs, herbaceous perennials and alpines, including many rare varieties.

Leonardslee Garden Nurseries
Lower Beeding
Horsham
West Sussex, RH13 6PX
Rhododendrons, rare and unusual varietes. Site visits and garden planning service also available.

Lewdon Farm Alpine Nursery
Cheriton Bishop
Devon, EX6 6HF
Alpines, miniature shrubs and herbaceous plants. Mail order service available.

Lincluden Nursery
Bisley Green
Bisley
Woking
Surrey, GU24 9EN
Dwarf, slow growing and unusual conifers.

McBeans Orchids Limited
Cooksbridge
Lewes
Sussex, BN8 4PR
Orchid hybrids.

Mallet Court Nursery
Curry Mallet
Taunton
Somerset, TA3 6SY
Rare trees and shrubs plus a range of acers, quercus and fagus. Catalogue available.

Maltocks Roses
The Rose Nureries
Nuneham
Courtenay
Oxford, OX9 9PY
Roses.

S.E. Marshall
Regal Road
Wisbech
Cambridgeshire, PE13 2RF
Vegetable seeds.

J. & D. Marston Fern Specialists
'Culag'
Green Lane
Nofferton
East Yorkshire, YO25 OLF
Quality pot-grown ferns for greenhouse and outdoors. Catalogue available.

Meadowcraft Fuchsias
Church St Nurseries
Woodhurst
Huntingdon
Cambridgeshire, PE17 3BN
Fuchsias and pelargoniums.

Merlin Rooted Cuttings
Little Drym
Praze
Camborne
Cornwall, TR14 ONU
Specialist propagators of interesting and unusual garden plants. Mail order service.

Millais Nurseries
Crosswater Lane
Churt
Farnham
Surrey, GU10 2JN
A unique collection of rare species and new hybrids, rhododendrons and azaleas.

Newington Nurseries
Newington
Wallingford
Oxon, OX10 7AW
A range of scented conservatory plants from around the world. Full advice service also available.

Orchard Nurseries
Foston
Tow Lane
Foston
Nr. Grantham
Lincolnshire, NG32 2LE
A wide selection of herbaceous plants and clematis, including Euphorbia 'Red Dwarf'.

Pantiles Nurseries Limited
Almners Road
Lyne
Chertsey
Surrey, KT16 OBJ
Large and unusual conifers, trees and shrubs. A full planting and landscaping servie, also a delivery service.

Priorswood Clematis
Priorswood
Widbury Hill
Ware
Hertfordshire, SG12 7QH
Propagators and growers of quality clematis plants and other climbers and shrubs.

PW Plants
'Sunnyside Nurseries'
Heath Road
Kenninghall
Norfolk, NR16 2DA
A range of plants including grass, shrubs, climbers, perennials, bamboos, conifers and streptocarpus. Mail service available.

Read's Nursery
Hales Hall
Loddon
Norfolk, NR14 6QW
Greenhouse and garden grapes.

The Romantic Garden Nursery
Swannington
Norwich
Norfolk, NR9 5NW
Specialist grower of topiary and ornamental standards, including plaitted stem oleanders, twisted stem bays, box spirals and animals, over 100 varieties of clematis, plus hardy and half hardy plants. Catalogue available.

Rougham Hall Nurseries
Ipswich Road
Rougham
Bury St Edmunds
Suffolk, IP30 9LY
Delphiniums, Iceland poppies and other hardy perennials.

Rushfields of Ledbury
Ross Road
Ledbury
Herefordshire, HR8 2LP
Herbaceous plants.

Southfields Nurseries
Lough Road
Holton-le-Clay
Grimsby
South Humberside, DN36 5HL
Cacti and succulents.

Southview Nurseries
Dept G
Chequers Lane
Eversley Cross
Hants, RG27 ONT
More than 200 choice perennials including a range of old-fashioned pinks, digitalis and penstemons. Mail order service available.

Stems
Mountpleasant
Gressingham
Nr. Hornby
Lancaster, LA2 8LP
Argyranthemums plus patio and bedding subjects: penstemons, gazania and others.

Suttons Seeds
Hele Road
Torway
Devon, TQ2 7QJ
Vegetables and annuals.

Thompson & Morgan
Poplar Lane
Ipswich, IP8 3BU
Mail order seedsmen. An extensive range of annuals, perennials, alpines, house plants, cacti, trees and shrubs and vegetables. Catalogue available upon request.

Tilegates Garden
Little Common Lane
Bletchingley
Surrey, RH1 4QF
A vast collection of magnolias, rhododendrons, maples, birches, conifers and more.

Philip Tivey & Sons
28 Wanlip Road
Syston
Nr. Leicester
Leicestershire, LE7 8PA
Dahlias and chrysanthemums.

Trehane Nurseries
Stapehill Road
Hampreston
Wimborne
Dorset, BH21 7NE
Camellias, azaleas, dwarf diamonds, glenn dales, satsukis and North Tisbury hybrids.

Tropical Rain Forest
66 Castle Grove Avenue
Leeds
West Yorkshire
LS6 4BS
Bromeliads and exotic plants.

Unwins
Mail Order Dept 529
Histon
Cambridge, CB4 4ZZ
A range of flower and vegetable seeds, including sweet peas, summer flowering bulbs, thornless bush roses, bedding plants and seedlings. Brochure available on request.

The Valley Clematis Nursery
Hainton
Lincoln, LN3 6LN
Mail order service; catalogue available.

The Veron Geranium Nursery
Cuddington Way
Cheam, Sutton
Surrey, SM2 7JB
Range of varieties including miniature geraniums. Mail order service available.

Water Garden Nursery
Wembworthy
Chulmleigh
Devon, EX18 7SG
Plants for all types of water gardening, sunny courtyards, shady moist woodlands, bog gardens and water meadows.

Woodfield Brothers
71 Townsend Road
Tiddington, Stratford-on-Avon
Warwickshire, CV37 7DF
Lupins.

Wyevale Gramphorn Garden Centres
Cressing Road
Braintree
Essex, CM7 8DL
A multiple retail group with 41 garden centres in the UK. Large range includes over 2,500 varieties of shrubs and trees. Also offer an international plant finding service and their own Good Plant Guide.

MISCELLANEOUS

Boswell Roberts
Dept GA2
46 Keyes Road
London, NW2 3XA
Hand-painted garden umbrellas in a range of sizes and designs.

Cons Co
62 Askern Industrial Estate
Askern
Doncaster, DN6 ODD
Decorative, rust-free, cast aluminium brackets in high quality stoned enamel.

Courtyard Pottery
Groundwell Road
Cricklade Road
Swindon, Wiltshire
Handmade, frost-proof terracotta pottery.

Dorset Weathervanes
284 Bournemouth Road
Charlton Marshall
Blandford Forum
Dorset, DT11 9NG
Over 30 different designs. Making one-off designs a speciality.

Eastman Vaughan Wire Products Limited
Stokes Croft
Bristol, BS1 3RD
Traditional Victorian rose garden arches. Made from woven wire mesh, weatherproof galvanized after manufacture.

English Basket and Hurdle Centre
Curload
Stoke St Gregory
Taunton
Somerset, TA3 6JD
Traditional wattle hurdles.

Good Directions Limited
Sarum House
6 Winchester Street
Botley
Hampshire, SO32 3EE
Aged copper weathervanes and fibreglass cupolas.

J.E. Homewood & Son
20 Wey Hill
Haslemere
Surrey, GU27 1BX
Manufacturers of high-quality cleft chestnut fencing. Available in four different styles and six heights.

Paddock Fencing
French Drove
Thorney
Peterborough, PE6 OPQ
Ornamental Victorian-style tree fences. Wide enough to stake trees inside, even large specimens.

Pamel
The Cottage
Sproxton
Melton Mowbray
Leicestershire, LE14 4QS
Timber tubs produced in solid hardwood to a traditional design. Available in natural wood or white and three sizes. Alternative sizes and rectangular troughs to order.

Roseney Farm Designs
Lanlivery, Bodmin
Cornwall, PL30 5DL
Makers of traditional style dovecotes, bird tables and planters. Several designs to choose from, kits also available.

Wells & Winter
Mereworth
Maidstone
Kent, ME18 5NB
Garden labels in zinc, copper, aluminium and also green plastic. Samples available.

West Meon Pottery
Church Lane
West Meon, Petersfield
Hants, GU32 1JW
Quality hand-thrown garden pots.

ACKNOWLEDGEMENTS

All photographs are by Andrew Lawson, with the following exceptions: A-Z Botanical 46 right, 47 centre and bottom left, 48 left, 50 right, 51 bottom left, 57 top right, 58 top left and bottom left; Sue Atkinson/Mitchell Beazley 8, 9 bottom, 29, 30 bottom left, 115 bottom; Paul Barker/Mitchell Beazley half title, 28, 40, 42, 103 top, 104 top, 115 top; Peter Beale 51 top; Eric Crichton 9 top, 10 bottom, 26 above centre, 27 bottom, 31 top, 33 bottom, 36 right, 44 top right, 46 bottom, 49 top left, 50 centre, 51 bottom right, 55 left, 56 top, 57 top left, 59 bottom left and below centre, 63 bottom left, 64 bottom, 76 top left and centre, 80 top left and centre, 81 right, 82 top right, 84 top right, 85 bottom left, 90 bottom right, 91 top left and bottom left, 96 top, 97 left, 103 bottom, 107 below centre, 110 top, 112 left, 113 top left; Garden Picture Library/Linda Burgess 86 /John Glover 88 bottom /Ron Sutherland 117 top; John Glover 22 centre, 25 above centre, 87 top and bottom, 88 top; Derek Gould 25 right, 39 left, 44 bottom right, 47 bottom; Jerry Harpur 31 bottom (Home Farm, Balscombe, Oxfordshire); 41 bottom (Dreamthorpe, Macedon, Victoria), 60 (Churchill, Campania, Tasmania), 96 bottom (D: Philip Watson, Fredericksburg, Virginia), 104 bottom (Royal Horticultural Society, Wisley, Surrey), 108 (D: Ann Griot, Los Angeles), 109 top (D: Victor Nelson, New York) and bottom, 110 bottom (Meadowbrook Farm, Philadelphia), 114 (D: Claus Scheinert, Alpes Maritimes), 117 bottom (D: Ernie Taylor); Marijke Heuff 30 top, 53 top, 54 top and bottom, 61; Clive Nichols title page, 10 top, 11, 41 top, 43 top left, 52, 66, 94, 95 top and bottom, 102; Hugh Palmer 68, 116; Photos Horticultural 22 top left, 26 bottom left, 34 top, 47 top left, 56 bottom left, 57 bottom right, 63 top right, 64 centre, 65 below centre, 70 bottom left and top right, 71 top, 85 top and right of centre, 90 right of centre, 106 top right, 107 top, 111 right, 113 centre; Reed Consumer Books/Michael Boys 77 left of centre, /Jerry Harpur 33 top, 37 bottom left, 112 top, /George Wright 77 top; Harry Smith Collection 47 bottom left, 51 top right, 65 top left, 75 bottom left, 84 centre, 107 bottop left, 118 top left, 119 right.